普通语言学概论

主　　编：陈佑林　何举纯
编　　者：陈佑林　何举纯　熊　兵
徐　泉　张国华

华中师范大学出版社
2024 年 · 武汉

新出图证(鄂)字 10 号

图书在版编目(CIP)数据

普通语言学概论/陈佑林,何举纯主编. —武汉:华中师范大学出版社,2010. 11
(2024. 7 重印)
(外语语言文学系列教材)
ISBN 978-7-5622-3876-8
Ⅰ. ①普… Ⅱ. ①陈… ②何… Ⅲ. ①普通语言学—高等学校—教材 Ⅳ. ①H0
中国版本图书馆 CIP 数据核字(2010)第 213384 号

普通语言学概论
© 陈佑林 何举纯 主编

责任编辑:廖国春 **责任校对:**刘 峥 **封面设计:**甘 英
编辑室:高校教材分社 **电话:**027-67867364
出版发行:华中师范大学出版社
社址:武汉市珞喻路 152 号 **邮编:**430079
发行电话:027-67861367
传真:027-67863291 **邮购:**027-67861321
网址: http://press.ccnu.edu.cn **电子信箱:**press@mail.ccnu.edu.cn
印刷:武汉市洪林印务有限公司 **督印:**刘 敏
字数:240 千字
开本:787mm×960mm 1/16 **印张:**15
版/印次:2024 年 7 月第 1 版第 5 次印刷
印数:5003—6002 **定价:**38.00 元
欢迎上网查询、购书

前　言

在华中师范大学出版社的大力支持和帮助下,《普通语言学概论》这本书终于得以面世,这是一件值得庆贺的事。

多年以来,我们几位从事语言学教学工作的教师就一直想为师范院校英语专业的本科生编写一本语言学导论性质的教材,并就教材的内容、重点、编写原则等问题进行过多次讨论。经过仔细的讨论和协商,我们就编写原则形成了以下共识:

1.本教材以介绍语言学的基本概念和知识为主,不进行详细的阐述和讨论。

2.本教材应反映语言学研究的最新动态与成果。

3.本教材在介绍基本概念和知识时,主要以英语语言为例进行阐述,偶尔也可使用汉语或其他语言的例证。

4.本教材的英语撰写,语言应简单明了、通俗易懂。

后来又在仔细分析了师范院校英语专业本科生职业需求的基础上确定了教材的内容与重点,并制定出了该教材的所有章节内容及重点。

该书的出版得到了出版社领导的大力支持。他们不仅提出了许多宝贵的修改意见,同时还将该教材纳入了出版计划。另外,江汉大学外国语学院的李磊老师曾为本书的出版做出过贡献,我们也在此表示谢意。

尽管我们在教材的编写过程中付出了很多努力,但是由于我们的水平有限,书中肯定还有一些我们尚未发现的错误和不妥之处。希望读者在使用过程中发现后能转告我们,以便该书在修订时能够得以更正。

编　者

2010 年 5 月

Contents

Chapter 1 Introduction

1.1 What is language?

Hardly can we imagine a human world without language. We have been on this earth for millions of years, and we have always been depending on language to develop for this long. When we speak, we use language. When we write, we also use language. Indeed, language is essential to mankind. Today, even machines are "learning" to use language. It is language, so to speak, that makes the world go round.

Up to now, we have known much more about things around us (the sun, the moon, the earth, etc) than those things inside our brains. Language comes to every normal person so naturally that we seldom stop to ask any basic questions about language. For example, "What is language?" "Where does language come from?" "How does language work?" "What language did the first group of human beings speak?" "Why do people in the world speak different languages?" "What is language like in the future?" "Why does language change?" Obviously, we cannot answer these questions easily, though we use language every day, if not every minute.

Some people are quite interested in these questions and have been trying to work out the answers. Their work brings about the birth of a discipline that is called "linguistics"—the science of language. These people are called "linguists".

1.1.1 Definition of language

As said above, the question "What is language?" seems so simple that few of us would want to think about it. Yet, this everyday phenomenon is far more complex than most of us could imagine, and thus it is rather difficult to give a satisfactory definition.

When we define "language", like to define a flower, we have to find out its distinctive characteristics, i. e. , what is it like? These characteristics must best describe what language (the "flower") actually is. The problem is that while the "flower" is a concrete, natural thing, language is man-made (though it is called "natural language") and abstract.

Some linguists, philosophers and psychologists have tried to define "language", but they observe language from different angles, and cannot make a "perfect" definition that covers all characteristics of "language". When we try, in our effort, to describe what language is, the following aspects cannot be neglected:

1) Any language is governed by some "rules". For example, in English, we always put the definite article "the" before a noun or an adjective, as in "the apple" and "the rich". This is one of the many "rules" of the English language. According to this rule, we may say,

Ex. 1-1 The apple is red.

Ex. 1-2 The rich should help the poor.

So, the following "sentences" are not correct although they have the same words:

Ex. 1-3 * Apple the is red.

Ex. 1-4 * Rich the help should poor the.

From these examples we may see that language is a rule-governed system.

2) We use language to express ourselves and understand others. So, language is for communication. This is the most important function of language. Take the telephone conversation as an example. The message goes from the speaker's mouth to the hearer's ears through the line. The speaker produces the message in a certain language. On the other side of the line, the hearer shares the same language and so he understands what the speaker says. This process of communication continues till the end of their conversation.

3) There is no necessary relation between a word and the notion it stands for. Different languages use different words to refer to the same thing. Take the chemical substance "H_2O" as an example. It is *water* in English, "水" in Chinese,

and *eau* in French. If the ancient English had used * *awter* to mean "H_2O", we would have been using this word ever since. We may conclude, therefore, that language is arbitrary. This example also shows that different languages associate objects, actions, ideas, etc with different "symbols".

4) There is no doubt that the written form of language came much later than its spoken form. The written form was "invented" to record the spoken language when there was the need. Moreover, even today, some languages do not have their written forms. On the other hand, every normal child is a "born listener". He listens and learns to speak before he can read and/or write. So, language is, first of all, a system of sounds, i. e. , a vocal system.

After we have discussed the above features of language, we can define "language" as a system of arbitrary vocal symbols used for human communication.

1.1.2 Distinctive features of language

If you carefully think about the definition of language, perhaps you will ask, "Why is language only for human communication?" or "Do animals have languages?" These questions raise another interesting issue in the study of language.

Maybe none of us would believe that a cat can "talk" with a mouse except in cartoon shows of Disney. But it seems that the same kind of animals can "talk" among themselves. When you are walking your dog in the park and meet another dog, they might bark at each other. They appear to be saying "Hello!" or "Shut up, you fool!" or anything that can only be understood by dogs. Naturally you will think the dogs have their own language as "Dog-ish" or "Dog-ese". Whatever you call it, it is obvious that they can communicate with each other. And the dog is not the only animal that "talks". You may also find bees, ducks, and lions "talking", or "buzzing", or quacking, or roaring.

A lot of scientists want to find out how animals communicate among their own kinds. The "bee-dance", for example, arouses their interest. Some other scientists make a research of "the dolphin's signals". However, up to now, we have not found out much about the animal's communication systems. This field leaves much room for further study.

On the other hand, however, linguists know more and more about human language. Their research has proved that language has its own features that distinguish it from any animal communication system. In other words, "being able to use language" is one of the human characteristics that separate man from animals. (Other human features are walking erectly, being able to use tools, etc.)

Charles Hockett, an American linguist, named these distinctive characteristics of language "design features". These design features distinguish language from any "animal communication system". That is to say, these features are "human specific". In this part, we shall discuss some of them so as to reach a better understanding of the nature of language.

1. Arbitrariness

As mentioned earlier, language is arbitrary. This means there is no logical connection between meanings and sounds. Why should we use the sound [biː] (bee) in English to refer to the dancing, honey-collecting insect? No reason at all. Why should we use the similar sound [bǐ] (笔) in Chinese to mean the tool for writing? No reason, either.

We live in this world with a lot of things around us. When we meet anything new, we first build up a "notion" of it. And then we need to give a "name" or "label" to this "notion". This is the process of connecting meanings with symbols. Such a process, in most cases, without any significant reason, occurs at our free will, so to speak, quite arbitrarily. The feature of arbitrariness is obvious in all human languages. It is the arbitrariness of language that enables man to create numerous symbols to meet the needs in the social development of human beings.

You may find, however, that language is not completely arbitrary. First, every language has certain words which imitate natural sounds, such as *bang*, *meow* and *wow-wow* in English, "砰", "喵", and "汪汪" in Chinese. These words are in accordance with the sounds they imitate. Therefore, they are not arbitrary. Second, some compound words are not entirely arbitrary, either. For example, since there already exist the words "news" and "paper", then the paper on which news is printed is called "newspaper". The reason for how such words and names camc into being is obvious.

Also, we can easily find non-arbitrary examples in Chinese. Take the symbol "木" for example. It looks like the shape of a tree and means "wood" which comes from the plant "tree". In this sense, the symbol "木" is not arbitrarily made. And then, if we put two such symbols together, we have another symbol "林", which means "woods". Furthermore, when three such symbols are combined, as in the shape of "森", the meaning becomes "a forest".

From this example we can see that when we are creating a name for a notion, sometimes, there does exist some logic or reason instead of arbitrariness.

Again, we have to point out that these "logically made" symbols only form a small portion of the vocabulary of a language. Let's put it more clearly with the following example:

In Chinese, a single horizontal line "一" means "one", two horizontal lines "二" means "two" and three horizontal lines "三" means "three". But, we cannot make an analogy that four horizontal lines means "four" or ten horizontal lines means "ten". This example shows that by form/shape, such symbols as "一", "二", and "三" are not arbitrarily made. However, if we think about their sounds, we cannot find any reason why they are pronounced [yī], [èr], and [sān] respectively. So, these symbols are not completely arbitrary in that they are arbitrary in sound (phonologically arbitrary) but non-arbitrary in form (morphologically non-arbitrary). Thus, with the feature of arbitrariness of language, we may come to the conclusion that language is arbitrary in nature, with more or less non-arbitrary elements.

It is the arbitrariness of language that enables man to create an infinite number of "names" for countless "notions", no matter how abstract the notions are. But animals are not as able. However loudly a dog may bark, he cannot tell you his father, an old male dog, is poor but honest. Nor can a lion sadly tell you that he is old and lonely and needs a new wife.

2. Productivity

Language is productive in the sense that language users can understand and produce sentences they have never heard before. Much of what we say and hear happens for the first time, but we can understand these messages perfectly well, even if some messages may be beyond our knowledge.

As a matter of fact, not only can we deal with messages about our daily life, we are also able to produce and understand sentences in strange contexts. If we read or hear such a sentence as "The three-eyed horse is smoking in Mr. Black's bedroom closet", we may feel this sentence is surely "new", only possible in a fairy tale. However, there seems to be no problem of understanding. This also owes to the productivity of language. With this feature, we are able to publish new books, tell new stories, enjoy new songs, teach new lessons, etc.

Productivity is unique to human language. In other words, no animal communication system has such a feature. Although animals can transmit messages among themselves in one way or another, the messages they send and receive are quite limited in number. Their "topics" of communication, if any, are highly restricted by their basic needs as searching for food, warning of danger, desire for mating, etc. We do not believe that a dog is able to ask his baby, "Is this bone long enough to make a rafter of our new house?"

3. Duality

As said earlier, language is a system made up of sounds, i. e. , a vocal system. Our speech organs, including the tongue, the lips, the teeth, the nose, etc, can produce a lot of sounds. But, in any language, only SOME of them are used, no matter how complex that language is. And, certain sounds are used in one language but not in another. For instance, [tr] and [dr] are used in English, but not in Chinese. We have [nja] and [gja] in Japanese, but they are not found in English. This is one of the basic concepts we should bear in mind. Therefore, basic sound units in a language are limited in number, and these sound units, such as [tr] and [dr], do not have any meaning. They are just vocal symbols. Language is based on these fundamental sound units. In other words, these basic units of sound combine to form larger, meaningful units, by certain "rules", so as to make up a language.

Let's take the English language as an example. Though it is very complex as a system, it has only 48 basic sound units such as [iː], [t], [m], etc. These sound units themselves are meaningless. They are lying at the "lower level" of the language system, according to linguists. If the English language only stayed at this "lower level" and gave each of the 48 sounds a meaning, for example [i:]=I, [t]= love, [m] = you, etc, then English would have only 48 meaningful units! Obviously, these 48 units can never completely express all that we want to say.

Fortunately, however, the 48 basic sound units at the "lower level" can be put together, according to some rules, to form larger meaningful units. The three sound units in the above example can be combined in the following ways:

[i:]+[t]⟶[i:t] *eat*

[t]+[i:]⟶[ti:] *tea*

[m]+[i:]⟶[mi:] *me*

[t]+[i:]+[m]⟶[ti:m] *team*

[m]+[i:]+[t]⟶[mi:t] *meet*

These "rule-governed" combinations arrive at the "higher level". Thus, English, as a system, has "two levels of structures". The meaningful units at the "higher level", such as "teach" and "cheat", may also be arranged and rearranged, by certain "rules", into as many sentences as we need. It is the same case with any other languages. This feature of language is what we mean by "duality".

Animals do not enjoy this feature in their communication system. They can transmit some information with different kinds of signals, but their signals are always at the "lower level", i. e. , they cannot set up a "rule" or "rules" to arrange their signals to fit in with the "higher level". To be more exact, there is only "one level" of signals in animals' communication system.

4. Displacement

Young parents often amuse their babies with stories. Many of the stories are fairy tales. Some of the stories begin like this, "Long, long ago, there was a small rabbit in the forest. He was clever but naughty. And his mother loved him very much..."

Obviously, those details in such stories are not real in life. They are imagined. However, a normal child has no difficulty in understanding them and is always carried away to some wonderful fairyland. On the other hand, children sometimes create stories by themselves. And, when they make mistakes, they even tell lies!

Also, they can tell each other what happened before and what may happen in the future.

So, language can be used to refer to things that are present or not present, real or unreal, or anything in far-away places. This is what "displacement" means. "Displacement", together with the above-mentioned "arbitrariness", "productivity", and "duality", enables man to talk about a surprisingly wide range of things.

In contrast, no animal communication system has this feature of "displacement", for animal calls are only in relation to present situations. Again, take the dog for example. Usually, the dog barks when a stranger is approaching. The nearer the stranger is, the louder he barks. When the stranger goes away or disappears, the bark stops. No dog can tell his father, "A fool wanted to get in our house five minutes ago, daddy!" Nor can he tell a lie to his mother, "I swear I never did hide that bone!"

5. Cultural transmission

All of us are born with the ability to acquire language. This capacity of language, according to scientists, is determined by human genes. In linguists' terms, such a capacity has a "genetic basis". But, it would be horrible if a baby had been able to say hello to his parents the moment he was born. That is to say, no one is born with a language already in mind though he is armed with a genetic basis for language. So, linguists believe that the details of any language system are not genetically or biologically transmitted, but have to be taught and learned. The child who is brought up by a wolf can not speak any language at all.

Man acquires language in a language/culture environment or a certain culture. He listens before he speaks. A child speaks English if what he hears is only English; he speaks Japanese if brought up in a Japanese environment. In fact, what he turns out to speak has nothing to do with his nationality or colour of the skin.

Since a human being is born with a "genetic basis" for language, he has language potential. But the "genetic basis" alone is not enough. The process of acquiring a language relies on both this "basis" and a certain language/culture environment. Therefore, language is "culturally transmitted". No one is a "born speaker of language", not even Shakespeare.

However, animals' call systems are genetically transmitted. A dog does not need to learn how to bark when he is born. Namely, he is able to bark by nature. And, we do not believe that a dog in Britain produces an "English bark" while one in China comes up with a "Chinese bark". Actually, they share the same "bark system" and thus can understand each other in their "dog communication". Their dog calls differ from one another, perhaps, only in volume and quality.

1.2 What is linguistics?

1.2.1 Definition of linguistics

Generally, linguistics is defined as the scientific study of language. To be more exact, linguistics is a branch of science that studies language rules.

It is important to pay close attention to the three key words "language", "study" and "scientific" in such a definition.

We do not put an article "the" or "a" before the word "language", because linguistics studies not just one particular language as English, Chinese, or French. Instead, it studies languages in general, i. e., all languages of human beings. Here, the word "language" is in an abstract sense. There are thousands of languages used in different places of the world everyday. These languages differ from one another in various ways. However, they have some features in common. When we discuss languages in general, we are concerned with what all these natural languages share. And, we cannot talk about language in general without referring to a particular language. In addition, "language" in this definition only refers to "natural human language". Therefore, we do not discuss any artificial language such as "Basic" used on computer or any sign language that is soundless.

The word "study" does not mean "learn" but "investigate" or "examine". Linguistics tries to answer the basic questions "What is language?" and "How does language work?". It also tries to find out what all languages have in common, why languages change, what is the relationship between language and society, how language relates to thought, and so on.

Then what is meant by "scientific"? It refers to the way in which language is studied. A scientific study of language is based on systematic investigations. Such investigations try to form linguistic theories out of linguistic facts/data. So, first of all, the linguist has to observe language facts, i. e. , to see how language is actually used; then he brings forth some hypotheses according to what he has observed. But the hypotheses thus formed have to be tested again and again. If the hypotheses can pass all tests, they are accepted as "theories".

The whole process of linguistic study can be better explained as follows:

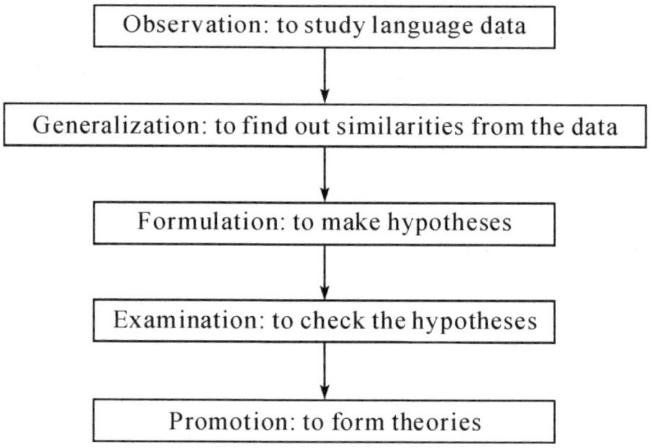

Theories are formed from linguistic facts, checked against linguistic facts, supported by linguistic facts, and are used to explain linguistic facts.

1.2.2 Principles for linguistic study

In order to make his analysis as scientific as possible, the linguist must be guided by four principles:

1. Exhaustiveness

Language is extremely complex. The linguist cannot expect to describe all aspects of language at once. Usually, he may examine one aspect at a time. Whichever aspect he examines, he should gather all the materials related to his investigation and give them an adequate explanation. This is what we mean by "exhaustiveness". If he chooses to study syntax, for example, he should collect all materials concerning syntax and explain them adequately. Otherwise, his study will not be regarded as "exhaustive" and his conclusion will not be accepted as scientific.

2. Consistency

By "consistency", we mean there should be no contradiction in a theory. The linguist cannot say "A is B" in one place and "A is not B" in another place. That is, he should be "consistent" in what he says. For example, if he declares "no verb in its base form can be used as the subject of a sentence", he must insist on this statement throughout his theory.

3. Economy

Good statements for a theory should be as short as possible and can most fully explain all facts involved. This is what "economy" means. Two points here deserve our attention. On the one hand, other things being equal, a shorter statement is better than a longer one. On the other hand, if the short statement leaves many facts unexplained, it is of no scientific value either, because too many exceptions will make it invalid.

4. Objectivity

A linguist should be as objective as possible in his description and analysis of data. No prejudice is allowed to influence his study, and every part of his analysis can be checked, not only by himself, but also by anyone else. Therefore, he should not omit any language facts only because he himself considers them to be "not elegant" or "not standard". Nor should he conceal facts that disagree with his theory. In short, he should respect language facts and make his theory acceptable to all others.

1.2.3 The scope of linguistics

The study of language as a whole is often called general linguistics. This includes the basic concepts, theories, descriptions, models and methods in the analysis of language. It is used in contrast to those branches of study which relate linguistics to the research of other areas.

As mentioned above, it is not quite possible for the linguist to study all aspects of language at once. To make his study scientific, the linguist often concentrates on one aspect at a time. Thus appear different branches of general linguistics.

1. Phonetics

Phonetics is the study of the phonetic medium of language, i. e. , it studies the production, transmission, and perception of the speech sounds. Phonetics is divided into three sub-branches:

a. Articulatory phonetics, the study of the production of speech sounds

b. Acoustic phonetics, the study of the transmission of speech sounds

c. Auditory phonetics, the study of the perception of speech sounds

2. Phonology

Phonology studies sound patterns of languages. Man can make a wide range of sounds, but only a small number of human sounds are used in speech. Phonology describes how these speech sounds are arranged into meaningful units.

3. Morphology

Morphology studies the form of words. It identifies the smallest meaningful units of a language which are called morphemes and how these morphemes are arranged to form words.

4. Syntax

Syntax studies the internal structure of sentences and the rules by which sentences are formed. Sentences are not strings of words arranged at random order. Change in the sequence affects the meaning of the sentence. So syntax identifies the acceptable sequences in a language and the relationships between elements in sentence structure.

5. Semantics

Semantics studies the meaning of language. It tries to explain what meaning is, how meaning really works and the change in meaning in language forms. Some other scopes of semantics include the relationship between language forms and approaches of semantic analysis.

6. Pragmatics

Pragmatics is the study of the meaning of language in context. It deals with how language users use the language to achieve communicative effects.

7. Historical linguistics

Historical linguistics is the study of language change.

The study of all these aspects of language forms the core of linguistics. Then, language is not an isolated phenomenon, it is a social activity carried out in a certain social environment by human beings. Naturally, in the course of time the study of language has established close links with other disciplines of social science, resulting in "interdisciplinary branches" of linguistic study.

8. Sociolinguistics

Sociolinguistics is the study of language and linguistic behaviours as influenced by social and cultural factors. It regards language as a social phenomenon. It's more concerned with investigating the relationships between language and society for a better understanding of the stucture of language and of how languanges function in communication.

9. Psycholinguistics

Psycholinguistics is the study of language in relation to the mind. It is viewed as the intersection of linguistics and psychology.

Findings in linguistic studies can often be applied to the solution of practical problems. The study of such applications is generally known as applied linguistics. But in a narrow sense, applied linguistics refers to the application of linguistic theories and principles to language teaching, especially the teaching of foreign language and second language.

Other related branches include anthropological linguistics, neurological linguistics, mathematical linguistics, and computational linguistics.

1.2.4 Some basic distinctions in linguistics

We introduce some basic distinctions in this part, because they are so essential to language study that they will quite often appear throughout this course.

1. Descriptive and prescriptive

If a linguistic study describes and analyses the "actual use of language", it is **descriptive**; if it tries to lay down rules for "correct usage of language", it is **prescriptive.** In other words, if a linguist talks about "what people actually say", he is descriptive. If he tells people "what should and what should not be said", he is prescriptive.

Linguistic study before the 20th century was largely prescriptive. It was based on a Latin framework known as "traditional grammar". In the past, traditional grammarians set classical literary or religious written records as "models" for language users to follow. They thought it was their duty to maintain the "correct" or "standard" usage of language.

But a modern linguist does not agree with traditional grammarians on this point. He prefers to be an observer of language facts, but not a "judge". He is interested in what is said, not what he thinks ought to be said. He describes language in all its aspects, but does not prescribe rules of "correctness". And, he regards the changes in language and language use as the result of a natural and continuous process, not something to be denied. For example, traditional grammarians tell people not to say "It's me", but say "It's I" in answer to the question "Who is it?". But people do say "It's me" in their daily life and this kind of usage has become part of their language. A modern linguist believes that whatever occurs in natural speech should be described in his analysis. That is, language changes should not and cannot be stopped; they must be explained. This is also required by "objectivity", which we have discussed. Therefore, modern linguistics is mostly descriptive.

2. Speech and writing

In the past, grammarians over-emphasized the importance of the written language basically for two reasons. First, written language has the quality of permanence. Before the invention of sound recording, it was difficult for people to deal with speech sounds that could exist only for seconds. Second, people insisted on learning to use language in accordance with the usage of the "best authors" of the classical times, and these authors existed only in written form.

But, in modern linguistics, priority is given to the spoken form of language. Linguists regard speech as primary, not writing, for a number of reasons. First, the spoken form exited long, long before the written form came into being. The writing system of any language is always a later invention, used to record the speech. Second, the spoken form is much more common than the written form. Even today many well-developed languages do not have a writing system yet, while all languages are vocal. Third, as mentioned earlier, the spoken form comes before the written form in the process of man's acquisition of his first language. Moreover, scientific study proves that blind children have no difficulty in learning to speak but deaf children have great difficulty in learning to read. This shows that the channel of sight is not as important as the channel of sound in learning a language. And fourth, the acquisition of spoken form is universal while that of written form is relative. That is to say, every normal person is able to speak but not all people are able to read and or write.

3. Synchronic and diachronic

Language exists in time and changes through time. The description of a language at some point in time is a **synchronic** study; the description of a language as it changes through time is a **diachronic** study. To be more exact, a diachronic study of language is a historical study. It studies the historical development of language over a period of time. Modern linguistics mainly takes a synchronic approach. Because if we could not analyze various states of a language successfully, it would be difficult to describe the changes that have taken place in its historical development. And most modern linguists are studying languages of the present time.

But we do not mean that synchronic and diachronic studies can be absolutely separated, for language is dynamic, i. e. , there is never a moment when a language stops changing for our description. In fact, we often need to know what the language was like before in order to describe, with insight, what it is like today.

4. Langue and parole

The distinction between langue and parole was made by the Swiss linguist F. de Saussure (1959) early in the 20th century. Langue refers to the abstract linguistic system shared by all the members of a speech community, and parole refers to the realization of langue in actual use.

Langue is abstract in that it is not the language people actually use; it is a set of conventions and rules which language users abide by. So, langue is relatively stable, i. e. , it does not change frequently. Parole, on the other hand, is concrete and natural language events and varies from person to person.

We all speak Chinese, for example. In this sense, "Chinese" is langue, like an "agreement" we all have signed. We are using the same system for communication. But when we actually say something in Chinese, none of us speaks exactly the same as another in pronunciation, vocabulary and grammar. What we actually say is "parole". That is, we produce different paroles under the guidance of the same langue. The relationship between langue and parole is that between the abstract and the concrete and that between the universal and the individual.

For Saussure, parole is a mass of confused facts, thus not suitable for systematic investigation. What a linguist should do, according to Saussure, is to abstract langue from instances of parole, i. e. , to discover the regularities/rules governing all instances of parole and make them the subject of linguistics. The langue-parole distinction is of great importance. It influenced many linguists later on.

5. Competence and performance

Norm Chomsky, the American linguist, made the distinction between competence and performance in late 1950's(Chomsky, 1968), which is similar to Saussure's distinction between langue and parole. According to Chomsky, **competence** refers to the ideal language user's knowledge of the rules of his language, and **performance** is the actual realization of this knowledge in linguistic communication. Competence, as the knowledge about the rules of the language, enables a speaker to produce countless sentences and recognize grammatical mistakes and ambiguities. A language user's competence is stable while his performance is often affected by psychological and social factors. Therefore, a speaker's performance does not always match his competence. A person's knowledge about the language might be perfect, but on certain occasions, he may not perform well for one reason or another. For example, we may often make grammatical mistakes in speech, but that does not mean we do not know the rule at all. If we are given an ungrammatical sentence, we can easily recognize the sentence as wrong. Misuse of language is caused by social and psychological factors such as stress, anxiety or embarrassment. Similar to Saussure, Chomsky thinks linguists should study the speaker's competence, not his performance. Although the speaker is always guided by the rules of language when he speaks the language in communication, he cannot tell exactly what these rules are. So the task of the linguists is to discover and specify the rules settled in the speaker's mind.

Though very similar to each other, Chomsky's competence-performance distinction is not exactly the same as Saussure's langue-parole distinction. Saussure's "langue" is a social product, a set of conventions for a speech community. Chomsky regards competence as a property of the mind of each individual. Saussure looks at language more from a sociological point of view while Chomsky looks at it more from a psychological point of view.

Exercises

1. Fill in the blanks with the most suitable words. Each blank represents ONE word.
   1) Language is a system of ________ vocal symbols used for human communication.
   2) F. de Saussure looks at language more from a sociological point of view while Chomsky looks at it more from a ________ point of view.
   3) A person who studies linguistics is usually referred to as a ________.
   4) So far as function is concerned, language is for ________.
   5) Charles Hockett's term of the distinctive characteristics of language is ________ features.
   6) We can produce and understand sentences that we have never heard before. This is meant by the ________ of language.
   7) Linguistics is the ________ study of language.
   8) The study of language as a whole is called ________ linguistics.
   9) ________ is the branch of linguistics which studies the meaning of language.
   10) The description of a language as it changes through time is a ________ study.
2. Tell whether the following statements are true or false.

1) Any language is governed by some rules.
2) The written form and the spoken form of language came into being at the same time.
3) All languages in the world have both spoken and written forms.
4) Animals are able to communicate with their own languages.
5) With the feature of arbitrariness of language, we may come to the conclusion that any language is completely arbitrary.
6) Different people look at language from different points of view and the definition of language is not yet perfect.
7) We can talk about things that happened before or in far-away places. This is what "productivity of language" means.
8) Historical linguistics studies those languages used in human history.
9) Most modern linguists believe that it is their duty to maintain the standard usage of language.
10) Modern linguists mainly take a synchronic approach in their study of language.

3. Define the following terms.
   1) morphology
   2) syntax
   3) pragmatics
   4) sociolinguistics
   5) psycholinguistics
4. Mark the correct choice for each of the following statements.
   1) Modern linguists give priority to speech because ________.
      A. speech sounds are derived from writing systems
      B. they can use recording devices
      C. speech precedes writing everywhere in the world
      D. writing precedes speech in English
   2) Modern linguists regard the changes in language and language use as ________.
      A. unnatural

B. natural

C. something to be feared

D. abnormal

3) The feature of arbitrariness of language means ________.

A. we can say whatever we want to say

B. we can talk about those things that are real or imagined

C. there is no necessary relation between symbol and meaning

D. we can understand any new sentences

4) Which of the following is NOT a design feature of language?

A. Cultural transmission.

B. Displacement.

C. Duality.

D. Consistency.

5) Which of the following is NOT a principle for linguistic study?

A. Productivity.

B. Objectivity.

C. Economy.

D. Exhaustiveness.

6) ________ is the branch of linguistics which studies language in actual use.

A. Syntax

B. Pragmatics

C. Morphology

D. Semantics

7) Which of the following words can prove that language is not completely arbitrary?

A. Dog.

B. Black.

C. Board.

D. Blackboard.

8) Linguistics is the study of ________.

A. the English language

B. the Chinese language

C. all languages

D. the linguist's native language

9) As a principle for linguistic study, "economy" means that a linguist should ________.

A. use the shortest possible statements to fully explain all facts involved

B. spend little time in his study because language changes quickly

C. only study language as an abstract system

D. only study the spoken form of language

10) According to Chomsky, "competence" refers to ________.

A. the linguist's ability to describe language rules

B. the linguist's ability to analyze language data

C. the ideal language user's knowledge of the rules of his language

D. the ideal language user's ability to use his language

5. Answer the following questions.

1) What is meant by "duality"?

2) What makes linguistics a science?

3) What is the difference between langue and parole?

Chapter 2 Phonetics

2.1 Study of speech sounds

Knowledge of a language includes that of the different components of the language: the morphemes, words, phrases, and sentences. It also includes knowing what sounds are in the language and how these sounds are put together to form meaningful units.

Different terms can be found in describing the sound system of language. Traditional terminology puts phonetics and phonology at a paralleled level. In this terminology, phonetics is the study of separate speech sounds, while phonology is concerned with the system of combination of sounds. According to the terminology in some books, however, the study of speech sounds in a general way is termed as phonology. It is concerned with all the aspects of the speech sounds and sound system of a language. Its subdivisions are phonetics and phonemics. Phonetics deals with speech sounds in isolation, and phonemics studies the system of speech sounds.

To avoid confusion, the traditional terminology is adopted in this book. Chapter 2 discusses phonetics and Chapter 3 mainly deals with phonology.

2.2 Definition of phonetics

2.2.1 Analysis of speech sounds

The study of phonic medium of language in isolation is the level of phonetics, attempting to describe all the sounds that occur in human language. It's mainly concerned with the production, transmission, and perception of the speech sounds.

Analysis of speech sounds can be approached from the following 4 levels.

Level 1: anatomy and physiology—referrs to speech organs and their functions

Level 2: articulatory phonetics—studies how to produce speech sounds

Level 3: auditory phonetics—studies how the sounds are perceived by the hearer

Level 4: acoustic phonetics—studies the way speech sounds are transmitted in the air (using spectrographs, analyze sound waves)

2.2.2 Process of speech production and perception

Suppose a speech sound is produced by Person A, employing his sufficient speech organs. It will be transmitted in the air (or in water) and then reaches the ear of Person B, the hearer, who will try to perceive the sound. Involved in the process are the following three steps:

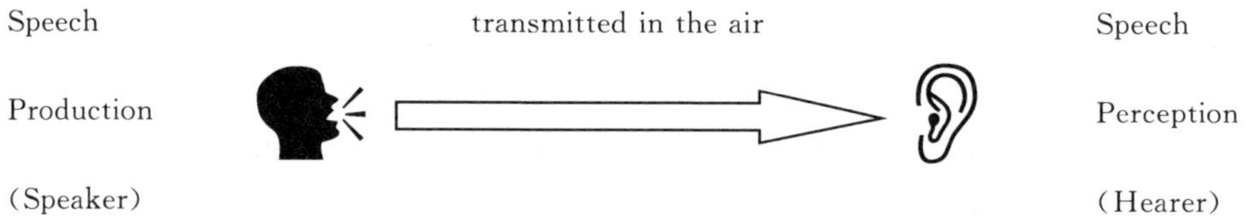

Diagram 2-1 The process of speech production and perception

Accordingly, the study of speech sounds is divided into three main areas, each dealing with one part of the process:

Articulatory phonetics studies the sounds from the speaker's point of view, i. e. , how a speaker manipulates his speech organs to produce speech sounds. This branch is the longest established and the most highly developed, and is also the primary concern of language learners and educators, since it is the most closely related to language learning and teaching.

Auditory phonetics studies the way listeners perceive the speech sounds. Research in this area is much concerned with the psychological and cognitive faculties of the hearer.

Acoustic phonetics studies the way sounds travel by looking at the sound waves (by using spectrographs), the physical properties of sounds in the process of its transmission through the air from the speaker to the hearer.

2.3 Speech organs

Speech organs, or vocal organs, are those parts of the body involved in the production of speech. The articulatory apparatus of human beings consists of three important areas or cavities.

The pharyngeal cavity—the throat. It contains the vocal cords—two membranes which can open and close. The opening through the vocal cords is called the glottis and is located in the larynx—"voice box". The tube through which the air coming from the lungs travels in the throat is called the pharynx.

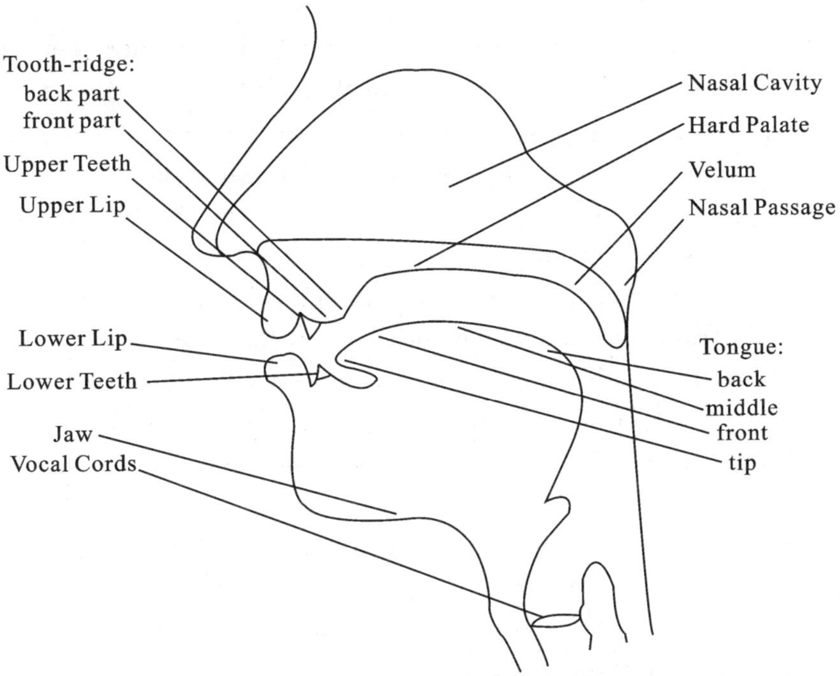

Diagram 2-2 The organs of speech

The oral cavity—the mouth. The greatest modification of the air stream takes place in the oral cavity. It contains such main places as the back, the front, and the blade of the tongue, and the extreme front—the tip of the tongue, the uvula, the soft palate (the velum), the hard palate, the teeth ridge(the alveolus), the teeth and the lips.

The nasal cavity—the nose. The nasal cavity is connected with the oral cavity. The velum, the soft part of the mouth, like a switch, can be drawn back to close the passage so that all air existing from the lungs can go through the mouth. Sounds produced in this manner are oral sounds. In contrast, if the passage is left open to allow air to pass through the nose, nasal sounds are produced. There are three nasal sounds in English: [m] [n] [ŋ].

2.4 Production of a sound

Speech sounds are produced with an air stream as their energy. The air stream starts from the lung, and then it goes upward through the windpipes. Sounds that are produced in this way are called pulmonic sounds, and since the air is pushed out, they are called egressive. Most sounds used in languages in the world are produced by a pulmonic egressive air stream mechanism, and all the sounds in English are articulated in this manner.

The first pass that the air stream goes through is the larynx, in which can be found the vocal cords, two thin membranes that can be closed and opened. When the vocal cords are apart, the air can pass through easily and the sounds produced is said to be VOICELESS. Consonants [p], [s] are produced in this way. When the cords are close together, the air stream causes them to vibrate against each other and so the VOICED sounds are made. When the vocal cords are totally closed, no air can pass between them. The result is the articulation of the glottal stop [ʔ](as in *button*).

The next pass that the air stream goes through is the glottis in the larynx. Together with the velar, it may switch the air into the oral cavity, thus making the oral sounds, or into the nasal cavity, producing the nasals.

The oral cavity contains uvular, tongue (back, blade, tip), palate (hard, soft), alveolar (or teeth ridge), teeth, lips.

2.5 Transcription of speech sounds

Speech sounds can be written down in a systematic and consistent way—phonetic transcription by using letter-symbols. It serves as an aid not only to phonetic study but also to language learning and teaching.

In the earliest stage of English, the sound was strictly consistent with the form, that is, the speech was represented much more faithfully than it is today, observing the rule of one letter one sound. With the development of the language, more and more differences have occurred between the two. The result is that a sound may be represented by different forms. For example, the sound [iː] may be represented by **e**, **ie**, **ae**, **ee**, **eo**, **ei**, **ea** as in the sentence:

Ex. 2-1 Did h**e** bel**ie**ve that C**ae**sar could s**ee** the p**eo**ple s**ei**ze the s**ea**s?

Because of the discrepancies of the letters from the actual sounds, it is necessary to establish a set of symbols to accurately represent the sounds for language teaching and learning and for the academic study of phonetics.

1. International Phonetic Alphabet (IPA)

In order to record the sounds in speech some symbols are created and agreed upon in linguistics. Until present, many systems of phonetic transcription have been invented. One of these systems is the **International Phonetic Alphabet (IPA)**—a standard and internationally accepted system of phonetic transcription. The main principles settled when the system was made were that there should be a separate letter for each distinctive sound, and that the same symbol should be used for the sound in any language in which it appears. Most IPA symbols are borrowed from the English alphabet, such as [b] [p] [d] [t] [f] [v]. Some are variations of alphabet letters, such as [ɔ], which is a reversed *c*; and [ŋ] is a combination of *n* and *g*; and [ʃ] is an elongated form of *s*. There are a few from other languages, such as [θ] from the Greek alphabet.

Table 2-1 International Phonetic Alphabet (IPA)

International Phonetic Alphabet (IPA) ˌɪntə ˈnæʃnəl fə ˈnɛt ɪk ˈælfəˌbɛt

Consonants

	Bilabial	Labiodental	Dental	Alveolar	Postalveolar	Retroflex	Palatal	Velar	Uvular	Pharyngeal	Glotal
Plosive	p b			t d		ʈ ɖ	c ɟ	k g	q ɢ		ʔ
Nasal	m	ɱ		n		ɳ	ɲ	ŋ	ɴ		
Trill	ʙ			r					R		
Tap or flap				ɾ		ɽ					
Fricative	ɸ β	f v	θ ð	s z	ʃ ʒ	ʂ ʐ	ç ʝ	x ɣ	χ ʁ	ħ ʕ	h ɦ
Lateral Fricative				ɬ ɮ							
Approximant		ʋ		ɹ		ɻ	j	ɰ			
Lateral approximant				l		ɭ	ʎ	ʟ			
Ejective stop	p'			t'		ʈ'	c'	k'	q'		
Implosive	ɓ̥ ɓ			ɗ̥ ɗ			ʄ̊ ʄ	ɠ̊ ɠ	ʛ̥ ʛ		

Diacritics Diacritics may be placed above a symbol with a descender, e. g. ŋ̊

̥ Voiceless	n̥ d̥	̤ Breathy voiced	b̤ a̤	̪ Dental	t̪ d̪
̬ Voiced	s̬ t̬	̰ Creaky voiced	b̰ a̰	̺ Apical	t̺ d̺
ʰ Aspirated	tʰ dʰ	̼ Linguolabial	t̼ d̼	̻ Laminal	t̻ d̻
̹ More rounded	ɔ̹	ʷ Labializde	tʷ dʷ	̃ Nasalized	ẽ
̜ Less rounded	ɔ̜	ʲ Palatalized	tʲ dʲ	ⁿ Nasal release	dⁿ
̟ Advanced	u̟	ˠ Velarized	tˠ dˠ	ˡ Lateral release	dˡ
̠ Retracted	i̠	ˤ Pharyngealized	tˤ dˤ	̚ No audible release	d̚
̈ Centralized	ë	̴ Velarized or pharynqealizde ɫ			
̽ Mid-centralized	e̽	̝ Raised e̝ (ɹ̝ voiced alveolar fricative)			
̩ Syllabic	ɹ̩	̞ Lowered e̞ (β̞ voiced bilabial approximant)			
̯ Non-syllabic	e̯	̘ Advanced Tongue Root e̘			
˞ Rhoticity	ə˞	̙ Retracted Tongue Root e̙			

Where symbols appear in pairs, the one on the right represents a voiced consonant, while the one on the left is unvoiced. Shaded areas denote articulations judged to be impossible.

Non pulmonic consonants

Clicks	Voiced implosives	Ejectives
ʘ Bilabial	ɓ Bilabial	ʼ as in:
ǀ Dental	ɗ Dental/alveolar	pʼ Bilabial
ǃ (Post)alveolar	ʄ Palatal	tʼ Dental/alveolar
ǂ Palatoalveolar	ɠ Velar	kʼ Velar
ǁ Alveolar lateral	ʛ Uvular	sʼ Alveolar fricative

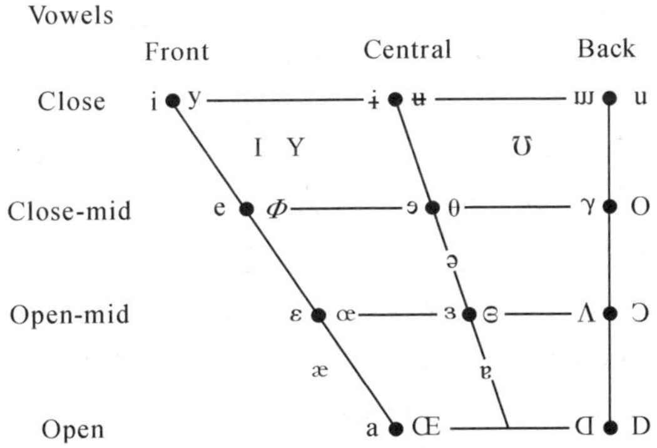

Where symbols appear in pairs, the one on the right represents a rounded vowel.

Other symbols

ʍ Voiceless labial-velar fricative

w Voiced labial-velar approximant

ɥ Voiced labial-palatal approximant

ʜ Voiceless epiglottal fricative

ʢ Voiced epiglottal fricative

ʡ Epiglottal plosive

ɕ ʑ alveolo-palatal fricatives

ɺ alveolar lateral flap

ɧ simultaneous ʃ and x

Affricatives and double articulations can be represented by two symbols joined by a tie bar if necessary: k͡p t͡s

2. Revised phonetic alphabet

The original IPA phonetic alphabet, made by the International phonetic Association in 1888(胡壮麟等,2002), was the primary one used all over the world by phoneticians, language teachers, speech pathologists and linguists. In 1989, about 120 members of the association met to work on revisions. The phonetic alphabet system used today is mostly from the revised version. The differences in the phonetic system can be found in British English and American English, and in textbooks and dictionaries published in different countries.

The following is a system used in the English Chinese dictionary (上海译文出版社, 1989) and also popularly used in many other dictionaries and teaching textbooks available in China.

Table 2-2 English vowels (monophthongs and diphthongs)

i: beat	i bit	e bet	æ bat	ə another	ɜ: burn
u: moon	ʊ put	ɔ: sword	ɒ lot	ɑ: car	ʌ but
ei say	ai buy	ɔi boy	əu so	aʊ noāw	iə peer
eə pair	ʊə poor				

Table 2-3 English consonants

p pill	b ball	t till	d desk	k kiss	g gap
m member	n name	ŋ ring	f feel	v veal	s so
z zoo	θ thin	ð thy	ʃ shy	ʒ measure	tʃ chain
dʒ Jill	l letter	r reef	w wait	j yard	

Speakers of different dialects pronounce some words differently from those of other speakers. Differences of speech sounds between American English and British English are evident in the phonetic alphabet. For example, in the following chart of phonetic alphabet for American English (Fronkin and Robert, *An Introduction to Language*, 1998), some symbols are different from those of IPA.

Table 2-4 Vowels of American English

i beet	I bit	e bait	ε bet	u boot	U foot
o boat	ɔ bore	æ bat	ʌ butt	ɒ pot/bar	aj site
ə sofa	ɔj boy	aw/æw bout			

Table 2-5 Consonants of American English

p pill	b ball	t till	d desk	k kiss	g gap
m member	n name	ŋ ring	f feel	v veal	s so
z zoo	θ thigh	ð thy	ʃ/š shy	ʒ/ž measure	č chain
ǰ Jill	l letter	r reef	w wait	ʍ which	j yard

3. Broad transcription and narrow transcription

In addition to the basic phonetic symbols, linguists often use supplementary marks to show slight variations in articulation. For example, two dots as in [u:]

indicate length; a very small *h* following the symbol indicates aspiration, that is, uttering the second with a slight puff of air, like [p^h] as in [p^hit] (pit). This set of symbols is called diacritics, which can be added to the letter-symbols to make finer distinctions than the letters alone make possible.

Accordingly there are two ways available to transcribe speech sounds. The phonetic transcription with diacritics to show the exact quality of the sounds is called **narrow transcription.** The other way is called **broad transcription**, with each symbol to represent a phoneme (check Chapter 3 for phoneme). Broad transcription is more practical and suitable for teaching the pronunciation of a foreign language and is generally used in dictionaries and textbooks, while the narrow transcription is often used by the phoneticians in their study of speech sounds. The diacritics can faithfully represent as much of the fine details as it is necessary for their purpose.

2.6 Classification of English speech sounds

The sounds of all languages can be put into two major natural classes—consonants and vowels, and English is no exception. The distinction between vowels and consonants lies in the obstruction of the air stream. Consonantal sounds are produced with some restriction or closure in the vocal tract as the air travels through the glottis out of the mouth, while vowels are produced with the air stream passing freely in the windpipe and out of the mouth.

Speech sounds { Vowels (with no obstruction through the speech organs)
Consonants (with obstruction through the speech organs)

2.6.1 Classification of English consonants

One important task of phonetics is to classify consonants. There are two major criteria in the description of English consonants: places of articulation and manners of articulation.

1. Places of articulation

Different consonantal sounds result when we change the shape of the oral cavity by moving the lips and tongue, the articulators, and the place of articulation in the oral cavity.

Bilabials: [p] [b] [m] [w] Bilabials are produced by bringing both lips together.

Labiodentals: [f] [v] These sounds are articulated by touching the bottom lip to the upper teeth, as in *fine* and *vine*.

Dental/Interdentals: [θ] [ð] These sounds are produced by inserting the tip of tongue between the upper and lower teeth. Examples are *thin* and *then*.

Alveolars: [t] [d] [s] [z] [n] [l] [r] Alveolar sounds are articulated by raising the front part of the tongue to the alveolar ridge. We can feel our tongue touch or almost touch the bony tooth ridge as we produce these sounds. The initial sounds in the following words are examples of alveolars: *two*, *do*, *so*, *zoo*, *now*, *lot*, and *rat*.

To produce the **lateral** [l], we raise the tongue to the alveolar ridge with the sides of the tongue down, permitting the air to escape laterally over the sides of the tongue.

The sound [r] can be produced by curling the tip of the tongue back behind the alveolar ridge. It is also called a **retroflex** sound. In some languages, it becomes a **thrill**, as in Russia when people produce this sound by vibrating the tip of the tongue against the roof of the mouth. And French speakers vibrate the uvular to articulate this sound as in the word *rouge*.

Palatals: [ʃ] [ʒ] [tʃ] [dʒ] [j] When we produce palatals we raise the front part of the tongue to a point on the hard palate just behind the alveolar ridge, as the sounds that begin or end the following words: *shy*, *pleasure*, *church*, *judge*, *yes*. Many Chinese learners cannot distinguish [ʒ] from [j] in their real language practice. For example, they often pronounce usual wrongly as [ˈju:juə:l] rather than [ˈju:ʒuə:l].

Velars: [k] [g] [ŋ] This class of sounds is produced by raising the back of the tongue to the soft palate or velum. The initial and final sounds of the words *kick*, *gun*, *back*, *bag* and *bang* are produced in this way.

Glottal: [h] When this sound is produced, the glottis is open, and no other modification of the air stream mechanisms occur in the mouth. The tongue and lips are usually in the position for the production of the following vowel as the air stream passes through the open glottis. Such sounds as those starting the following words are glottal sounds *house*, *high* and *who*.

2. Manners of articulation

Places of articulation are very important features in the description of consonants. But they are not sufficient in distinguishing the members of each group, for example, in distinguishing [p] from [b], or [b] from [m], which are all bilabial sounds. We need to differentiate consonants by the way the air stream is affected as it travels from the lungs up and out of the mouth and nose: by manners of articulation.

Voiced (voicing) and voiceless sounds

When the vocal cords are apart when the air stream passes, the air is not obstructed at the glottis and it travels freely into the supraglottal cavities (the parts of the vocal tract above the glottis). The sounds produced in this way are voiceless sounds.

If the vocal cords are together, the air stream forces its way through and causes them to vibrate. Such sounds are voiced.

Aspirated and unaspirated sounds

In our discussion of the voiceless bilabial stop [p], we do not distinguish the initial sound in the word *pit* from the second sound in the word *spit*. There is, actually, a phonetic difference in these voiceless stops. When we produce voiceless sounds the glottis is open and the air passes freely through the opening between the vocal cords. For example, when we produce the word *pit*, there is a brief period of voicelessness immediately after the sound [p] is released. Such sounds are called **aspirated** because an extra puff is produced. When we produce the sound [p] in *spit*, however, the vocal cords begin vibrating as soon as the lips are open. Such sounds are called **unaspirated.**

Stops (plosives): [p] [b] [t] [d] [k] [g] [m] [n] [ŋ] The production of stops involve complete closure of the articulation, so that the air stream, after entering the oral cavity for a brief period, may be completely stopped. [p] [b] [t] [d] [k] [g] are oral stops because the air stream goes through the oral cavity and the nasal cavity is closed. On the contrary, if the air is stopped in the oral cavity but the soft palate is down so that it can go out through the nasal cavity, the sound produced is a nasal stop. [m] [n] [ŋ] are nasal stops, which are often called nasals by phoneticians.

Fricatives: [f] [v] [s] [z] [θ] [ð] [ʃ] [ʒ] Fricatives are made by narrowing the air passage at some point in the mouth so that the air rushes out to cause a slight friction or rubbing.

Affricates: [tʃ] [dʒ] They are produced by a stop closure followed immediately by a slow release of the closure characteristic of a fricative.

Liquids: [l]—**lateral sound** [r]—**retroflex** In the production of the sounds [l] and [r], there is some obstruction of the air stream in the mouth, but not enough to cause any real obstruction or frication. These sounds are called liquids. [l] is called a lateral liquid because in the production of this sound, the surface of the tongue, instead of being more or less flat, is made slightly convex and causes stoppage in the centre of the roof of the mouth while allowing air to pass at the side. In the production of the other liquid [r], the tip of the tongue is curled back and the air passes over it. It is also called **retroflex.**

Glides: [w] [j] These two sounds are produced with little or no obstruction of the air stream in the mouth. The tongue moves rapidly in gliding fashion either toward or away from a neighbouring vowel, hence the term **glide.** Glides are transition sounds that are sometimes called semivowels, since they are formed in the same manner as the vowels [i] and [u], with a narrower passage between the tongue and the hard palate or between the lips.

3. Description of consonants

When we describe or name a consonant in English we check the following three criteria:

1) Vibration of vocal cords-voiced or voiceless

2) Places of articulation

3) Manners of articulation

In Table 6 all the consonants of English are presented in these three criteria.

Table 2-6 Classification of English consonants

(Source: Fronkin et all, 2003)

	Bilabial	Labiodental	Dental	Alveolar	Palatal	Velar	Glottal
Stops(oral)							
Voiceless	p			t		k	
Voiced	b			d		g	
Nasals(stops)	m			n		ŋ	
Fricatives							
Voiceless		f	θ	s	ʃ		h
Voiced		v	ð	z	ʒ		
Affricates							
Voiceless					tʃ		
Voiced					dʒ		
Glides							
Voiced	w				j		
Liquids				l r			

2.6.2 Classification of vowels

Vowels are more difficult to describe or classify than consonants because they are produced without any articulators touching or even coming very close to the points of articulation. The quality of a vowel is determined by the particular configuration of the vocal tract when the vowel is produced. The articulation of vowels has much to do with the two articulatory organs: the tongue and lips. Different parts of the tongue may be raised or lowered. The lips may be spread or pursed. Therefore, the criteria according to which vowels are classified are mostly connected with the position of the tongue and the shape of the lips.

1. Tongue position

The tongue may be put in different parts of the mouth: front, centre, back, hence the three classes of vowels:

Front vowels: [iː] [i] [e] [æ]

Central vowels: [ə] [ɜː] [ʌ]

Back vowels: [uː] [ʊ] [ɔː] [ɔ] [ɑː]

2. Shape of the lips

Vowels also differ as to whether the lips are rounded or unrounded. In English all the front vowels and the central vowels are unrounded vowels, i. e. , without rounding the lips, and all the back vowels except [ɑː] are rounded.

3. Openness of the mouth

According to how wide our mouth is opened, we can classify English vowels into four groups:

Close vowels: [iː] [i] [ʊ]

Semi-close vowels: [e] [ɜː]

Semi-open vowels: [ə] [ɔː]

Open vowels: [æ] [ɒ] [ʌ] [ɑː]

4. Monophthongs and diphthongs

Monophthongs are simple vowel sounds. A monophthong has an unchanged quality. When we produce a monophthong, the articulatory organs do not move. There are twelve monophthongs in English. Many languages, including English, have vowels called diphthongs which are produced as a sequence of two sounds, vowel + glide. The organs involved must move from one position to another. Usually, the first element is long and clear, and the second one is short, weak and unclear. There are eight diphthongs in English.

Monophthongs: [iː] [i] [e] [æ] [ə] [ɜː] [ʌ] [uː] [ʊ] [ɔː] [ɔ] [ɑː]

Diphthongs: [ei] [ai] [ɔi] [əu] [aʊ] [iə] [eə] [ʊə]

5. Length of the vowels

Vowels are also classified according to duration or length of articulation. Long vowels are distinguished by two dots: [iː] [ɜː] [ɔː] [ɑː].

6. Tense vowels and lax vowels

Tense vowels are produced with greater tension of the tongue muscles than the lax ones and are often somewhat longer in duration. Long vowels are tense vowels while short vowels are lax vowels.

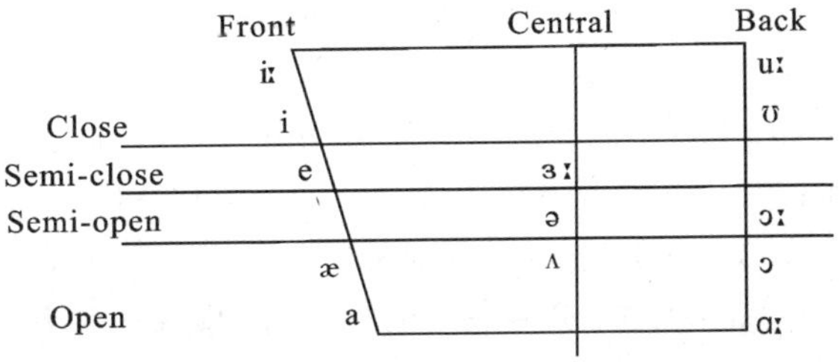

Diagram 2-3 Classification of English vowels

Exercises

1. Fill in the blanks with the most suitable words. Each blank represents ONE word.

1) ________ and ________ are the two major media used by natural languages for communication.

2) Phonetics is the study of phonic medium of language, i. e. , the study of the ________, ________ and ________ of speech sounds.

3) Phonetics studies speech sounds from three different angles. Accordingly, it can be further classified into three sub-branches: ________ phonetics, ________ phonetics and ________ phonetics.

4) The speech organs are contained in three important areas or cavities: the ________, the ________ and the ________.

5) There are two ways to transcribe speech sounds. One is ________ transcription; the other is ________ transcription.

6) ________ are sounds produced by some form of obstruction of the air stream and may be either voiced or voiceless.

7) For ________ consonants, the obstruction takes place between the lower lip and the upper teeth.

8) ________ consonants are made by completely shutting up the air passage at some points in the mouth and lowering the soft palate to let the air go out through the nose.

9) ________ vowels are made by raising the back of the tongue towards the soft palate.

10) ________ are produced by moving from one vowel position to another.

2. Decide whether the following statements are true or false.

1) Phonetics also studies the sound of one's cough.

2) Phonetics is concerned with all the sounds that occur in the world's languages.

3) The branch of phonetics which studies the perception of speech sounds is called acoustic phonetics.

4) The lungs are the power organ of speech.

5) When the vocal cords are held tightly, there is only a narrow passage between them. This is the position when one is breathing normally.

6) All vowels and no consonants are produced with the vibration of vocal cords.

7) Glottal stop occurs in the English language.

8) The English spoken sounds, like the sounds of any other language, are generally divided into two main classes: vowels and consonants.

9) Semi-vowels are not vowels.

10) The International Phonetic Alphabet is the only way to transcribe speech sounds.

3. Answer the following questions.

1) What is the scope of phonetics?

2) What is phonetic transcription?

3) How do we classify the English consonants according to the place of articulation?

4) How do we classify the English consonants according to the manner of articulation?

5) How do we classify the English vowels according to the position of the tongue?

6) How do we classify English vowels?

Chapter 3 Phonology

3.1 Phonetics and phonology

Before discussing the principles of phonology, it is necessary to make a clear distinction of the terms in question. Phonetics and phonology, with the same root *phono-*, which means *sound*, are both related to the study of speech sounds, but they have different focus and approach to the subject. Phonetics is of a general nature; it studies all the speech sounds used in all human languages, dealing with the characteristics of speech sounds and providing methods for their description, classification and transcription. Phonology is the general knowledge of speech sounds of a language, concerned with the linguistic patterning of sounds in human languages, with its primary aim being to discover the principles that govern the way sounds are organized in languages, and to explain the variations that occur.

Phonology is concerned with the system of sounds of a particular language. What applies to one language may not apply to another. Ways of combining speech sounds can be different across languages. With sufficient phonological knowledge of a certain language, a speaker is able to produce sounds that form meaningful utterances, to recognize a foreign accent, to make up new words, to add the appropriate phonetic segments to form plurals and past tenses, to produce aspirated and unaspirated voiceless stops in the appropriate context, to know what is or is not a sound in one's language.

3.2 Phone, phoneme and allophone

1. Phone

When people talk, their vocal tract produces continuous sounds which form words, phrases, sentences, and so on and forth. To analyze and describe speech sounds it is necessary to know what an individual sound is and how each sound differs from all others. The first task is, of course, to segment the speech utterance into individual units. And these segmental units of speech are the phones of the language.

A **phone** is a phonic unit or segment. Phones are the actual sounds we produce. For example, the utterance "Good morning!" consists of the following individual phones: [g], [u], [d], [m], [ɔː], [n], [i], [ŋ].

2. Phoneme

As discussed in earlier chapters, knowing a word means knowing both its form (its sound) and its meaning. Most of the words in a language differ both in form and meaning, sometimes just by one sound. We can change one word into another simply by changing one sound. Consider the following English words: *pit—bit*, *light—night*, *bit—bat*.

Each word differs from the other in the pair in both form and meaning. The difference between *pit* and *bit* is shown by the fact that the initial sound of the first word is [p] and the initial sound of the second word is [b]. So the two words are identical except for the initial consonant sound. [p] and [b] can therefore distinguish or contrast words. They are distinctive sounds in English. Such sounds that are of distinctive value are called phonemes.

We can see from the contrast between *light* and *night* and between *bit* and *bat* that [l], [n], [i] and [æ] must also be phonemes in English for the same reason—substituting [l] for [n] or [i] for [æ] results in a different word, a different form with a different meaning.

A **phoneme** is the smallest unit of sound that can distinguish meaning in a language. It is not a physical sound that can be pronounced but rather an abstract unit. It is a collection of distinctive phonetic features. Phonemes are usually put between two slashes: /p/, /b/, /i/, /e/.

3. Allophone

Phonemes are abstract units and cannot be read out. Its realization in certain phonetic environments results in allophones, variants of the phoneme. An allophone is therefore a predictable phonetic variant of a phoneme. In English, each vowel phoneme has both an oral and a nasalized allophone. Allophones are put between two square brackets: [p] [p^h], [t][t^h], [k] [k^h].

Allophones are variants of the same phoneme. The choice of allophone is rule-governed. Its occurrence is restricted by the neighbouring sounds. Allophones of one phoneme never occur in the same context. For example, the bilabial stop /p/ may have at least two variants [$p^=$] and [p^h]. [$p^=$] occurs after [s] while [p^h] always occurs in some other places. We can represent this rule as:

/p/⟶[$p^=$] in [s_] ("[s_]" is the environment in which /p/ appears.)

[p^h] elsewhere

Another example is the phoneme /l/. This sound is pronounced differently in *lead* and *deal*, where in the second case the tongue is curled a little backwards towards the hard palate (palatarization). We often call this a "dark l" and use the symbol [ɫ], and [l] as in *lead*, is called "clear l". The rule for this variation is: the phoneme /l/ is pronounced as [l] before a vowel and as [ɫ] after a vowel. They can be represented as:

/l/⟶[l] in [_V]

[ɫ] in [V_]

3.3 Distinctive features

A native speaker of English can tell by intuition that the following sound combinations all carry different meanings: [men] [ten] [ben] [ken]. This is because they all contain a different phoneme. The features that a phoneme possesses, making it different from other phonemes, are its **distinctive features.** The importance of phonology can be seen by the fact that one can change one word into another simply by changing one sound.

Distinctive features are language-specific. What distinguishes meaning in one language does not necessarily do so in another language. For example, aspiration does not distinguish meaning in English, so it is not a distinctive feature in English. But it can be a distinctive feature in Chinese. The difference between "ba" (爸) and "pa"（怕）is caused by the feature of aspiration.

Many distinctive features are binary features, that is, we can group them in two categories: one with this feature (denoted by +) and the other without (denoted by −). For example,

	p	b	m
Stop	+	+	+
Labial	+	+	+
Voiced	−	+	+
Nasal	−	−	+

3.4 Minimal pairs

If two words are identical in form except for one sound segment that occurs in the same place in the string, they form a **minimal pair**, for example, *fine* vs. *vine*; *crick* vs. *creek*, *bowl* vs. *dole*; *lobe* vs. *load*; *thigh* vs. *thy*. The substitution of one sound for the other makes a different word. *Seed* [siːd] and *soup* [suːp] are not a minimal pair because they differ in two sounds, the vowel and the final consonants. The definition of minimal pairs is of important value for linguists, because it helps them to decide whether a sound is an independent phoneme or just an allophone of some phoneme. There are many minimal pairs in English, which makes it relatively easy to determine what the English phonemes are.

For the following group of words—*beat*, *bit*, *bait*, *bet*, *bat*, substituting one central vowel for another changes both the phonetic form and meaning. These words form a minimal set.

3.5 Complementary distribution

If two or more phones never occur in the same phonological context, they are in **complementary distribution**. Allophones of one phoneme are usually in complementary distribution. In English the velar nasal /ŋ/ and the glottal glide /h/ are in complementary distribution; /ŋ/ is not found in a word initially and /h/ does not occur in a word finally.

3.6 Phonological rules

The phonological system determines which phonemes can begin a word, end a word, and follow each other. If we are asked to arrange the following sounds k, i, b, l, results may be [lbki], [ilbk], [bkil],[ilkb],[blik],[klib],[kilb]. The first four are not possible words in English, because they violate the rule of arranging sounds in English.

Furthermore, phonological rules also suggest possible changes to sounds when they become neighbours.

1. Sequential rules

The rules that govern the combination of sounds in a particular language are called **sequential rules.** They decide which sounds can go with each other. One of the sequential rules in English concerns consonant cluster.

If three consonants should cluster together at the beginning of a word, the combination should obey the following rules:

1) The first phoneme must be /s/.

2) The second phoneme must be /p/ or /t/ or /k/.

3) The third phoneme must be /l/ or /r/ or /w/.

Words like *spring*, *strict*, *square*, *splendid*, *scream* are typical examples of sequential rules.

Another familiar sequential rule in English says that affricates [tʃ] and [dʒ] and the sibilants [s], [z], [ʃ], [ʒ] are not to be followed by another sibilant. This explains why sometimes we add -s to a noun to form plurals and to a verb infinite to form the third personal singular, but sometimes we have to add -es to some words in this use. Hence: *teach—teaches*, *ooze—oozes*, *kiss—kisses*, but *stomach—stomachs*.

2. Assimilation rules

The **assimilation rule** assimilates one segment to another by "copying" or "spreading" a feature of a sequential phoneme on to its neighbouring segment, thus making the two phones more similar. Assimilation rules are mostly caused by articulatory or physiological process. Speakers tend to make articulation easier, or make it easier to move the articulators.

For example, according to nasalization rule, a vowel becomes or is nasalized in the environment before a nasal segment, for example, *bomb* [bām]. We can use a formula to show the changes:

V ⟶ [+nasal] / __ [+nasal]

The following are two more assimilation rules:

Dentalization rule: [− dental] ⟶ [+ dental] / __ [+ dental] A sound becomes a dental if it occurs before a dental. C. f. *tent* [tent] vs. *tenth* [tenθ]

Velarization rule: [−velar] ⟶ [+velar] / __ [+velar] A sound becomes a velar if it occurs before a velar. C. f. *since* [sins] vs. *sink* [siŋk]

More examples of sound assimilation: the alveolar prefix in- may become different sounds in *indiscrete*, *incorrect*, *impossible*, *irregular*, *illegal*.

3. Deletion rule

Another phonological rule deals with the deletion of segments in certain sound strings. Sometimes a sound is deleted although it is orthographically represented. For example in *gnostic*, *sign*, *design*, and *paradigm*, there is no [g] sound although it is represented in spelling by the letter g. The rule can be stated as:

Delete a /g/ when it occurs in a word initially before a nasal consonant (as in *gnostic*) or before a word-final consonant (as in *sign*, *design*, and *paradigm*).

The phoneme /g/, however, will be regained in the corresponding forms of the above words: *signature*, *designation*, and *paradigmatic*.

3.7 Suprasegmental features

It is self-evident that phoneme can distinguish meanings, and that the replacement of one segment for another in a word may change it into a totally different word. But many significant differences in meaning may be caused by some other factors than phonemes. These distinctive features may be in evidence running over a sequence of two or more phoneme segments. The phonemic features that occur above the level of the segments are called **suprasegmental features**, which mainly include pitch, stress, tone and intonation.

3.7.1 Stress

Stress is the degree of emphasis or accent given to some syllables in relation to others. The stressed syllable receives more force in articulation than the unstressed ones. There are two kinds of stress in English: word stress and sentence stress.

1. Word stress

If a word contains two or more syllables, one of the syllables receives more force or energy of articulation. This is called **word stress.** Some languages have regular word stress, that is, the stress always falls on a certain syllable. For example, in French, the word stress unexceptionally falls on the last syllable. In English, the word stress may fall on any syllable.

Stress in English is phonemic, that is to say, it distinguishes meaning. The same word form, if read with different stresses, results in a difference in meaning or grammatical functions. For example, if the word *bluepencil* is read as [ˈbluːˈpensil], it is a verb, meaning "to cross out anything not suitable from a piece of writing", while it is a noun, meaning a pencil in blue color if it is read as [bluːˈpensil]. This can be exemplified by more words: *ˈabstract adj.* —*abˈstract v.*, *ˈcombine n.* —*comˈbine v.*, *ˈcontract n.* —*conˈtract v.*, *ˈcontrast n.* —*conˈtrast v.*, *ˈdesert n.* —*deˈsert v.*, *ˈexport n.* —*exˈport v.*, *ˈimport n.* —*imˈport v.*, *ˈinsult n.* —*inˈsult v.*, *ˈobject n.* —*obˈject v.*, *ˈpresent n. adj.* —*preˈsent v.* (For convenience, the symbol ˈ is used directly to show where the stress falls on the word)

Sometimes word stress helps to distinguish a compound from a phrase in English. For compounds, the first element is stressed, while for phrases, the stress falls on the second element. For example, *ˈblack bird* is a compound noun, referring to a special kind of bird whose colour may not necessarily be black, but *black ˈbird* is a phrase which means a bird whose colour is black. A *hot dog* with the first element stressed is a kind of food consisting of a sausage in a bread doll, while with the second element stressed it is an overheated animal. The same difference is shown in green house. A ˈ*green house* is a building with glass roof and sides and often heated, used for growing plants which need heat, light and freedom from winds, while a ˈ*green* ˈ*house* is a house which is green in colour.

2. Sentence stress

A sentence is a sequence of words formed according to syntactic rules. The words in a sentence are not equally important in meaning. In oral presentation of a sentence, the word that receives more emphasis in the speaker's mind is to be uttered with more energy. This is where the sentence stress goes.

Sentence stress is usually determined by the notions of words in the sentence. Content words, like *car*, *green*, *slight*, *quickly*, are often stressed, while functional words, like *from*, *the*, *or*, are not to be stressed. The principle, however, is sometimes violated when the speaker stresses a functional word so as to make it sound more prominent. Some other factors may also affect the normal occurring of sentence stress. For example, rhythm in English has considerable influence upon the stress.

3.7.2 Tone

When we speak the levels of highness and lowness varies in accordance with the contents. These levels of change are called pitch. Pitch variations, phonologically referred to as contrasting tones, may be distinctive like phonemes, that is, they may become phonemic features that can distinguish meaning. In such Asian languages as Chinese and Thai, the tone has a meaning-distinctive function. These languages are called tone languages. Take Chinese as an example. It has four tones. The first tone is level (阴平), the second rise(阳平), the third fall-rise (上声), and the fourth fall (去声).

English is not a tone language, and the first obstacle facing an English native speaker when he begins to learn Chinese is the tone variation, since the same string of sounds meaning totally different things in the four tones: dā—搭, dá—达, dǎ—打, dà—大.

3.7.3 Intonation

When all the phonological features of pitch variations, stress and tones are realized at the sentence level rather than separate words, it constitutes intonation. In English syntactic differences may be shown by different intonation. There are four basic types of intonation in English, known as the four tones: the falling tone, the rising tone, the fall-rise tone, and the rise-fall tone. The four tones are not of equal importance in the conveying of the speaker's meanings. Generally speaking, the falling tone is used for confirmation, or to state a fact, often applied to declarative sentences; the rising tone is used for doubts or inquiring, suitable for questions; the fall-rise tone indicates implication; the rise-fall tone suggests hesitation in certain sense.

Consider the sentence *This is not the book he wants*. In a falling tone, this sentence just tells the fact that he does not like the book. In a rising tone, the speaker of the sentence is doubtful or uncertain about whether he likes the book or not. And in a fall-rise tone, the sentence indicates that apart from what is directly said, there is an implied message—He likes some other books.

Exercises

1. Fill in the blanks with the most suitable words. Each blank represents ONE word.
   1) Phonology studies the ________ ________ of a particular language.
   2) The speech sounds which can be used to distinguish meaning are called ________.
   3) ________ of the same phoneme are in complementary distribution.
   4) The process of producing one phoneme by "copying" the features of a neighbouring phoneme is called ________.
   5) The features above the level of basic phonemic segments are called ________ features.
   6) ________ ________ refers to the fact that a certain syllable of a word is

pronounced with greater force than other syllables.

7) ________ are pitch variations, which are caused by the differing rates of vibration of the vocal cords.

8) When pitch, stress and length of sound are tied to a sentence rather than to a word, they are collectively known as ________.

2. Decide whether the following sentences are true or false.

1) Phonology is concerned with the speech sounds which distinguish meaning.

2) Phones are speech sounds we actually produce, while phonemes are of an abstract nature.

3) Phonetics and phonology study speech sounds in the same way.

4) Phonetic knowledge enables a speaker to recognize a "foreign accent", to make up new words, to know what is and what is not a possible sound in his language.

5) The words "speak" and "peak" share a same phone.

6) Phonetically similar sounds are in "phonemic contrast" if they represent different phonemes that distinguish meaning.

7) Sequential rules are language specific.

8) English is a tone language.

9) Monosyllabic words cannot be said to have word stress.

10) Intonation can be used to distinguish meaning in English, but not in Chinese.

3. Answer the following questions.

1) How do phonetics and phonology differ from each other?

2) How is a phone different from a phoneme?

3) What is "allophone"?

4) Explain the assimilation rules in English.

5) Why do we say "stress" is a suprasegmental feature?

Chapter 4 Morphology

4.1 Definition of morphology

Morphology is a branch of linguistics which studies the internal structure of words and the rules by which words are formed. Words are not just random strings of letters, but built on the basis of some basic building units, and the construction of words is governed by rules. Morphology studies those building units and governing rules. For example, if such words as *baker*, *owner*, *customer*, *leader*, *messenger*, *prisoner*, *philosopher*, and *manufacturer* are put together, they may be found similar in some way, i. e., they all end with "-er". If analysis is made on that similarity, the following rules can be worked out:

1) They all refer to people;

2) They are all nouns;

3) They are formed by either "noun+-er" or "verb+-er".

These are the morphological rules, and they can account for the existence of a set of nouns with "-er" ending.

Ex. 4-1 a. *garden*(n.)+*er*=*gardener*(n.)

b. *London*(n.)+*er*=*Londoner*(n.)

c. *mill*(n.)+*er*=*miller*(n.)

d. *produce*(v.)+*er*=*producer*(n.)

e. *murder*(v.)+*er*=*murderer*(n.)

f. *command*(v.)+*er*=*commander*(n.)

In order to achieve a better understanding of the concept of morphology, it's beneficial to make a comparison between phonology studied in the last chapter and morphology to be examined in this chapter.

Phonology studies the sounds of a language. Morphology studies the forms of a language. There are many parallels between them, such as the terms employed in each discipline. The basic unit for the study in phonology is phoneme, while it is morpheme in morphology. Both phoneme and morpheme are abstract units, neither is used in actual speech. Phoneme is realized by phone in actual speech, and morpheme by morph. One phoneme is embodied by different phones in different situations, and those phones are called allophones. Similarly, one morpheme is embodied by different morphs, and those morphs are called allomorphs.

4.2 Classification of morphology

Morphology is generally divided into two categories: inflectional morphology and lexical morphology.

Inflectional morphology studies the expressions of grammatical inflections and grammatical meanings. **Inflection** is the manifestation of grammatical relationships through the addition of inflectional affixes. This kind of addition does not change the grammatical class of the stem. The grammatical relationships manifested by inflections are like the following: number, case, person, finiteness, time, aspect etc.

Ex. 4-2 The underlined parts in the following words indicate different grammatical relationships:

a. number: *ball*(singular)—*balls*(plural); *box*(singular)—*boxes* (plural)

b. case: *Tom*—*Tom's* (possessive); *company*—*company's*(possessive)

c. person: *play* (the first and second person in simple present tense)—*plays* (the third person singular in simple present tense)

d. finiteness: *be* (the basic form)—*am* (first person singular in simple present tense)—*is* (third person singular in simple present tense)—*was* (first person singular in simple past tense)

time: *play* (the basic form)—*played* (past time)

aspect: *do* (the basic form)—*does* (third person singular in simple present tense)—*doing* (continuous tense)—*done* (perfect tense)

Lexical morphology is also referred to as derivational morphology or word-formation. It studies the process of word formation and the signalling of lexical relationships. Word formation can be further classified into compositional type (compounding) and the derivational type (derivation).

Compounding is a way of forming new words by putting two or more free morphemes (words) together, and new words produced by compounding are called compounds. Thus, a **compound** is a lexical unit consisting of more than one free word or free morpheme and functioning both grammatically and semantically as a single word. Compounds mainly consist of three categories according to word classes: noun compounds, adjective compounds and verb compounds.

Noun compounds may be composed in the following ways:

noun+noun: *piano-keys*, *cartwheel*, *fireman*

noun+verb: *earthquake*, *rainfall*, *headache*, *nightfall*

verb+noun: *watchdog*, *push—button*, *playboy*, *call-girl*

adjective+noun: *darkroom*, *blackboard*, *blueprint*

Adjective compounds may be composed in the following ways:

noun+v-ing: *breathtaking*, *lip-sucking*, *record-breaking*

noun+v-ed: *self-employed*, *self-appointed*, *self-styled*

noun+adjective: *carsick*, *fireproof*, *tax-free*

adjective/adverb+v-ing: *easy-going*, *far-fetching*, *good-looking*

adjective/adverb+v-ed: *fresh-bred*, *dry-cleaned*, *new-laid*

Verb compounds are mainly composed by "noun+verb". For example, *house-keep*, *sleep-walk*, *sightsee*. Besides the nouns, adjectives and verbs, the prepositions, pronouns, adverbs also have compounds, e. g. *within*, *into*, *anyone*, *everybody*, *however*, *somehow*, etc.

Derivation is also known as affixation. It's a way of forming new words by adding affixes to stems or bases. The new words produced by derivation are derivatives.

The major distinction between infection and derivation lies in (1) inflection is concerned with grammatical function, while derivation with the creation of new words; (2) inflection draws morphology to syntax, while derivation to lexis.

4.3 Morpheme and allomorph

4.3.1 Morpheme

Morphemes are the smallest meaningful units of language.

A discourse may consist of paragraphs and sentences, and a sentence can be divided into words. In communication, people always base their utterances on words. It seems that words are the basic units by which people deliver their ideas and express the meanings. Are words the smallest meaningful units? Can they still be further divided to an even lower level without destroying or drastically altering the meaning? If so, what is the lowest level? Actually words are not the smallest meaningful units of language. They can still be divided into a lower level, that is, morphemes. A morpheme is the minimal unit of meaning. For instance, *book* and *books* are used at different situations though they both bear the meaning "collection of sheets of paper fastened together as a thing to be read, or to be written in", our choices are governed by a grammatical rule, *books* is to be used if a plural concept needs to be specified, and *book* is to be used when a singular concept needs to be specified. That is because the word *books* consists of two morphemes: *book* and "-s", and the "-s" here is a morpheme marking plural form to express plural meaning, and it can be used in the forming of other words, for example, *dogs*, *cats*, *persons*, *trees* and so on. From that we can see that *books*, though being a word, is not the minimal unit of meaning.

Morpheme has two kinds of meanings: lexical meaning and grammatical meaning. A morpheme may have either of them. Here lexical meaning means the semantic "content" of messages of morphemes, while grammatical meaning means the grammatical functions of morphemes. Let's look at some examples.

Ex. 4-3 The word *face* consists of only one morpheme *face*, it means "the front part of the head (forehead, eyes, nose, mouth, cheeks, chin)", that is the lexical meaning, and the morpheme *face* only has lexical meaning.

Ex. 4-4 a. *I want to go swimming*, b. *Who would you like to see?* In this example, there is the same word *to* in both sentences, *to* is a morpheme, it does not have lexical meaning, but only grammatical one, that is, an infinitive marker.

Ex. 4-5 Words like *cups*, *teaches*, *rained*, *cooking* consist of two morphemes in each of them, among them the morphemes *cup*, *teach*, *rain*, *cook* have lexical meanings, while *-s*, *-es*, *-ed*, *-ing* have grammatical meanings, the *-s* means plural, the *-es* means third person singular in simple present tense, *-ed* means past tense, *-ing* means progressive aspect. From the examples we can see a morpheme can not possess both lexical meaning and grammatical meaning at the same time. A morpheme has only one meaning.

Morphemes are units by which words are formed. Many simple words consist of only one simple morpheme.

Ex. 4-6 *man*, *cat*, *bad*, *text*, *cup* and *book*. Other words are more complex. They may contain two morphemes, three morphemes, or even more morphemes.

Ex. 4-7 *bookish* (book+-ish, two morphemes), *unfinished* (un-+finish+-ed, three morphemes), *objectivity* (ob-+ject-+ive+ity, four morphemes).

4.3.2 Morpheme and phoneme

A **morpheme** is the minimal unit of meaning, it distinguishes one meaning from another; and a phoneme is the minimal unit of sound, it distinguishes one sound from another, and they are terms used in different branches of grammar. A single phoneme may represent a single morpheme, but they are not identical. The phoneme /s/ in [luks] (looks) means the third person singular present tense morpheme, but /s/ appears frequently when it has noting to do with this specific morpheme, such as the ones used in the following examples.

Ex. 4-8 a. *books*, /buks/; b. *Mark's*, /maːks/; c. *case*, /keis/

In a the phoneme /s/ means the plural morpheme, while in b, it means possessive case, and it does not mean anything in c.

4.3.3 Allomorph

Some morphemes remain a single form in every circumstance, for example, *disc*, *walk*, *nice*, *very*, *in* and so on. Some other morphemes have variations, that is, they may change their forms in different circumstances. Those variations do not change the meaning of the morpheme, and each of them is an **allomorph** of the morpheme. Take the plural morpheme in English for example. In English the plurality may be attached to a number of morphemes to produce structures like *cat* +plural, *bus*+plural, *sheep*+plural, and *man*+plural, *tooth*+plural. Though the structures are the same "noun+plural", the actual forms of morphs indicating the "plural" morpheme may turn out to be different as shown in *cats*, *buses*, *sheep*, *men*, *teeth*. Here {-s, -es, -ø, -e, -ee} are all the **allomorphs** of the plural morpheme.

It is worthy of notice that there is a phenomenon which seems to be just the opposite of allomorph. In allomorph, one morpheme is embodied by different actual forms, that is, morphs. Sometimes, one morphemic shape represents different morphemes, that is, it can be treated as different morphemes in different context. For example, *-s* may represent plurality in *books*, possessive case in *Mark's*, third person singular in simple present tense in *laughs*, and so on.

4.3.4 Types of morphemes

In the above section, the definition of morpheme has been presented and explained. In this section, we will discuss the classification of morphemes, that is, the types of morphemes. Generally, morphemes can be classified into two types: free morpheme and bound morpheme.

1. Free morphemes

A **free morpheme** is the one that can stand by itself as a single word. A free morpheme can be an independent word.

Ex. 4-9 *tour*, *file*, *open*, *run*, *good*, *hot*, *how*, *very*, *in*, *to*. It can also be a part of a word, but the part can be extracted out as an independent word.

Ex. 4-10 *overcoat*, *roommate*, *underestimate*, *coexist*, *Microsoft*, *misprint*, *beloved*, *surface*, *internet*, *restless* and so on. Each one of these words consists of more than one morpheme, but there is at least one free morpheme in each of them. They are *over*, *coat*, *room*, *mate*, *under*, *estimate*, *exist*, *soft*, *print*, *love*, *face*, *net* and *rest*.

2. Bound morphemes

A **bound morpheme** is one that cannot normally stand alone, but is typically attached to another form. A bound morpheme appears with at least another morpheme, and they are combined together to form a word, and thus can be used independently. A bound morpheme cannot be used independently as a word. Bound morphemes such as *-es* in *boxes*, *-ful* in *colourful* and *en-* in *encourage* cannot be used as independent words. The bound morpheme *-es* has to be used together with *box* as in this example, and with countable nouns ending with *-s*, *-es*, *-ch*, *-sh* and some countable nouns ending with *-o*, such as *bus*, *tax*, *watch*, *wish* and *tomato*. The morpheme *-ful* has to be used together with other morphemes to form words like *beautiful*, *wonderful*, *roomful* and so on. The morpheme *en-* has to be used as one part in words like *enforce*, *endanger*, *encode* and so on. The word *compromise* consists of three bound morphemes: *com* (meaning "together"), *pro* (meaning "forth") and *mise* (meaning "throw").

Based on the above discussion, one generalization can be made: a word may consist of only one free morpheme, which is called a mono-morphemic word, such as *jump* and *chair*; a word may consist of two or more free morphemes and is called a compound, such as *godfather* and *sunflower*; a word may also consist of free morphemes and bound morphemes, such as *pager* and *pointed*; a word may also consist of bound morphemes only, such as *geology* and *maintain*. The last three types are called poly-morphemic words. The words of the last two types are composed of roots and affixes.

A **root** is the base form of a word that cannot be further divided without total loss of identity. In other words, it is the part of a word that remains after all affixes are moved away. It is the basic unchangeable part of a word.

A root can be either a free morpheme or a bound one. A free root morpheme is the one that can stand by itself. For example, the word *transaction* is made up of "an affix+a root+an affix", that is, *trans-*(meaning "through")+*-act-*(the root, meaning "to act")+*-ion*(an affix indicating a noun). The root *act* in this word is a free root morpheme. Most of the roots are of this kind, and theoretically speaking, the number of this type of roots is unlimited. A bound root morpheme is the one that cannot form a word by itself. It has to occur in combination with roots or affixes. For example, the word *incessant* is also made up of "an affix+a root+an affix", i.e., *in-*(meaning "not")+*-cess-*(the root, meaning "yield")+*-ant*(an affix indicating an adjective). The root *cess* in this word is a bound morpheme. The number of this type of roots is relatively fewer, such as *semi-*, *manu-*, *-ceive* and *-tain*.

A root, whether it is free or bound, generally carries the main component of meaning in the word. Look at these three words: *revive*, *vitamin*, *vivacious*. Although we may not know the meaning of every word, we can see they are similar in some way, that is, each consists of the Latin root *vit-* or *viv-*, meaning "life" or "to live", which is related to the meanings of the three words. If we consult a dictionary, we will find that is true. *Revive* means "to live again", *vitamin* means "any of a number of organic substances which are present in certain food stuffs and are essential to the health of man and other animals", and *vivacious* means "full of life; lively; high-spirited".

Affix is the collective term for the type of formatives that can be used only when added to another morpheme. Affixes, therefore, are bound morphemes. They are generally divided into two types: inflectional and derivational.

An inflectional affix or inflectional morpheme does not form a new word with new lexical meaning when it is added to another word. Nor does it change the word class of the word to which it attaches. Its major function is grammatical, i.e., to mark various grammatical relations or grammatical categories such as number, tense, degree, and case.

Ex. 4-11 a. Number: *boys*, *torches*(*-s* and *-es* indicate plurality in number)

b. Tense: *played*, *making*(*-ed* indicates past tense, *-ing* indicates progressive tense)

c. Degree: *cooler*, *likeliest*(*-er* indicates comparative degree, *-est* indicates superlative degree)

d. Case: *Tom's*, *baby's*(*-'s* indicates possessive case)

Inflectional affixes always come at the end of words in English and usually no other morpheme can be added after an inflectional morpheme.

A **derivational affix** is the one that is added to another morpheme and derives a new word. This is a frequently used way to create new words in English. For example: the underlined parts in the following words are derivational affix: *sleepy*, *national*, *distinction*, *endanger*, *dissatisfy*. This way of word formation is called derivation, and the new words formed by derivation like the above examples are called derivative. A derivative is formed by "an existing form+derivational affix". This "existing form" to which the derivational affix is attached is called stem. A stem may be a free morpheme, the combination of several free morphemes, a bound morpheme, or the combination of free morpheme and bound morpheme. *Man* in *manly*, *withdraw* in *withdrawal*, *-ment* in *comment* and *preposition* in *prepositional* are examples of stem.

The affix may appear at either the beginning or the end of a word. The affix that appears at the beginning of a word is called **prefix** and the affix that appears at the end of a words is called **suffix.**

There are more than one hundred prefixes in English and the following are some examples.

Ex. 4-12 a. *bi-*: as in words *bicycle*, *bilingual*, *bimonthly*

b. *de-*: as in words *debate*, *declare*, *deflate*

c. *en-*: as in words *encourage*, *enrich*, *envelope*

d. *pro-*: as in words *prolong*, *propose*, *prospect*

e. *sub-*: as in words *submarine*, *subway*, *submit*

f. *un-*: as in words *unconscious*, *uncomfortable*, *undefined*

The prefixes can modify the meaning of the stem, but most do not change the part of speech of the original word. Exceptions are like *a-*, *be-*, *en-* and so on. *A-* can be added to a verb and forms an adjective, as in *alive*; and it also can be added to an adjective to form an adverb, as in *anew*. *Be-* and *en-* can be added to an adjective or a noun to form a verb as in words *belittle*, *enrich*, *embody*.

The number of suffix is larger than prefix. The suffixes can be attached to a stem, and in most cases, they change the part of speech of the stem and make them a noun, an adjective, an adverb or a verb. The following are some examples.

Ex. 4-13 a. *-er*: as in *baker*, *producer*, *leader*

b. *-en*: as in *strengthen*, *fasten*, *tighten*

c. *-ary*: as in *imaginary*, *voluntary*, *customary*

d. *-ite*: as in *favourite*, *polite*, *infinite*

e. *-ly*: as in *costly*, *timely*, *friendly*

f. *-some*: as in *burdensome*, *tiresome*, *meddlesome*

Derivation is a most frequently used method in new word formation.

3. Distinction between root, stem and base

A root is the base form of a word that expresses its essential meaning, a meaning that never changes, no matter how many affixes are added to it and where they may occur. Root is the foundation of a word. For example, *use* is the root of *unusually* and *tele-*is the root of *telegram.*

A **stem** is the main part of a word to which suffixes or case endings are added, e.g., *short* in *shortly* and *boy* in *boy's.*

The term *base* is disputable. Some linguists regard it as the equivalent term of *root.* For example, *press* is the base of *pressing*, *pressure*, *compress*, *compression*, *depress* and so on. Other linguists look at it as the part of a word on which an affix is added. It is dynamic and needs not necessarily to be the root. For example, *beauty* may be regarded as the base of *beautify*, which is regarded as the base of *beautification.*

So the three terms may coincide, i.e., to refer to the same part of a word. For example, the *short* in *shortly* and *man* in *manly* can be regarded as roots, stems or bases.

4.4 Morphological rules—compounding

Morphological rules mainly refer to the rules that govern the formation of new words by derivation, that is, the rules by which the affixes are added to stems to form new words. For example, *un-* can be added to an adjective to form an adjective which means just the opposite, as in *uncommon*, *uncomfortable*, *unconscious*, *unfortunate* and *unreliable.*

The morphological rules are very useful in word formation and the identification of the part of speech of a word. But the rules can only be employed on the basis of the experience of the accumulation of plenty of words, that is, the rules cannot be used randomly. For example, *un-* can not be added to all adjectives to change their meanings to the opposite. There are not such words as *unsad*, or *unbrave*. The suffix *-ly* can be added to the end of nouns to form adjectives, as in *friendly*, *kingly* and *lovely*, but there are not such words as *boyly* or *girlly*. The adjective forms of *boy* and *girl* are *boyish* or *boy-like* and *girlish* or *girl-like*.

An English learner should obtain the knowledge of morphological rules, so that his vocabulary can be enlarged. But on the other hand, the rules can not be over-generalized or over-used in case words that do not exist are produced.

4.4.1 Compounding

As discussed in Section 4. 2, compounding, paralleling with derivation, is a kind of very important means to form new words in English. Derivation is to form new words by "root + derivational affix", that is, by "free morpheme + bound morpheme" or "bound morpheme + bound morpheme". **Compounding** is to form new words by "word+word", that is, by "free morpheme+free morpheme".

4.4.2 Types of compound words

A compound is a lexical unit consisting of more than one base and functioning both grammatically and semantically as a single word. Compounds can be categorized into different groups according to different standards. The brief classification made in Section 2 is to classify the compounds according to their parts of speech. In this section, we will classify them according to the parts of speech of their components so that we can achieve a better understanding of compounds formation. The most frequently used types are the following.

Ex. 4-14 a. noun+noun: *workbook*, *sunset*, *watermelon*

b. adjective+noun: *blackboard*, *blackbird*, *deadline*

c. adjective+noun+-ed: *white-haired*, *dark-eyed*, *well-meant*

d. verb+noun: *searchlight*, *playboy*, *watchdog*

e. adverb+noun: *downtown*, *overburden*, *upgrade*

f. noun+verb: *daybreak*, *headache*, *rainfall*

g. verb+adverb: *warm-up*, *crackdown*, *kick-off*

h. noun+adjective: *tax-free*, *throat sore*, *carsick*

i. -ing +noun: *waiting room*, *washing machine*, *walking stick*

Besides the above forms, some other forms can also be found. One point which is worthy to be mentioned here is that the way of compound formation has been used to connect the words of a sentence and make it a word functionally, for example, the underlined part in the following sentence functions as an adjective: *Women has outgrown the jump-onto-a-chair-at-the-sight-of-a-mouse era*.

4.4.3 Features of compounds

The compounds may obey different forming rules, but they share some common characteristics. The following part will discuss those characteristics at orthographical, syntactical, semantic and phonological levels.

Orthographically, compounds are written in three ways: solid, hyphenated or open. A solid compound is written as one word, that is, there is no hyphen or space between its components for example, *bedtime*, *armchair*, *playboy*. A hyphenated compound is written with a hyphen between them, for example, *touch-me-not*, *kick-off*, *tax-free*. An open compound is written as separate words, for example, *sleeping car*, *reading comprehension*, *on the contrary*. In English, which form should a compound take is not fixed sometimes, for example, *flowerpot*, *flower-pot* and *flower pot*. But it is generally accepted that according to the sequence solid > hyphenated > open, the degree of people's acceptance of compound as Standard English word decreases. Regardless of its orthographical form, a compound word is treated as one word in grammatical features and meaning. As the cited example compound *flowerpot*, no matter it appears in solid form, hyphenated form or open form, it's taken as one word by its users. In grammar it takes all features of a countable noun, in meaning it refers to "one kind of pot used for planting flowers".

Syntactically, compounds are mainly categorized into three groups: nouns, verbs and adjectives. Besides those, there are also compound prepositions, compound pronouns, compound adverbs and so on, but their numbers are relatively few. The most difficult point about compounds is to determine their syntactical functions, to be specific, to distinguish their part of speech. Generally, the part of speech of a compound falls into the last element, such as *playboy*, *duty-free*, *house-keep* and so on. However, this rule is not recapitulative enough because there are many exceptions to it. For example, the compounds ending with a verb, an adverb or preposition often violate the rule. Such examples as *warm-up*, *fall-down*, *kick-off* seem to be adverbs according to the rule, but factually, they are verbs; the compounds *birth-control*, *haircut*, *dress-design*, *self-control* seem to be verbs according to the rule, but factually, they are nouns. Some compounds have more than one part of speech, such as *crackdown*, *telephone call* etc.

Semantically, the meanings of compounds are generally idiomatic, they are related to the meanings of their constituting elements, but are not the addition of them. For example, *darkroom* is not only used to mean "a room where it is dark", but more frequently used to mean "a room used for photographic processing". Some linguists argue that it is a noun phrase when it is used in the first sense, and it is taken as a compound when it is used in the second sense. A *greenhouse* does not refer to a house that is green, but a special building in a garden or park which has glass walls and roof and in which you grow plants that need to be kept warm, or protected from winds or frost. The *sugar-coated bullet* does not means that the bullet is really wrapped with sugar, but a metaphoric usage which means to attack in a roundabout way or to attack with a fake "seem-to-be-hospitable" disguise. So we'd better treat compounds as idioms. When pinning down the meanings, we should consult the dictionary when we don't know, rather than guess them out subjectively.

Phonologically, the main stress of a compound often lies on its first element, and the second stress on its second element. For example, the main stresses of such compounds as *blackberry*, *black-current*, *blackboard*, *blackguard*, *blackjack* are all on the first element. This rule can help to identify whether a combination formed by free morphemes is a compound or a free phrase. For example, when the word *blackbird* has its stress on its first element, that is, *black*, it is a compound, which refers to a special kind of bird; when its stress is on the second element, it refers to the birds whose colour is black. The rule can also help us to distinguish whether a "-ing+noun" structure is a compound or the former part is just used to modify the latter noun. For example, when the main stress is on the first element of *dancing-girl*, that is, on *dancing*, it is a compound, which means a girl whose job is to dance; when the main stress is on the second element, it is a subordinate phrase, *dancing* is used to modify *girl*, and it refers to the girl who is dancing. So though this structure can be pronounced in two ways, but their meanings are different. *Running dog* may be counted as another example, when primarily stressed on *running*, it is a compound, which metaphorically means a person who follows another person obediently in his wrong doings; when stressed primarily on *dog*, it is a phrase, which means a dog that is running. Many similar example can be cited, for example, *diving board*, *swimming suit*, *living room*, *sewing machine*, *walking stick*, *sleeping car*, etc, it is unnecessary to elaborate on them here.

The above features are approximately the general features shared by most of the compounds, but they are not absolute and cannot be used as strict defining criteria of English compounds because there are exceptions as well. All of them have drawbacks. The orthographic feature manifests that different orthographic forms can indicate their degree of standardization as English word, but one compound may appear in different forms in different places or even in different dictionaries. It is in lack of uniformity. The syntactical feature generalizes the way by which the part of speech of the compound is determined, but there are many exceptions as discussed in the above paragraph. The semantic feature claims that meanings of compounds are idiomatic, and cannot be guessed from their components, but it is not always so. For example, the words like *sunrise*, *headache*, *snow-white* are compounds, but their meanings can be inferred from the meanings of their component elements. The phonological rule claims that the main stress of a compound should be put on the first element; otherwise, it is not a compound, but free phrase. In fact, such words as the following have been accepted as compounds: *cold-war*, *inverted commas*, *split infinitive*.

Exercises

1. Decide whether the following statements are true or false.
   1) Although the vast majority of prefixes do not change the original word class, there are prefixes that are class-changing: a-, be-em-/en.
   2) Suffixes are basically class-changing morphemes.
   3) The function of a prefix tends to be semantically oriented, that is, it adds new meaning to a base.
   4) Morphemes vary in size. Neither syllables nor length are any guide to their identification. The essential criterion is that a morpheme cannot be cut up into smaller syntactic segments.
   5) Inflectional endings can be added to derivational ones, but not vice-versa.
   6) A morpheme cannot be made up of one phoneme.
   7) The syllabic structure of a word and its morphemic structure must correspond.
   8) Derivations can make the word class of the original word either changed or unchanged.
   9) The following words contain some derivational morphemes which change the part of speech or class of the words: expresident, profiteer, booklet, undo, disobey, tallish.
   10) A language may have more phonemes than morphemes.
2. Divide the following words into morphemes.

retroactive	befriended	televised	margin	unforgettable
endearment	psychology	unpalatable	holiday	grandmother
morphemic	mistreatment	deactivation	airsickness	saltpeter

3. Match the proper description in Column B with the italicized part of each word in Column A.

A	B
a. terroriz*ed*	1. free root
b. un*civil*ized	2. bound root

c. terror*ize*
d. *luke*worm
e. *im*possible

3. inflectional suffix
4. derivational suffix
5. inflectional prefix
6. derivational prefix
7. inflectional infix
8. derivational infix

4. The following infinitive and past participle verb forms are found in Dutch.

Root	Infinitive	Past Participle	English equivalent
wandel	wandelen	gewandeld	walk
duw	duwen	geduwd	push
zag	zagen	gezagd	saw
stofzuig	stofzuigen	gestofzuigd	vacuum-clean

1) State the morphological rules for forming an infinitive in Dutch.
2) State the morphological rules for forming the Dutch past participle.

5. Answer the following questions.

1) Draw a diagram to show how the morphemes are classified in English.
2) How many inflectional suffixes are there in English? What grammatical functions do they have?
3) What are the main features of the English compounds?

Chapter 5 Syntax

5.1 Definition of syntax

In this chapter, we will study **syntax**, the structure of sentence. It is very clear that if we are to make sensible sentences, we need to know how to put words together. The sentence *Tom played football* does not have the same meaning as *Football played Tom*, and *Played Tom football* or *Played football Tom* doesn't make any sense though the words in them are all the same. A sentence requires a certain structure. The study of that structure, that is, the study of the rules governing the ways words, word groups and phrases are combined to form sentences in a language, or the study of the interrelationships between elements in sentence structures, is called syntax. Syntax is a word derived from two Greek elements which means "together" and "arrangement".

The syntactical theories are very complex and are still under development. In this chapter, it is to be discussed in this order: first, a general introduction to syntax as a system of rules; then, sentence structure and category; next, the grammatical relations in a sentence; still next, the structural rules and movement rules in a sentence; and finally, a brief introduction to Universal Grammar, a notable school in syntactic research.

5.2 Syntax as a system of rules

Syntax is a system composed of limited abstract rules. Sentences are formed by combination of words. This combination is governed by syntactical rules. The number of both words and syntactical rules is limited; however, the sentences generated by them are limitless. People can use their limited vocabulary and syntactical rules to produce and understand uncountable sentences, whether they have ever spoken them or not, or whether they have ever heard them spoken or not. This is called *Productivity*, one of the most distinguished features of language.

The function of syntactic rules is to make the language users produce grammatical sentences, and to have the ability to judge whether a sentence is grammatical or ungrammatical. Generally, a sentence is considered grammatical when it accords with the grammatical knowledge in the native speakers' mind. That grammatical knowledge is shared by all the members in the speech community. They are a set of natural linguistic habits rather than artificial rules made by people. For example, the Chinese grammatical knowledge is shared by all the people who speak Chinese. This knowledge enables us to produce sentences which can be understood by other Chinese speakers. The acquisition of this knowledge does not need any special efforts. It is built in the natural language. If we can use a language correctly, we have obtained the grammatical knowledge, consciously or unconsciously. For example, we Chinese can speak Chinese, and that implies we know the Chinese grammatical rules, even if we do not clearly know where they are and how they work in making utterance and understanding meaning.

The syntactic rules can not only help the speakers produce sentences which conform to grammatical rules, that is, sentences which are considered normal, natural or standard by the native speakers, they can also enable the native speakers to understand the sentences. All the sentences that accord with syntactic rules can be understood by the native speakers; if they violate the rules, they can not be understood, or understood properly by the native speakers.

Ex. 5-1 a. *The boy bit the dog.*

b. *The dog bit the boy.*

c. *Bit the dog the boy.*

Sentence a and b are grammatically well formed, but differ in meaning, while sentence c is unacceptable. Sentence c is against the English syntactic rule, and cannot be regarded as a correct sentence. It may be spoken by a little child who is learning language, but can not be possibly spoken by a normal English speaker, even it is spoken, it can not be understood.

5.3 Sentence structure

In terms of sentence structure, we will discuss it from two perspectives. One is inside the sentence, the other one is outside the sentence. Inside the sentence, the sentence components and the way in which they are arranged are to be studied in Section 5.3. Outside the sentence, sentence types are to be studied in Section 5.4.

Sentence is a grammatical unit which is independent in structure and self-contained in meaning. As we know, grammatical unit has different levels, such as phoneme, morpheme, word, phrase, clause, and sentence. In these strata, sentence lies on the top level, so in structure it is independent and not subordinate to a larger linguistic form. In meaning, different from separate words, a sentence can express a complete thought.

Sentences can perform many functions. The most frequently used ones are to deliver a statement, to raise a question or to give a command.

Ex. 5-2 a. A statement: *I like playing computer games.*

b. A question: *Do you like computer games?*

c. A command: *Don't play computer games!*

Sentences are usually composed of subjects and predicates. The core of a sentence is predicate. There may be no subject, no object, no attributive, no adverbial or else in a sentence, but there cannot be no predicate; otherwise, it is not a sentence. Some sentences may contain only one word, such as "Yes.", "No.", "Delicious!", etc, but most sentences consist of at least one subject and one predicate.

Subject refers to the word or words that represent the person, object, event or concept that is being talked about and is performing the action expressed by the verb in a sentence. In active voice, subject is the producer of the action; in passive voice, subject is the receiver of the action. For example, *Tom* is the subject in both of the following sentences: *Tom hit the ball* and *Tom was hit by the ball*, but "He" is the producer of the action *hit* in the former, and the receiver in the latter. The subjects of sentences may be nouns, pronouns, gerunds, infinitives and so on, but the most frequently used ones are nouns or noun phrases. Predicate refers to the part in a sentence which is said about the subject, it may be the action, the expression, the judgment, etc of or about the subject. Some linguists argue that a sentence is composed of two parts: the subject and the predicate, so the predicate refers to the part which is left after the subject has been taken away. For example, in *I decided what to do*, *decided what to do* is the predicate. The predicates of sentences may be finite verbs, verb phrases, adjectives, infinite verbs and so on, the most frequently used ones are verbs and adjectives. Let's take another example to analyze the subject and predicate.

Ex. 5-3 *Mr. Wang has been to America before.*

In this sentence, *Mr. Wang* is a nominal phrase, it is the doer of the action *going to America*, and functions as the subject of the sentence. *has been to America* is the action performed by *Mr. Wang*, it is the predicate; *before* indicates the time, it functions as adverbial, but according to the rough division, both *has been to America* and *before* belong to the predicate part because they are the left part after the subject has been taken away. The structure of the sentence can be expressed as the following diagram.

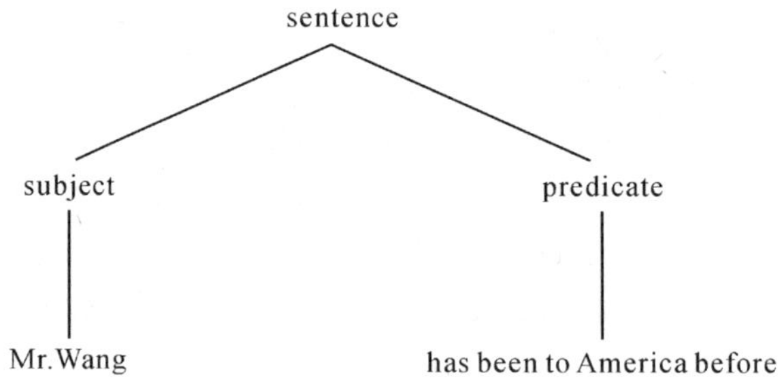

Diagram 5-1

5.4 Types of sentences

Traditionally, sentences fall into two types: simple sentence and non-simple sentence, and the latter can be sub-classified into compound sentence and complex sentence.

1. Simple sentence

Before we discuss the simple sentence, one term, "clause", should be introduced. Generally speaking, a clause is a group of words with its own subject and predicate. Just like sentence, in a clause, predicate is the central and necessary element, the subject may be dropped. The predicate is mainly formed by finite verb. Clause can be classified into finite and non-finite clauses, the latter including the traditional infinitive phrase, participle phrase and gerundial phrase.

A **simple sentence** is a complete sentence which contains only one clause. That is, a simple sentence contains only one finite clause, a clause that takes a subject and a finite verb, and at the same time stands structurally alone.

Ex. 5-4 a. *Tom is a boy.*

b. *Mary was appointed the chairperson of the committee.*

c. *There are a lot of beautiful cars on the parking plots.*

d. *It is impossible for Jack to finish his homework in one hour.*

The above four sentences are all simple sentences because on the one hand, they can stand structurally independent, on the other hand, each of them contains only one subject and finite verb. One point needed to be paid attention to is in sentences like example d, there are two verbs, *is* and *finish*, but only *is* is used finitely, *finish* is used in *to finish* and it is infinitive use. So the sentence also belongs to simple sentence.

2. Coordinate sentence

A **coordinate sentence** contains two clauses which are linked together by such conjunctions like *and*, *or*, *but*, *moreover*, etc.

Ex. 5-5 a. *John loves Mary and Mary loves John.*

b. *You do it well, or you quit.*

c. *It's raining, but they still play football.*

d. *I don't like skating; moreover, the ice is too thin.*

The above four sentences are coordinate sentences. Each sentence consists of two clauses. Those two clauses are structurally independent and semantically complete, but they are connected together by various conjunctions to express different meaning relationships.

3. Complex sentence

A **complex sentence** contains two or more clauses, and the relation between the clauses is that one is subordinate to another instead of being coordinate. In complex sentences, the clauses are not equal in position and function. A complex sentence generally includes a main clause and one or more subordinate clauses. The main clause sets up the main frame of the sentence, and the subordinate clauses grow in the main clause to act as or modify one part of the main clause structure. The main clause is called Matrix Clause, the subordinate clause is called Embedded Clause. The subordinate clauses can function as subject, objective, predicative, adverbial and so on.

Ex. 5-6 a. *[What he told you] is true.*

b. *Do you think [it is possible to learn English with the help of computer]?*

c. *The boy [that is smiling at her] is her son.*

d. *They were watching TV [when the telephone rang].*

From the above examples we can see that the matrix clause and embedded clause are inter-dependent, and cannot be separated without loss or identification of the meaning. Unlike coordinate sentence, the clauses in a complex sentence are not structurally independent and semantically complete, they are combined together to function as different parts of a sentence and form a complete meaning.

5.5 Linear and hierarchical structures of sentences

Under the government of syntactical rules, words are combined into sentences. The combination of words is not at random. The grammatical sentences share two features in structure: linear and hierarchical.

5.5.1 Linear word order of a sentence

The linear feature of a sentence means that there is only one dimension, or one direction in a sentence. In spoken utterances, the words are spoken one after another, they are arranged in a sequence and cannot be folded, and their dimension in delivery cannot be changed. This kind of linear feature is determined by time in spoken utterances because the words of a sentence have to be uttered successively with the elapse of time. If the sentence is written in paper, this linear feature becomes more apparent. In paper, the sentence goes in one direction, the words in a sentence cannot be overlapped or folded, otherwise, it will become undistinguishable, and cannot be understood. Look at the following examples and try to understand the linear feature of sentence.

Ex. 5-7 a. *The boys shyly touched the ball.*

b. *Jane is loved by John.*

c. *You are the brightest student in this class.*

5.5.2 Hierarchical structure of a sentence

The words in a sentence are arranged in a linear sequence, this is the linear feature. Beside that, there is another feature shared by all sentences, which is not as superficial as linearity and underlies in the sentences, that is, the hierarchical. The hierarchical feature means that the sentences are hierarchical constructions which are formed in word groups, or sense groups, to be exact, in groups of "noun phrase (NP) + verb phrase (VP)". Let's illustrate this feature by observing three example sentences.

Ex. 5-8 a. *The monkey ate a banana.*

b. *John loves Mary and Mary loves John too.*

c. *She was very beautiful when she was young.*

The above three sentences are linearly structured. If we divide them into groups according to the following way, they will sound unnatural.

Ex. 5-9 a. *The, monkey ate a, banana.*

b. *John loves, Mary and, Mary loves, John too.*

c. *She, was very, beautiful when, she was young.*

The reason why the above division is unnatural is because the division does not accord with the hierarchical order, that is, if we just join words into sentences in that way, the sentences will be unnatural, both in speaking, listening and in written form. The natural division is like the following.

Ex. 5-10 a. *The/ monkey/ ate a banana.*

b. *John/ loves Mary/ and/ Mary/ loves John.*

c. *She/ was very beautiful// when/ she was quite young.*

From the above analysis, we know that sentences are organized with words of the same syntactic category, such as NP, or VP.

5.5.3 Tree diagrams of sentence structure

In order to express the hierarchical order existing in sentences and show the syntactic relations between the components, linguists tend to employ the "constituent tree diagram" or "labelled tree diagram". The constituent structure of the above three sentences can be shown in the following diagram trees in the following columns.

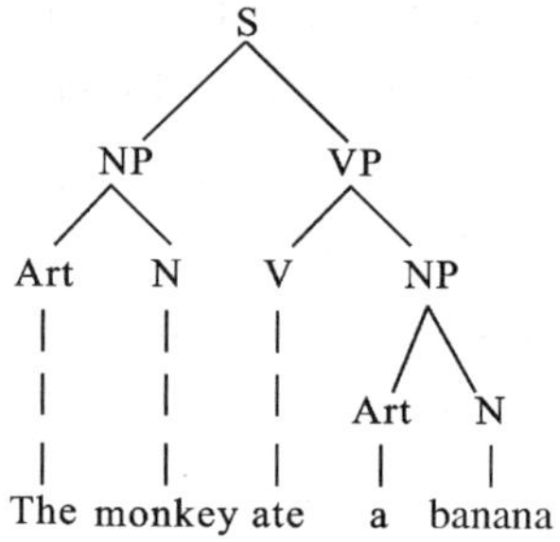

Diagram 5-2

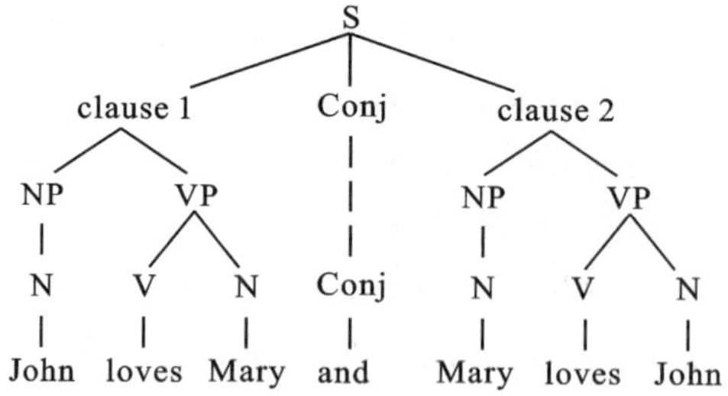

Diagram 5-3

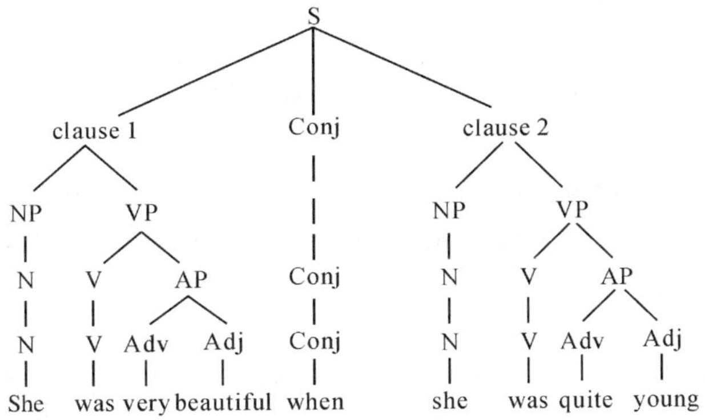

Diagram 5-4

This tree diagram can be used to analyze the various ambiguous meanings of a sentence. For example, in the sentence *The young man and woman came*, the word *young* can be a modifier either of the word *man* or of *man and woman*. If we analyze the hierarchical structure of the sentence as shown in the following two tree diagrams, the ambiguity can be clearly demonstrated and the reason which causes the ambiguity can be clearly uncovered.

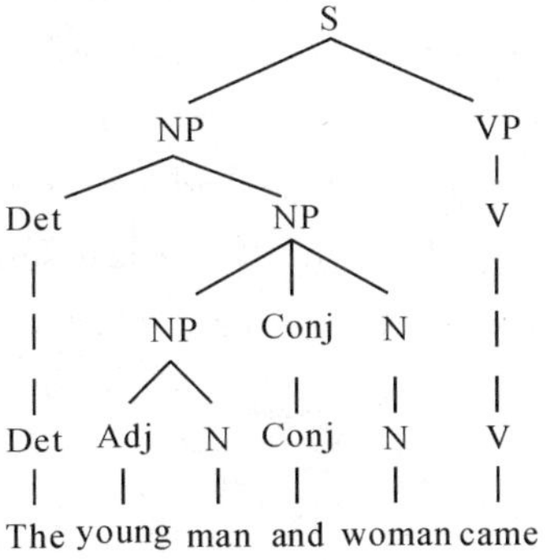

Diagram 5-5

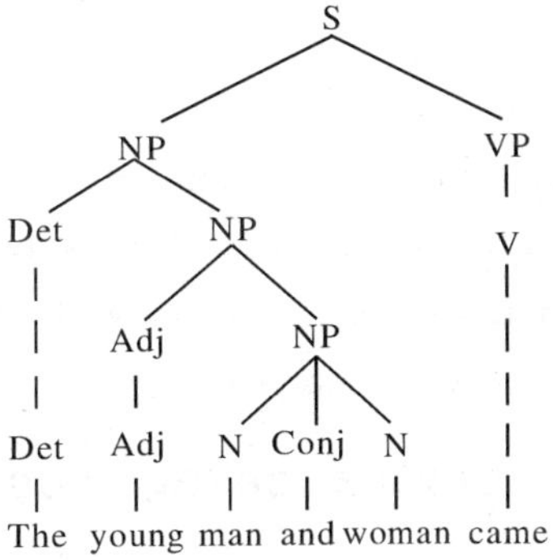

Diagram 5-6

Besides using the tree diagram, linguists also use brackets to show sentence structures.

Ex. 5-11 a. (((*The*) (*monkey*)) ((*ate*) ((*a*) (*banana*)))).

b. (((*John*) ((*loves*) (*Mary*))) (*and*) ((*Mary*) ((*loves*) (*John*)) (*too*))).

c. (((*She*) ((*was*) ((*very*) (*beautiful*)))) ((*when*) ((*she*) ((*was*) (*young*))))).

d. (((*The*) (*young*) ((*man*) (*and*) (*woman*))) (*came*)). [*young* describing *man and woman*] Or: ((((*The*) ((*young*) (*man*)) (*and*) (*woman*)) (*came*)) [*young* describing *man*]

Comparing the above two methods, we can see that the tree diagram method can more clearly show the syntactic structure of a sentence, particularly in analyzing the sentence structure which bears ambiguous meanings when being structurally analyzed differently. So the method is more preferred by linguists.

5.6 Syntactic categories

Sentences are constituted by words and phrases according to syntactic rules. The rules govern what kind of words can be used in the sentence and which part of the sentence they should be used in, i. e. , the function they can perform in the sentence. Syntactic category can be understood from two perspectives: the narrow sense and the broad sense. In the narrow sense, it refers to classes and functions of syntactic components, e. g. , noun, verb, verb phrase, subject, predicate, etc. In the broad sense, it refers to the defining properties of these components: the category of noun, for example, involves number, gender, case and countability, the category of verb, involves tense, aspect, voice, and so on. Since the sentence component includes words and phrases, the syntactic categories include lexical category and phrasal category.

5.6.1 Lexical categories

Every word belongs to a certain kind of lexical category. The **lexical category** refers to the part of speech of words. Lexical category is subdivided into major group and minor group. The classification of categories is based on the meanings that they signify or the functions that they perform in larger structures.

The major group includes:

a. noun (N), such as *book*, *computer*, *panda*;

b. verb (V), such as *go*, *run*, *drink*;

c. adjective (Adj), such as *beautiful*, *pleasant*, *funny*;

d. adverb (Adv), such as *quickly*, *hurriedly*, *hardly*.

The minor group includes:

a. determiner (Det), such as *a*, *an*, *the*, *this*, *that*;

b. auxiliary (Aux), such as *will*, *be*, *must*;

c. preposition (Prep), such as *in*, *on*, *at*;

d. pronoun (Pron), such as *I*, *your*, *you*;

e. conjunction (Conj), such as *and*, *or*, *but*;

f. interjection (Int), such as *Ah*, *Oh*, *Eh*.

From the above classification and exemplification, it can be understood that the major group contains the lexical words, or content words, and the minor group contains the functional words, or empty words. The number of the words in the major group will grow with the development of the society and physical world, thus it's an open group, while the words in the minor group are relatively fixed, thus it's a close group.

5.6.2 Phrasal categories

Phrase is formed by combination of individual words which belong to different lexical categories. The **phrasal category** refers to the part of speech of the phrase. According to the function of the phrase, phrasal categories mainly include four types:

a. noun phrase (NP), such as *a handsome boy*, *the girls*, *the dolls*;

b. verb phrase (VP), such as *hit the boy*, *play with a cat*, *walk in the street*;

c. preposition phrase (PP), such as *under the tree*, *on the tree*, *under the guidance of*;

d. adjective phrase (AP), such as *very hot*, *quite good*, *terribly sorry*.

Phrase is a syntactic concept. It can be composed of one or more than one word, e.g., a VP can be either a verb or the combination of a verb and a noun, both *play* and *play the ball* are VPs. Whatever category the phrase belongs to, it includes word or words which belong to this category, e.g., a NP should consist of at least one noun in it, a VP should consist of at least one verb in it, so are the cases to PP and AP. Among the four phrasal categories, the NP and VP take the majority.

5.6.3 Grammatical relations

From the discussion in the above section, we know that a sentence is formed with combination of words or phrases of different categories. A typical sentence follows the structure of "NP+VP". Grammatical relations deal with the relations between the "NP" and the "VP" in one sentence, i. e. , **grammatical relations** refer to the relations between the functions performed by the NP and VP.

In grammar, names of functions are expressed in terms of subjects, predicates, objects, attributes, complements, etc. Among them, subjects, predicates and objects are the main ones. We will discuss them in this section.

In English, the subject can be divided into two types: the structural subject and the logical subject. The structural subject usually precedes the verb, and the verb is often followed by object, accordingly, the structural object. The structural subject and object are just the formal ones of a sentence.

Ex. 5-12 a. *Tom kicked the dog.*

b. *The dog was kicked by Tom.*

In sentence a, the subject is *Tom*, the object is *the dog*; while, in b, the subject is *The dog*, the object is *Tom*. They are defined so just because of their positions in the sentences.

The logical subject, which is also named semantic subject, refers to the "doer of the action". Accordingly, the logical object refers to the recipient of the action. For example, the logical subjects of both the above two example sentences are *Tom* because he is the *doer* of the action *kick*, and the *dog* is the object in them because *dog* is the recipient of the action *kick*.

The logical subject and object may be in accordance with the structural subject and object as the following example sentences show.

Ex. 5-13 a. *I have had my dinner.*

b. *John played basketball.*

In sentence a, *I* is both logical and structural subject, *my dinner* is both logical and structural object. In b, *John* is both logical and structural subject, and *basketball* is both logical and structural object.

The logical subject and object may also be different from the structural ones.

Ex. 5-14 a. *The apple was eaten by me.*

b. *Tom was punished by his teacher.*

In a *the apple* is the structural subject and *me* is the structural object; while *me* is the logical subject and *the apple* is the logical object. In b, *Tom* is the structural subject and *his teacher* is the structural object, while *his teacher* is the logical subject and *Tom* is the logical object.

5.6.4 Combinational rules

The number of words and phrases is limited, but the sentences made out of them are unlimited. This is because of the magic power of combinational rules. It is these finite rules that govern the creation of infinite grammatical sentences.

1. Phrase structure rules

In Section 5. 5. 3, the tree-diagrams are introduced to analyze and demonstrate sentence structures. Actually, we can view this tree-diagram format in two different ways. In one way, we can simply treat it as a static representation of the structure of the sentence at the bottom of the diagram. The alternative view is to treat the diagram as a "dynamic" format, in the sense that it represents a way of "generating" not only one sentence, but a very large number of sentences with similar structures. This alternative view is very appealing since it enables people to generate a large number of sentences with only a small number of rules. These rules are usually called **Phrase Structure Rules**, and they present the information of the tree diagram in an alternative format. So instead of the tree diagrams, we can use the notation shown as: "S→NP VP". The rule is then read as "A sentence consists of a noun phrase followed by a verb phrase".

In addition to rules of this type which generate structures, we can also have lexical rules which indicate the words to be used for constituents such as N. For example: "N→{boy, girl, dog...}". This means that N is rewritten as "boy", or "girl", or "dog".

We can create a set of extremely simple phrase structure rules which can be used to generate a large number of English sentences:

S→NP VP;

NP→(Det) (Adj) N (PP) (S); e. g., "the beautiful girl with sun-glasses that I called".

VP→V (NP) (PP) (S); e. g., "tell the person in the room that he needn't to wait".

AP→A (PP) (S); e. g., "curious that no one was here".

PP→P NP; e. g., "in the room".

The rule NP→(Det) (Adj) N (PP) (S) is read as: "A noun phrase consists of, or is written as, an optional determiner, an optional adjective, an obligatory noun, an optional prepositional phrase, and/or an optional sentence." The rule VP→V (NP) (PP) (S) is read as: "A verb phrase consists of, or is written as, an obligatory verb, an optional noun phrase, an optional prepositional phrase, and/or an optional sentence." The rule AP→A (PP) (S) is read as: "An adjective phrase consists of, or is written as, an obligatory adjective, an optional prepositional phrase, and/or an optional sentence." The rule PP→P NP is read as: "A prepositional phrase consists of, or is written as, an obligatory preposition and an obligatory noun phrase."

These rules will ensure the generation of the grammatical sentences shown below as a to g, but will not yield the ungrammatical sentences shown as h to j:

Ex. 5-15 a. *The girl followed the boy.*

b. *A boy helped the dog.*

c. *The dog saw a girl.*

d. *Mary helped George recently.*

e. *George saw a dog yesterday.*

f. *A small dog followed Mary.*

g. *The small boy saw George with a crazy dog recently.*

h. *Boy the Mary saw.* *

i. *Helped a girl.* *

j. *Small dog with girl.* *

The phrase structures like NP, VP, AP, PP discussed above can be categorized into Lexical categories. Generative grammar recognized that phrase structures also contain Functional categories; the major types include IP, CP and DP.

As for IP, I is shorted from INFL, and INFL stands for inflectional or infinitival. Inflectional here refers to such words as auxiliaries and modal words because they are inflected for expressing tense, aspect or agreement in function. Infinitival refers to the particle "to" (the infinitive marker). Thus, IP refers to the type of phrase structure containing auxiliaries (e. g. will, shall, shall, should, was, were, did, have, etc), or modal words (e. g. must, may, might, can, could etc), or particle "to". For example, the underlined part in the following sentence are IP.

Ex. 5-16 a. *We will play the game.*

b. *He has won.*

c. *Tommy wants to eat.*

As for CP, C is shorted from complementizer, referring to a category of clause introducing words like "that, if, for". The underlined part in the following sentences are examples of CP.

Ex. 5-17 a. *He promised that he would come back.*

b. *The mother is not sure if her son can finish his homework alone.*

c. *It's time for us to get on the move.*

As for DP, D is shortened from determiner, referring to articles like *a*, *an*, *the*, demonstrative pronouns like *this*, *that*, *these*, *those*, quantifiers like *some*, *any*, *all*, *both*, etc and personal pronouns like *my*, *your*, *his*, etc. Example of DP are like *my school*, *this building*, *some money*.

The phrase structure rules can explain the generating process of sentences, and they can also explain the infiniteness of sentence generation.

2. Recursiveness of phrase structure rules

According to the phrase structure rules, phrases and sentences can be combined infinitely to form sentences, and theoretically, the sentence length may also be infinite. This is because one sentence may be embedded into another, and there is not limit to the number of this kind of embedding. For example, an S consists of a VP that may consists of another S; a VP may include an S that contains another VP; a PP consists of an NP that may be followed by another PP; and an NP may include a PP that further includes an NP or an S.

The grammatical rules of any language are all a set of finite rules. However large the vocabulary is, it is still limited. However, the number of sentence is infinite, and the length of sentence may also be infinite. This property of infiniteness can be satisfactorily explained by the recursiveness of phrase structure rules.

3. X-bar theory

We have generalized the phrase structure rules for NP, VP, AP and PP, the formulas are like the following:

NP→(Det) (Adj) N (PP) (S);

VP→V (NP) (PP) (S);

AP→A (PP) (S);

PP→P NP.

If we observe these formulas closely, we may find they share a common feature, that is, every type of phrase consists of at least one word which belongs to the same category as the phrase. For example, an NP consists of an N, a VP consists of a V, an AP consists of an Adj, a PP consists of a Prep. It is also the very word which gives the phrase its name. It is called the Phrasal Head.

Actually, we can further generalize the above four phrase structures on the basis of their common feature. The more generalized and more abstract formula may go like this:

XP→... X...

In this formula, XP may refer to either of the above four types of phrases. X refers to the correspondent word, such as N, V, Adj, Prep, it is the phrasal head; P means phrase. If on the right side of the formula, there are something more than X, the part which precedes X is called Specifier(Spec), the part which follows X is called Complement (Compl). For example, the NP *a young man who has long hair* contains Det, N and S, so "a young" functions as the specifier, "man" is the phrasal head, and "who has long hair" is the complement. So accordingly, the above abstract formula may be rewritten as:

XP→(Spec) X (Compl)

On the basis of the universal properties of the XP rule, a format using the symbol ″ (read as Double Bar) and ′ (read as Single Bar) is applied in tree-diagram and formula expression as shown in the following:

(1) Formula: X″→Spec X′

X′→X Compl

(2) Tree diagram:

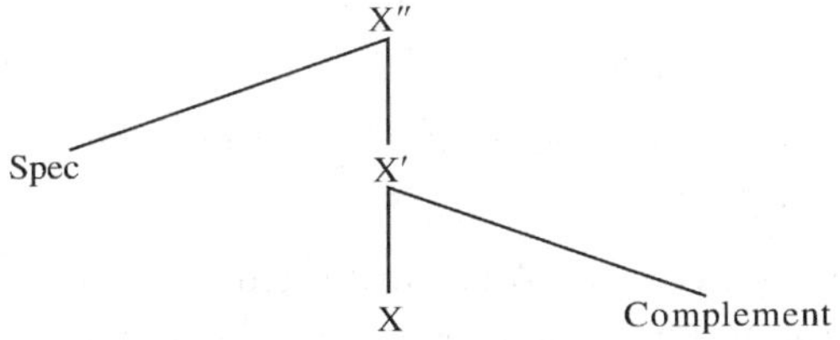

This is called **X-bar theory** and this X-bar schema is capable of reducing the redundancies of individual phrasal structure rules and may well generalize the basic properties shared by all phrasal categories across the languages of the world.

5.7 Syntactic movement and movement rules

Syntactic movement means a constituent in a sentence moves out of its original place to a new position. For example, the sentence *George helped Mary yesterday.* is changed into *Yesterday George helped Mary.* This kind of movement is governed by rules named Transformational rules. The movement may change the syntactic construction. In English, the major types of syntactic movement are NP movement and WH-movement.

5.7.1 NP-movement and WH-movement

The NP-movement refers to the syntactic phenomenon that a noun phrase is moved from its original position to a new position.

The NP-movement can be shown through the change of a sentence from active voice to passive voice.

Ex. 5-18 a. *Charlie broke the window.*

b. *The window was broken by Charlie.*

The above two sentences appear to be different, but in fact, they express the same meaning: a man named Charlie broke a window. We can say b is the result of NP-movement of a. In b, "Charlie" is post-posed and "the window" is pre-posed.

The NP-movement can also be shown through sentences like the following.

Ex. 5-19 a. *It seems that Tom is a competent manager.*

b. *Tom seems to be a competent manager.*

The above two sentences have identical meaning though they appear to be different in syntactic structure. We may regard b as the result of NP-movement of a. In b, "Tom" is pre-posed.

Apart from NP-movement, the WH-movement also occurs frequently. It means words initialized with "wh", such as "what", "when", "who", "where", are moved from their original position to another position. In English, the movement of "wh-" words to the initial place of a sentence is a necessary condition to change a statement into an interrogative sentence.

Ex. 5-20 a. Statement: *George helped Mary yesterday.*

b. Interrogative sentences: *Who did George help yesterday?*

When did George help Mary?

5.7.2 Other types of movement

Other types of movement include AUX-movement and Adj-movement. The AUX-movement is a necessary condition to change a statement to a question.

Ex. 5-21 a. *She has suffered a lot.*

→ *Has she suffered a lot?*

How much <u>has</u> she suffered?

b. *He picked up the book from the floor.*

→ *Did he pick up the book from the floor?*

What did he pick up from the floor?

The employment of Adj-movement is mainly for stylistic purposes, for example, for emphasis.

Ex. 5-22 *Though he is poor, he strives on very diligently.*

→*Poor as he is, he strives on very diligently.*

5.7.3 Move α—a general movement rule

Just as the X-bar schema can highly generalize various kinds of phrase structure rules, there is a rule, named **Move α rule**, which is a universal rule governing syntactic movement. It generalizes all kinds of syntactic movement and can account for the syntactic movement existing in every language. In this rule, α is a Greek symbol used here to represent any constituent, the rules means "move any constituent to any place".

However, this rule is too powerful. If a constituent could move to any place, ungrammatical sentences would then be generated. So the operation of these rules needs to be restrained by some conditions. In fact, any specific movement operation is always carried out under certain constraints.

5.8 D-structure and S-structure

D-structure is deep structure; S-structure is surface structure. This is related to transformation and proposed by Noam Chomsky. Please look at the following two sentences.

Ex. 5-23 a. *Charlie broke the window.*

b. *The window was broken by Charlie.*

In traditional terminology, the first is an active sentence and the second is passive. The distinction between them, it can be claimed, is a difference in their surface structure, that is, the syntactic form they take as an actual English sentence. However, this difference in superficial form disguises the fact that the two sentences are very closely related, even identical, at some less "superficial" level. This other "underlying" level, where the basic components (categories and lexicon) shared by the two sentences would be represented, has been called their deep structure. The **deep structure** is an abstract level of structural organization in which all the elements determining structural interpretation are represented. So, the grammar must be capable of showing how a single underlying abstract representation can become different surface structures. So from the above discussion we can generalize that the D-structure is a kind of abstract syntactic structure underlying in the mind of speakers and interlocutors, it is the product of the combination of phrasal structural rules and lexical items; **S-structure** is the concrete syntactic structure that people can perceive or use in expression, it is the product of transformational components (rules)' influence on D-structure.

If there is syntactic movement in a sentence, the D-structure and the S-structure will be different; If there is no syntactic movement in a sentence, the D-structure and the S-structure will appear to be the same.

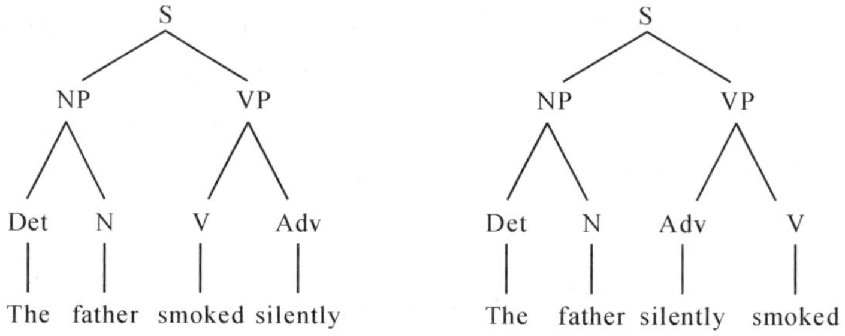

(a) (b)

Diagram 5-7 Diagram 5-8

Above, the (a) tree is the deep structure, underlying both sentences (a) and (b). The surface structure of (a) is the same as its deep structure because no transformation has been applied to it. The surface structure of (b), however, is the (b) tree because the adverb moving transformation alters its deep structure.

5.9 Theory of Universal Grammar

Chomsky, the founder of **Universal Grammar**, is much interested in the study of the similarities among languages rather than their differences. In other words, his theory is much more concerned with the findings of language universals. As the result of his research, Chomsky proposes that grammars of all human languages share a common framework, which he called a transformational grammar. This UG is a system of linguistic knowledge and a human species-specific gift which exists in the mind or brain of a normal human being. It is composed of two parts: a set of highly abstract principles (general principles) and a set of parameters. The former is responsible for generating phrases and restraining the power of Move α, the latter is responsible for the operation of general principles in certain ways, for example, according to which a particular grammar of natural language varies. This theory was developed by Chomsky and his followers, and is called **Principles-and-Parameters Theory**.

5.9.1 General principles of Universal Grammar

The general principles are a set of general conditioning items, such as Case Condition, Adjacency Condition and so on.

The case condition means that a noun phrase must have case and case is assigned by V (verb) or P (preposition) to the object position, or by AUX to the subject position. The case condition can account for the reason why NP can only appear in subject and object position. If they move, they can only move to the position where they can be assigned case.

The adjacency condition means that a case assignor and a case recipient should stay adjacent to each other. This condition can account for the reason why a verb and its direct object can not be intervened by other phrasal category. E. g., the following sentences are not regarded as well-formed.

Ex. 5-24 a. *They clapped happily their hands.* *

b. *Mother put in closet her clothes.* *

5.9.2 The parameters of Universal Grammar

Parameters are variables or options of UG which allow general principles to operate in one way or another on natural languages. Based on the general principles, the parameters that always acquire a particular value, by means of plus

[+] or minus [−], make adjustment and therefore allow the grammar of a natural language to behave in a way different from one of other languages. The following will take for example Adjacency Parameter and Directionality Parameter to have an analysis.

The adjacency parameter allows [+strict adjacency] or [−strict adjacency] on the adjacency condition, thus makes difference between different languages. For example, with English, the adjacency parameter is set to the [+strict adjacency] value; while with French, it is set to the [−strict adjacency] value. So English has stricter requirement on adjacency. And the different word order patterns between English and French can be accounted for.

Ex. 5-25 a. *Mary does quickly her homework.* *

b. *Marie fait lentement ses devoirs.*

Sentence a is ungrammatical in English because "quickly" cannot be located between "does" and "her homework" according to the [+strick adjacency] value. Sentence b is grammatical in French though "lentement" is placed between "fait" and "ses devoirs".

The directionality parameter is related to word order, i. e. , the directionality of case assignment. This parameter can account for the typological difference in the word order with the VP category between English and Japanese. For example, the following two sentences are the same in meaning.

Ex. 5-26 a. English VP word order: VP→V NP; e. g. ,

He {(VP) [(V) ate] [(NP) an apple.]}

b. Japanese VP word order: VP→NP V; e. g. ,

彼は{(VP) [(NP)りんご を 一つ][(V)食ました。]}

Now let's analyze how this difference happens on the basis of UG. Suppose in the directionality parameter, there is a parameter which has two directionality values [rightward directionality] and [leftward directionality]. According to the case condition principle, an NP must have case, and within the VP category, case is assigned adjacently to NP by V. Under the functioning of the directionality parameter on case assignment, the parameter is set to the value of [rightward directionality] for English VP and to the value of [leftward directionality] for Japanese VP, so the word orders of VP between English and Japanese are different.

This chapter provides a brief introduction to the knowledge of syntax. It begins with the explanation about what syntax is. Then it continues with the macro-structure of syntax: the basic components of sentence, the types of sentence and the linear and hierarchical structures of sentences. Next it turns to the micro-structure of sentence: the syntactic categories including lexical and phrasal ones; grammatical relations between sentence components; the combinational rules including phrase structure rules, the recursive feature of the rules and the X-bar theory; the syntactic movement and movement rules including the knowledge about deep structure and surface structure. Finally, the last section gives a very brief introduction to the Universal Grammar, including a slight touch on its general principles and parameters.

Exercises

1. Each of the following sentences may be understood in two different ways. Please paraphrase them in two different ways to show that you understand the ambiguity involved.

   1) Dick finally decided on the boat.
   2) The professor's appointment was shocking.
   3) The design has big squares and circles.
   4) That sheepdog is too hairy to eat.
   5) Could this be the invisible man's hair tonic?
   6) The governor is a dirty street fighter.
   7) I cannot recommend him too highly.
   8) Terry loves his wife and so do I.
   9) They said that they would go yesterday.
   10) No smoking section available.

11) Burning grass is dangerous.

12) The man watched the boy with a telescope.

2. Draw phrase structure trees for the following sentences.

1) The hot sun melted the ice.

2) The house on the hill collapsed in the wind.

3) Broken ice melted in the sun.

4) The guitar gently weeps.

5) A frightened passenger landed the crippled airliner.

6) Mary advised John to see the dentist.

7) Mary promised John to see the dentist.

8) The reporter realized that the senator lied.

9) A fast car with twin camps sped by the children on the grassy lane.

10) That the president realized that the headmaster lied surprised her.

3. Decide whether the following statements are true or false.

1) The syntactic rules of a language are finite in number, yet there is no limit to the number of sentences that could be produced.

2) Transformational rules account for sentences whose surface structures are different, but have the same meaning, such as Mary hired Bill and Bill was hired by Mary.

3) The D-structure of a sentence and S-structure of a sentence never look the same.

4) To form a grammatical sentence, a verb does not only select the right syntactic category to fill an argument position, it also needs to assign the right semantic function, or semantic role, to each NP argument it takes.

5) All languages are fundamentally of the same universal character, including the lexico-semantic and syntactic components of languages.

6) All human languages utilize a finite set of discrete sounds (or gestures) that are combined to form meaningful elements or words, which themselves form an infinite set of possible sentences.

7) The subordinator does not merely mark the beginning of a matrix clause but

more importantly, indicates the grammatical function of the embedded clause in the sentence.

4. Answer the following questions.
   1) What functions do syntactic rules play in language production and perception?
   2) What is the relationship between syntax and grammar?
   3) What is an adequate grammar according to Chomsky?
   4) What are the main troubles with transformations?

Chapter 6 Semantics

6.1 Definition of semantics

What we've learnt about phonology, phonetics, morphology and syntax mainly deals with the "form" of language, and the branch of linguistics that studies the "meaning" of language as a whole is semantics. We know people use language mainly to communicate, so the meaning of what people intend to convey through language is very important. What are the types of meaning or what meanings can language express? How are they related to each other? How can people express themselves through language? Semantics must answer these questions.

Philosophers, psychologists, rhetoricians, logicians and linguists have been interested in the study of meaning, but they study it from different angles. Their focuses of interest are different. For example, philosophers take interest in making out the relations between linguistic expressions and the phenomena in the real word which the expressions refer to. They are also interested in evaluating whether those expressions are true or false. Psychologists try to understand human brain through language. Our study of meaning of language is made from a linguistic point of view, so ours is linguistic semantics.

6.2 Some major views concerning the study of meaning

Many scholars have made their studies of meaning of language in different ways since ancient times. Let's look at some major ones.

1. Naming theory

It is the oldest and the most primitive theory dealing with the study of meaning. It was put forward by Plato. According to the theory, words are just names or labels that people use for things. The linguistic symbols are just used as names to refer to the objects they stand for.

It's easy for us to see the limitations of the theory. It seems that people can use such names only to refer to things in the real world, or things physical. And most of such words are nouns. But what about those things mental or spiritual, like "sincerity", "sadness" and "ambition"? What about verbs, adjectives and adverbs, like "pass", "worried" and "hastily"? And what about those things which are abstract or do not exist in the real world at all, such as "hell", "angel" and "happiness"?

2. Conceptual view

We must mention Ogden and Richards when we discuss the conceptualist view or conceptualism. They presented the classic "Semantic Triangle" or "Semiotic Triangle" which is manifested in the following diagram. According to them, a linguistic form or symbol (that is signifier) and what it refers to (that is referent or signified) are not directly linked to each other, but the two hold direct links to "thought" or "reference" (that is concept or notion) respectively. A linguistic element symbolizes a concept, and a concept refers to a referent, while the element only stands for the referent. So concept serves as a link between symbol and referent. A symbol signifies "reality or things" via the concept that is associated with the form of the word in the minds of a speaker, and the meaning of the element is just the concept in that sense.

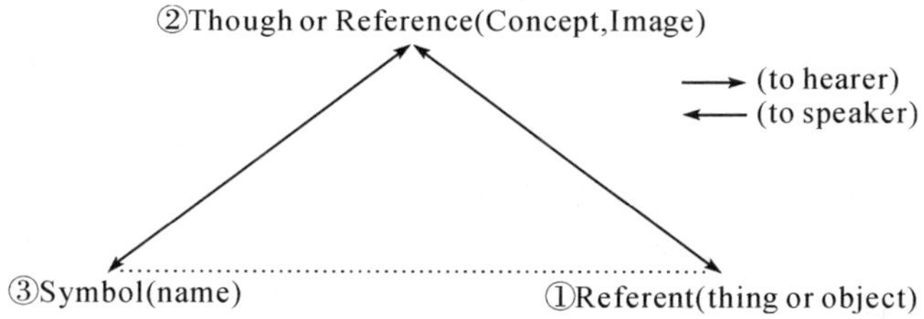

Diagram 6-1 Semantic Triangle

This view sounds good in some cases. Since there's no direct or necessary connection between a linguistic element and the object it refers to, the same object may have different forms or names. That accounts for why a letter is called "letter" in English, "*xin* or 信" in Chinese and "*tegami* or 手紙" in Japanese. But people do not think that the Triangle can sufficiently specify or make exact the "link" between the symbol and the concept and wonder how the meditation of the concept happens. We do not "think of" a concept so mechanically or as a rule each time we meet a linguistic element. Since the theory is far from being enough to describe or explain all possible cases or relations in the real world, it's been criticized ever since it was put forward.

3. Contextualism

How can we define the meaning of linguistic elements? Some people believe that meaning can be made out according to certain context that can be observed. That is to say, we can understand the meaning of a linguistic element through studying the context in which the element appears. There are two kinds of context: the situational context and the linguistic context. We know that people always use language in a certain space at a certain time. And together with the place and the time, the speaker and the hearer, the actions they do at that time, some deictic features and the environment or the things around including the events or the things happened there are also involved. We give a general term to cover all those factors, that is, situational context. Some people call the linguistic context co-text. That deals with the probability of what linguistic elements co-appear or collocate with a word, because that is also a part of the meaning (or the collocative meaning in other words), and the co-text also refers to the part of text which comes after and before a particular sentence.

The scholars of London School and the German philosopher Wittgenstein made most contribution to the establishment of the contextualism. They believe that the meaning of a word can only be determined through studying the company it keeps, or the use of the word determines the meaning of it. In other words, meaning is context-dependent, or context determines meaning.

Besides, in the broad sense, context means the whole vast social background under which some certain linguistic element is used. Obviously, that covers a lot, or everything that has something to do with the meaning we consider or discuss.

4. Behaviourism

It is also called behaviorist theory or behaviorist psychology. It is an American psychological theory. Behaviorists believe that the behaviors of human beings and animals can and should be studied according to some physiological and physical process. They think, for instance, when people are to interpret the process of language learning, they need only consider how external events or stimulus makes one change his behavior, and they need not consider such factors as personal psyche, concept or inner behavior. The American linguist L. Bloomfield used this theory in his attempt to determine the meaning of a linguistic form as the "situation in which the speaker utters it and the response it calls forth in the hearer". It sounds that the theory takes into consideration the context of an utterance. That is somewhat close to contextualism or supports it. But the psychological color of it is strong and obvious. Bloomfield's classical example is about the Jill-Jack story. He thought that the meaning just lies in the relation between the speech or the response of a hearer to the utterance of a speaker in their communication. This understanding of meaning is too dependent on or confined to one's psychological behavior, and it stresses the response or the effect of an utterance. But what about the communication without the so-called stimulus or response? Or what about the non-immediate communication? Similarly, it is too narrow in its coverage and is not sufficient to describe or explain all the possible cases of communication in the real world.

6.3 Lexical meaning

When we talk about the meaning of language, in most cases, we refer to word meaning and sentence meaning, because they are the basic ones. It's important for us to have a clear idea about the two notions which are related to word meaning: sense and reference.

6.3.1 Sense and reference

Meaning can be abstract in our discussion, and sense and reference are two different sides of meaning. Sense is not specific but a very general one. It refers to the inherent meaning of the linguistic element. It is abstract, and it doesn't hold relation to a certain context. It collects all the possible features of the element. We don't relate it to any other factors when we try to understand it. In other words, the part of meaning that is recorded in a dictionary is sense. For instance, when we find out the meanings of "book" or "clothes", they don't refer to anything specific or concrete, neither the book you are reading nor the clothes your roommate is wearing.

Contrary to sense, reference means something specific in the real world. It can be interpreted as the relationship between the linguistic element and the non-linguistic context in which the element is used. In other words, reference is the realization of sense in context, or it is meaningful only in a particular situation.

Let's take two sentences as examples:

Ex. 6-1 a. Do you read books?

b. Please bring me the books over there on the edge of the yellow desk.

The "books" in the first sentence refer to things that can be called "books", and that is the sense of "book". We don't know which books they refer to. The "books" in the second sentence refer to the ones both the speaker and the hearer know. That is the reference of the "books".

So, it's easy to understand that a linguistic element that has only one sense may have different references. Like the "books" in the preceding sentences, they may refer to the books sold in Shanghai Bookstore, or the ones in your house, or the ones in the library of your college, or whatever, because they refer to different things in different situations. But occasionally a linguistic element which has the same reference may have different senses. For instance, "morning star" and "evening star" refer to a one-and-only star with the same reference, but the same star has two different names. That shows they are different in sense.

6.3.2 Major sense relations

Sense relations between words can be classified into 5 types. They are synonymy, polysemy, homonymy, hyponymy and antonymy.

1. Synonymy

Words that share the same or very close meaning are synonyms. Synonymy refers to the relation of sameness or closeness of meaning between words. But people do not think that strict synonyms exist, because they differ from each either in one way or another, though the difference may be very small. Those synonyms that are completely interchangeable or can replace each other under all circumstances without changing meaning are rare. So synonymy is just a relative or loose concept. Synonyms can be divided into the following groups according to how they differ from each other.

Dialectal synonyms

They refer to the words that are used in different regions or dialects. People may say the same thing by using different words in their dialects. American English and British English have different names for the same things, like "elevator" vs. "lift" and "fall" vs. "autumn".

Stylistic synonyms

Words sharing the same or close meaning may be different in their styles or register, or degree of formality. Some words are only used in formal situations, others in informal situations, and still others in neutral ones. For example, we usually use "horse" in our daily life, but we use "geegee" when with children, and still we refer to it as "steed" in writing or reading poems.

Synonyms that differ only in their emotive meanings or evaluative meanings

Words bearing the same or close meaning may reflect different emotions of a user, and the choice of such words indicates the attitude or bias of the user toward what he is talking about. The emotional colour may be mainly neutral, derogatory or commendatory, which shows how the user evaluates what he is referring to. For instance, the use of "statesman" is usually commendatory, while that of "politician" is usually derogatory. Both words refer to someone who is engaged in political affairs.

Collocational synonyms

The collocation of words refers to the rule or fact that some words can only go together with some other words. That is to say, that some words are collocationally restricted. For example, we can say "deep sympathy" and "profound sympathy", and we can also say "deep waters" and "profound books", but we can't say * "deep books" or * "profound waters".

Semantically different synonyms

Some synonyms are in themselves different slightly from each other in their meanings. For instance, the words *amaze*, *astonish*, *shock*, *appal*, *startle*, *astound* and *surprise* share close meaning, but they somewhat differ from each other. We can consult an English-English dictionary so that we can clarify and understand the differences between them.

2. Polysemy

Different words may share the same or close meaning while the same word may have more than one meaning. This relation is called polysemy, and such a kind of word is a polysemic word. Polysemic words are often seen in the English language. Generally speaking, the more commonly a word is used, the more probable the word is polysemic. It's easy for us to find in any dictionary a word that has more than one meaning. People believe that a word may just have one single meaning when it was first used, which is called the primary meaning. Then the meaning of the word developed and grew and changed. People would not like to create new words to refer to new things, because that would be quite a trouble. So they use the words that they are familiar with instead. That's why new meanings are given to old words. However, the primary meaning of a word has become relatively less common or unknown to people. The words *board*, *head*, *paper* and *chicken* serve as examples.

3. Homonymy

Homonymy refers to the fact that words that share the same form are different in meaning. In other words, different words **happen to** have the same pronunciation, or spelling, or both (however, some believe that these words are possibly related to each other in this or that way). Words are homophones when they share the same pronunciation, and they are homographs when they share the same spelling. They are complete homonyms when they share the same pronunciation and spelling. We find it easy to get such examples in various textbooks and reference books.

Then we may wonder, when two or more forms share the same pronunciation and spelling, how we can tell if they are complete homonyms or just different meanings of the same polysemic word. First, if the senses under discussion are related historically, it's a case of polysemy; if not, they are complete homonyms. Second, we can check if the differences in meaning are regular and predictable to some degree. If so, it's polysemy rather than homonymy.

4. Hyponymy

The sense relation that a more general word is inclusive of one or more specific words is called hyponymy. The word that is inclusive of other word(s) in meaning is called the superordinate, and the more specific word or words hyponyms. A superordinate may have more than one hyponym at the same level, so those hyponyms are called co-hyponyms to each other (among themselves). So, a superordinate of other hyponyms may be a hyponym of another superordinate; a hyponym of a superordinate may be the superordinate of many other hyponyms. In this sense, hyponymy is a relation of inclusion in terms of meaning. A superordinate at higher level is inclusive of all its hyponyms at lower levels as illustrated in the following diagram. We know that co-hyponyms hold a horizontal relation, whereas a superordinate holds a vertical relation to all its hyponyms. Let's see the following diagram of hyponymy:

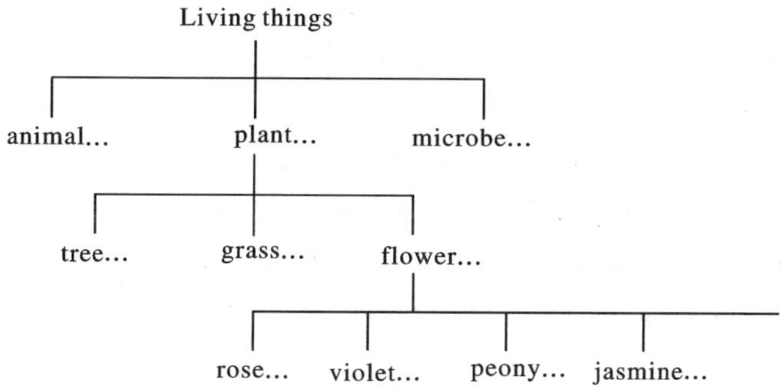

Diagram 6-2 Hyponymy

5. Antonymy

Antonymy refers to the sense relation of oppositeness of meaning between words. Words that are opposite in meaning are antonyms. Words may contrast each other on various dimensions. In other words, they may differ from each other in meaning in different ways. So we can distinguish the following types of antonyms.

Complementary antonyms

If a pair of antonyms is complementary, we are sure that the denial of one means the assertion of the other. It's not a matter of degree but an either-or relation. If it is not A, then it must only be B. Such examples include pairs like *dead* vs. *alive*, *married* vs. *single*, *female* vs. *male*, and so on. Since there are only two possibilities, like the two ends of a pole, such antonyms are also called binary antonyms.

Gradable antonyms

There are sometimes intermediate forms between pairs of antonyms, and those antonyms are called gradable antonyms. It's a matter of degree or a more-or-less relation. Let's compare the relation to the pole we just mentioned. There are possible points between the two antonyms on the pole. We can't say "not A, and not B" if they are complementary antonyms, but we can if they are gradable antonyms. For example, we can't say, "He is neither married nor single", but we can say, "The water is neither hot nor cold. It's lukewarm", or "She is neither old nor young. She is middle-aged". It's easy for us to find such gradable antonyms, like *big* vs. *small*, *open* vs. *closed*, and *good* vs. *bad*, and so on.

Since it's a matter of degree, we can make sure if they are gradable antonyms by seeing if they have sensible superlative and/or comparative degree forms. Generally speaking, only gradable antonyms can be used in sentence patterns making comparison, and they can be modified by such adverbs as *fairly*, *very*, *rather* and *how*. We cannot say, "How alive is he?" But we can say, "How long is the road?"

Relational opposites

Those words that show the reversal of relationship between them are relational opposites. It's important for us to know that there exists a certain kind of relation between the two antonyms. Some pairs of words like *buy* vs. *sell*, *lend* vs. *borrow*, *above* vs. *below*, *pupil* vs. *teacher* are examples of relational opposites.

Some relational opposites **may be** transitive. For instance, if A is above B and B above C, so A is above C. Some relational opposites **may be** symmetric. For example, if A is B's husband, then B is A's wife. If A is B's cousin, B is also A's cousin. The above-mentioned characteristics must be understood and treated with great care. We can't make hasty deductions because they are sometimes culture-dependent and vary among different cases.

6.4 Sense relations between sentences

As we have finished the talk on the topic of sense relations between lexical items, let's move on to the topic of sense relations between sentences. Sense relations exist between sentences and between constituents of the same sentence.

1. Entailment

Entailment is in nature a relation of inclusion of meaning between sentences. The relation of inclusion of meaning between words or phrases is called hyponymy. If sentence a's meaning is included in that of sentence b, sentence b entails sentence a, or sentence a is an entailment of sentence b. For instance,

Ex. 6-2 a1. She has been to Tokyo.

b1. She has been to Asia.

a2. She, a native Chinese, has never been abroad.

b2. She, a native Chinese, has never been to Tokyo.

When necessary conditions are satisfied, we can arrive at a conclusion that sentence a1(a2) includes sentence b1(b2), or sentence b1(b2) is an entailment of sentence a1(a2). So, if a is true, b is necessarily true; if a is false, b may be true or false; if b is true, a may be true or false; if b is false, a is false.

2. Presupposition

When writing or speaking, one may assume that other people have had the knowledge of or information on something. The process is called presupposition. It's first of all a matter of logic which presupposes a proposition. It means in other words that a sentence can be deduced from another sentence in terms of the information contained. If sentence a presupposes sentence b, sentence b is a prerequisite of sentence a. Let's look at an example.

Ex. 6-3 a. His brother is a lawyer.

b. He has a brother.

Presupposition can't be easily negated, and that's what it mainly differs from entailment. When a is true, b is true; when a is false, b is still true; when b is true, a can be either true or false; when b is false, we can't make any judgment about a in terms of its truth value.

Obviously, questions, commands and exclamations can all presuppose propositions. See the following instances:

Ex. 6-4 a. Did your son like the toy you bought for him yesterday?

b. Bring me the toy you bought yesterday.

c. How nice the toy you bought yesterday is!

The three sentences all presuppose that "You bought a toy yesterday".

3. Ambiguity

Ambiguity mainly refers to the fact that a sentence may be interpreted or understood in two or more than two ways. For example,

Ex. 6-5 a. *Visiting aunts* can be boring. (to visit aunts; aunts who are visiting)

b. I went to the *bank* yesterday afternoon. (river bank or bank from which money is drawn)

c. He *is ready for recording*. (to do recording for others or to be recorded by others)

d. He has a head for remembering historical *figures*. (numbers or well-known people)

e. He feels unhappy about the grade A. (It may sound like *gray day* in oral form.)

From the above-mentioned examples, we can conclude that ambiguity of sentences may be caused by ambiguous sounds, words (mainly polysemic words and homonyms) or phrases or ambiguous sentence structure. But ambiguous sentences can be disambiguated if they are put into a context.

4. Vagueness

Ambiguous sentences may have two or more than two **definite** meanings, but some linguistic items do not have definite meanings. In other words, their meanings cannot be made explicitly specific. We must make precise and clear statements in writing an academic paper on the topic of biochemistry, for example, but we needn't sometimes in our daily lives. We use those general words either consciously or unconsciously. For instance, we use such words as *around*, *about*, *somewhat*, *probably*, *in principle* quite a lot in daily communications. We cannot precisely define the differences between *mountain* and *hill*, *town* and *city*, *house* and *building*, etc. And we can't distinguish those words with high relativity, like *rich* and *poor*, *weak* and *strong*, *big* and *small*, *cheap* and *expensive*, etc. What does it mean by *Tom's book*? One cannot make sure who was looking for him if someone tells him, "Just now someone was looking for you". When we hear "He went on a holiday last week", we don't have any idea about how he went and what kind of holiday that was. In most cases, vagueness, unlike ambiguity, of sentences can't be eliminated even if they are put under some context.

5. Other relationships

We also recognize some other relationships between sentences or between constituents within a sentence.

1) a is synonymous with b, or the two sentences share the same meaning. If a is true, b is true; if a is false, b is false, and vice versa. For example,

Ex. 6-6 a. The hunter killed the rabbit.

b. The rabbit was killed by the hunter.

2) a is inconsistent with b. Only one of them is true, and the other one is false. For example,

Ex. 6-7 a. He is a bachelor all his life.

b. He married a woman.

3) a is a contradiction. That means a is in itself not true. For example,

Ex. 6-8 a. The correct answer you gave me is wrong.

4) a is semantically anomalous, or a is abnormal and/or absurd in its meaning.

For example:

Ex. 6-9 a. The chair smiled for a while and laughed to his heart.

An anomalous sentence in fact presupposes a contradiction. Since a chair is inanimate or lifeless, how could it "smile" or "laugh" "to his heart" like a person?

6.5 Semantic analysis

1. Componential analysis

People analyze meaning of words in different ways, and componential analysis is one of them. It was first proposed by some German Structuralist semanticists. People believe that the meaning of a word can be dissected into a group of features, and these features combine to make the word different from other words in meaning. They are called meaning components or semantic features. It's just like that a phoneme can be analyzed into distinctive features. We can use plus or minus signs to indicate whether a word has some feature or not. The symbols of those features are written in capitalized letters. For example,

Table 6-1

man	boy	woman	girl
+ADULT	−ADULT	+ADULT	−ADULT
+MALE	+MALE	−MALE	−MALE
+HUMAN	+HUMAN	+HUMAN	+HUMAN

So it is easy for us to see how these words are related to each other in meaning as we have specified the semantic features of these words. But people argue that they do not analyze every word in that way actually, and the analysis of the features is quite subjective. What's more, there are so many words that can't be analyzed in this way, and the basic features can only show the basic differences between words. Binarism is not enough to specify the subtle meanings of words.

2. Predication analysis

It's easy for us to understand that the meaning of a sentence, unlike that of a word, is not the sum total of all the meanings of its components. We can't work out the meaning of a sentence only by adding up all the meanings of its components.

The order of the components, for example, may change the meaning of the sentence.

The meaning of a sentence can be discussed in two senses: in grammatical sense and semantic sense. Grammatical meaning of a sentence means that how well the sentence is formed grammatically, and semantic meaning of a sentence refers to whether some lexical items can go with other ones so as to make sense. Sentences, though grammatically right, may not be necessarily semantically right. For example, * "My car is a red fool."

All the different ways to analyze the meaning of sentences aim to abstract it. One of them is called predication analysis. It was proposed by G. Leech. When we make grammatical analysis of a sentence, the sentence is the basic unit which is further analyzed into various grammatical components. But in semantic analysis, the basic unit is called **predication** or the content of proposition. It is the abstraction of sentence meaning.

A predication consists of argument(s) and predicate. An argument is an entity or a logical participant that is talked about or referred to in a sentence; a predicate refers to all those semantically significant parts said about an argument, or it states or describes the logical relation that is important to the argument(s) in a sentence. Grammatical forms don't play any role in semantic predication (analysis), so the same semantic predication may have various grammatical realizations. In other words, sentences in various grammatical forms may not share the same proposition, but they may share the same propositional content and the same predication analysis. For example, the following sentences share the same semantic predication:

Ex. 6-10 a. John is a fool.
b. John was a fool.
c. Is John a fool?
d. John has been a fool.
e. John is a fool?

The semantic predication can be written as "argument(s) + predicate". So the semantic predication of the above cited sentences can be written as "JOHN

(FOOL)". According to the number of arguments contained in a predication, we can classify the predications into three types: two-place predication (with two arguments), one-place predication (with one argument) and no-place predication (without any argument). Look at the following examples:

Ex. 6-11 Boys read books. →BOY, BOOK (READ) (with two arguments)

Ex. 6-12 He is reading. →HE (READ) (with one argument)

Ex. 6-13 It is hot. →(BE HOT) (without any argument)

It is a very complicated and highly abstract problem to analyze sentence meaning. What we have tried to do is just an attempt to give you a general idea. No method is good enough to solve the problem alone, but we can rely on componential analysis and predication analysis together as they can help us understand and describe the relatively greater part of sentence meaning.

Exercises

1. Fill in the blanks in the following passage by choosing the appropriate word form the four choices provided under each number.

Semantics is the study of ___(1)___ of language. It is one of the three components of ___(2)___. It focuses on the ___(3)___ between languages, rather than on the ___(4)___.

In most cases, the interpretation of language utterances depends on the ___(5)___ in which they are used, and most of them have a ___(6)___ range of meanings than first come to mind. It may seem to you that meaning is so vague, insubstantial, and elusive that it is impossible to draw any clear, concrete or tangible conclusions about it. We can say that many kinds of behavior can be described as ___(7)___, but the range, diversity and complexity of meaning expressed in language are unmatched in any other human or non-human communicative behavior. And linguistic ___(8)___, which studies meaning in language, was ignored considerably in the past because people felt that meaning was inherently ___(9)___ and at least temporarily beyond the scope of ___(10)___ investigation. Mainly as a result of Chomsky's theory of ___(11)___ grammar, and the technical advances made in linguistics, in logic and philosophy of ___(12)___, linguistic semantics is currently enjoying a revival of interest.

(1) a. grammar	b. structure	c. form	d. meaning
(2) a. linguistics	b. grammar	c. morphology	d. syntax
(3) a. form	b. similarity	c. differences	d. meaning
(4) a. substance	b. difference	c. similarity	d. grammar
(5) a. words	b. sentences	c. utterances	d. context
(6) a. wider	b. narrower	c. more accurate	d. clearer
(7) a. productive	b. effective	c. informative	d. communicative
(8) a. stylistics	b. syntax	c. logic	d. semantics
(9) a. stable	b. unstable	c. social	d. definite
(10) a. independent	b. philosophical	c. logical	d. human
(11) a. traditional	b. structural	c. systemic	d. transformational
(12) a. language	b. semantics	c. the world	d. human brain

2. Explain the meanings of words such as "mean", "meaning" in the following sentences.

   1) When she mentioned "the cute boy", she meant me. ____________

   2) The dark clouds mean rain. ____________

   3) What do you mean by saying that? ____________

   4) Fame and riches mean nothing to a true scholar. ____________

   5) Can you tell me the meaning of the word "dormant"? ____________

   6) I always mean what I mean. ____________

   7) I'm sorry, but I didn't mean to hurt you. ____________

   8) She never says what she really means. ____________

   9) "Craving" is a noun which means "strong desire". ____________

3. Can the following characteristics be applied to sentences (S) or utterances (U)?

   1) A kind of human physical behaviour or event, or product of such behaviour. U/S

   2) A string of words put together by the grammatical rules of a language. U/S

   3) Abstract, not to change in meaning according to different contexts. U/S

   4) A stretch of talk by a particular speaker. U/S

5) Dependent on the particular context for its meaning. U/S

6) Its meaning is predictable from the words it contains and its grammatical structure. U/S

7) It's context-free. U/S

8) It's used by a certain person at a certain time in a certain place. U/S

4. Pick out the arguments (or referring expressions) in the following sentences.

1) Tom's mother liked the dog.

2) Your books are under the bed.

3) Jacky sang very well.

4) Lu Xun was a great satire writer.

5) Premier Zhou En-lai was always among the workers, peasants, soldiers and intellectuals.

6) Hubei is between Henan and Hunan.

5. Decide whether the following statements are true or false.

1) In the case of sense inclusion, it is those words which have larger size of extension include those which have smaller size of extension.

2) There are very few perfect synonyms in a language.

3) If x is synonymous to y and y to z, then x is also synonymous to z.

4) "Man" is the only opposite to "woman".

5) A word may be incompatible or opposite to several words in different aspects.

6) The meaning of each expression can be defined in terms of its semantic components so as to contrast with the meaning of all the expressions in the same language.

7) The componential analysis of meaning was adopted from distinctive features analysis in morphosyntax which in turn had its own root in the methodology of Prague School phonology.

8) The presupposition of a particular statement is always true no matter the statement is true or false.

9) Many sentences require that certain culturally defined conditions or contexts be satisfied in order for an utterance to be understood.

10) Pragmatic presupposition has nothing to do with the meanings of the words

a sentence contains.

6. Give three hyponyms to the following words.
   1) automobile: ____, ____, ____
   2) emotion: ____, ____, ____
   3) flower: ____, ____, ____
   4) virtue: ____, ____, ____
7. Each of the following adjectives has at least three antonyms. Give them respectively.
   1) bright: ____, ____, ____
   2) rich: ____, ____, ____
   3) handsome: ____, ____, ____
   4) right: ____, ____, ____
   5) deep: ____, ____, ____
8. Use arrows "←", "→" to indicate the entailment relation between the sentences in the following pairs. For example, "A (→) B" means A is an entailment of B, or B entails A.
   1) There is a desk in the room. (   ) There is a piece of furniture in the room.
   2) All the cars here are red. (   ) All the cars here are coloured.
   3) All the children here are cute. (   ) All the girls here are cute.
   4) Tom wasn't dead. (   ) Tom didn't kill himself.
   5) Someone has stolen my computer. (   ) Someone has taken away my computer.

Chapter 7 Pragmatics

7.1 An introduction to pragmatics

7.1.1 Definition

Pragmatics is the branch of linguistics that studies language in use and linguistic communication. It is also a study of meaning, but it takes care of the part of meaning that semantics does not cover. People always use language in some situations, and the context of situation to a great extent affects or determines the meaning of the language use. That is why pure grammatical analysis of the language use alone cannot tell us all about the meaning. So pragmatics takes interest in studying the relationships between language use, context and specific situations in which the language use appears. To put it in another way, it studies how speakers of a language use sentences to effect successful communication.

7.1.2 Pragmatics vs. semantics

Since both the two branches study meaning of language, then how are they related, and what are the differences between them?

Semantics studies meaning of language as it is, or it gives no consideration to any extra-linguistic factor. People used to believe that meaning of language is stable, inherent and intrinsic, so they studied meaning in an isolated way. Later on, people came to realize that the context in which language is used actually determines the meaning of the language use. The meaning of language varies according to different context. So **pragmatics** studies the dynamic relation of meaning of language use to the context. Whether the context is considered in the study of meaning differs the two branches.

7.1.3 Context and meaning

Generally speaking, **context** is viewed as a set of knowledge that the speaker and the hearer share. The knowledge can be divided into two kinds: knowledge of the language in use and that about the world, which includes the general knowledge about the world and the specific knowledge about the situation in which communication takes place. For instance, if one does not know of the person deictics (used to identify "who" like "you" and "our"), place deictics (used to identify "where" like "this" and "that") or time deictics (used to identify "when" like "yesterday" and "next month"), he cannot make sure the specific meaning of the sentence "I will go to that town to visit you and our dog at this time next month". Look at another example. The sentence "How clever you are!" may mean a true praise or an irony in certain situation. In short, context contributes a lot to the meaning of language use.

7.1.4 Sentence meaning vs. utterance meaning

A sentence is discussed only in grammatical sense, and we do not consider the factor of context in studying the meaning of it. So its meaning is abstract, intrinsic, stable and has nothing to do with context. But if the meaning of a sentence is studied with the consideration of the context in which it is used, we call it an utterance. In this sense, the meaning of an utterance is concrete, specific and depends on context. Obviously, utterance bases its meaning upon sentence meaning.

There are many factors that produce influence on people's use of language for effective communication besides the rules of language itself. People's use of language, for example, may vary with where and to whom they speak and their purpose of communication. Pragmatics just studies those factors and sees how they affect the meaning of language use, or what to convey through utterances and how to interpret them in real situation of communication. As G. Leech puts it, semantics answers the question "What does X mean?" and pragmatics "What do you mean by X?"(Leech, 1983).

7.2 Speech act theory

This theory is important in the pragmatic study of utterance meaning. It was originated with the British philosopher John Austin (1962) and developed by the American philosophical linguist John Searle (1969). It aims to offer a philosophical explanation of the nature of linguistic communication by trying to answer the question: "What do we do when using language?"

Traditionally philosophers were interested in the truth-value of sentences, with a belief that a statement was used either to state a fact or to describe a state of affairs. However, Austin found that people use language not only to give information or to describe things, but also to do things or perform acts, because they discovered that there were utterances about which no truth-value could be said. According to them, statements that either state or describe are constatives, and people can check whether they are true or false. Sentences that neither state nor describe and are not verifiable are performatives. They are used to do something, and the performatives are important to performative sentences. Of course, other necessary conditions must be satisfied for the successful performance. For example, when a person in the proper position says at proper time and place according to proper procedure to the proper participants, "I hereby name this ship Red Flag", the ship is named, and the action is done.

7.2.1 Austin's model of speech acts

To illustrate his point, Austin (1962) cited the following four examples, which have become classical and are frequently quoted in the literature:

Ex. 7-1 I do.

Ex. 7-2 I name this ship Elizabeth.

Ex. 7-3 I give and bequeath my watch to my brother.

Ex. 7-4 I bet you sixpence it will rain tomorrow.

"I do" is used in the course of a wedding ceremony for the speaker to get married. "I name this ship..." is used by an authorized person to perform the act of naming a ship. Similarly, the utterance "I give and bequeath my watch to my brother", most probably occurring in a will, is used to perform the act of bequeathing. And when a speaker says "I bet you..." he is doing nothing else but betting. Therefore, when the speaker makes such utterances, he or she is actually performing certain acts rather than stating something. In addition to these conventionalized cases, non-conventional acts such as stating, promising, requesting, and suggesting are also identified. So the idea of doing something while speaking can be broadened to include very much and this feature is recognized as a common one. Hence the theory came to be known as the speech act theory, according to which we are performing actions simultaneously when we are speaking.

Later on, for a variety of reasons, Austin gave up his initial distinction between constatives and performatives and established another model to explain how people perform acts with language. According to this new model, a speaker might be performing three acts simultaneously when speaking: locutionary act, illocutionary act, and perlocutionary act.

A locutionary act is the making of utterance with definite literal meaning, i. e. the act of uttering words, phrases and clauses. An illocutionary act refers to what a speaker intends to express through the locutionary act, and it is the act that is done in saying something. A perlocutionary act is the act performed by or resulting from saying something, or in other words, it is the consequence or effect of the utterance, or the change brought about by it.

Take an example. Suppose someone says "It's quite stuffy in here". The locutionary act performed by the speaker is his utterance of all the words in this sentence. In other words, the saying of the sentence with the explicit literal meaning is its locutionary act. The illocutionary act performed by the speaker is that by making such an utterance he has expressed his intention of speaking, i. e., asking someone to open the window, or making a complaint, depending on the context. Therefore, the illocutionary act can be a request or an order. The perlocutionary act refers to the effect of the utterance. If the hearer gets the speaker's message and sees that the speaker means to tell him to open the window, the speaker has successfully brought about the change in the real world he has intended to; then the perlocutionary act is successfully performed. So, the perlocutionary act of it can be that the hearer opens the window or that he refuses to do that, or whatever.

From the aforementioned example, one can see clearly that the literal meaning of an utterance is fixed, and the consequence of the utterance varies according to situation, as it may accord or disaccord with the literal meaning, depending on contextual factors. The speaker's communicative intention implied in his utterance or the function it is intended to perform is the most important part to pragmatic study, and that is identical with the illocutionary act. In fact, speech act theory pays most attention to the study of illocutionary acts, i. e. , how a speaker conveys his intention and how his intention gets across or is recognized by the hearer.

7.2.2 Searle's classification of speech acts

Austin's theory provided great philosophical insight into the nature of linguistic communication. In the light of the speech act theory, people are doing something when they are speaking, and the process of linguistic communication is made up of a sequence of acts. This theory soon aroused great interest among many scholars, one of whom was the American philosophical linguist John Searle, who made notable contributions to it by classifying in general five types of illocutionary acts. According to Searle (1969), there are five general types of things we do with language. Specific acts that fall into each type share the same illocutionary point or communicative purpose, but differ in their strength. The illocutionary points are assertive, directive, commissive, expressive and declarative.

The illocutionary point of the assertives or representatives is to commit the speaker to something's being the case, to the truth of what has been said. In other words, when performing an illocutionary act of representative, the speaker is making a statement or giving a description which he himself believes to be true. Usually, stating, believing, swearing and making hypothesis are among the most typical of the assertives. Naturally, the degree of the commitment varies among assertive sentences. Take the following sentences as instances. We can clearly see that sentence A "I solemnly swear that he has taken the money" has stronger commitment than that of sentence B "I guess he has taken the money".

Directives are attempts by the speaker to get the hearer to do something. Usually, inviting, suggesting, requesting, warning, threatening, ordering and advising are typical examples of this type. For instance, "Lend me some money, please" is an attempt to get something (lending money) done by the hearer. And "Would you like to go to the picnic with us?" is a question in form but an invitation in function.

Commissives are those illocutionary acts whose point is to commit the speaker himself to some future actions, i. e. , when making such an utterance the speaker puts himself under a certain obligation to do something in future. Promises, vows and offers are generally characteristic of this type. For example, "I promise to apologize" and "I will bring you the book tomorrow without fail" are commissive.

The illocutionary point of expressives is to express in the utterance the specific psychological state of the speaker, like his feelings, attitude, etc. towards an existing state of affairs. Apologizing, thanking, welcoming, deploring and congratulating are typically expressive, e. g. , "We deeply regret for your loss of your men and plane" and "I'm sorry for the mess I have made".

"Declaratives" have the characteristic that the successful performance of an act of this type brings about the correspondence between what is said and reality. To put it in another way, they cause immediate change in the existing state of affairs when an utterance of this kind is made. Verbs often used in declarations are "name", "declare", "point", "christen" and "appoint". When a boss says "I fire you" to an employee, the latter loses his job. When a chairman says "I now declare the meeting open", the meeting begins.

As has just been mentioned earlier, acts sharing the same illocutionary point may have different force or strength. Meanwhile, all the utterances that can be made to perform the same act may vary in their syntactic form. For example, in order to get someone to open the door, we can use the imperative form "Close the door", but we still have many alternatives, like "Will you open the door!", "Can you open the door?", "Do you mind opening the door?", "I would be very grateful if you could open the door!", "The door please!" and so on. That's why we can have different patterns to express our uncertainty or request. Understandably, an utterance may not necessarily perform only one illocutionary act. Sometimes, it may perform two or more than two acts. For example, warning, like "If you don't tell me that, I'll break your neck", is both directive and commissive as it both urges "you" to "tell that" and commits the speaker to doing something ("breaking your neck").

7.2.3 Indirect speech act

When "there is a direct relationship between a structure and a function, we have a **direct speech act**" (Yule, 1996: 55). For instance, in the example "I beg you not to stay here for a long time", both the structure (literal meaning) and the function of the sentence are expressing a request. So, it is a direct speech act. And according to the previous discussion, the verb "beg" is called a performative verb. However, when "there is an indirect relationship between a structure and a function, we have an **indirect speech act**" (Yule, 1996: 55). In such cases a sentence that contain the illocutionary force indicators for one kind of illocutionary act can be uttered to perform, in addition, another type of illocutionary act (Searle, 1975b: 168). And that means, sometimes, some sentences perform their illocutionary acts in an indirect way. That is to say, they perform one by performing another. These are called indirect speech acts.

So, one must know how it is possible for a speaker to say something but mean something else, and how it is possible for the hearer to understand the indirect speech acts, or what actually the speaker means. See an example. "Can you take this book to Mr. Wu for me?" is first of all a question. It asks about whether the hearer **is able to** take the book to the person mentioned. It is also a polite request. The speaker asks the hearer to do the thing for him or her. Usually, it carries the second meaning, as a conventional indirect speech act. This shows how the illocutionary act is performed in an indirect way. Look at another example. Suppose X and Y are roommates.

Ex. 7-5 X. Can you play chess with me now?

Y. I'm now up to my neck with my thesis.

As has just been mentioned, X's utterance is actually an invitation rather than a question about Y's ability. And, Y's utterance is in fact a refusal, though it is assertive literally. Generally, people share background information, and they are rational or sensible. So it will be easy for them to make out the implied meaning. They usually make a conscious inference (i. e. what does he mean by saying that which sounds irrelevant to my question?), which is automatic. The more information they share in common, the easier it will be for them to understand each other. This demonstrates that a non-conventional indirect speech act could be much more flexible and difficult in interpreting than the conventional ones.

It is found that requests are often performed in an indirect way, mostly because people mean to be polite. It's interesting that requests can be made in different ways with different degrees of indirectness and characteristics. We classify such sentences into the following types:

Type 1: Sentences which are related to the hearer's ability to do something.

Ex. 7-6 Can you fetch me the book over there on the table?

Ex. 7-7 Could you open the door for us?

Type 2: Sentences which literally deal with the speaker's wish or want that the hearer will do something.

Ex. 7-8 I would like you to shut the door.

Ex. 7-9 I'd rather you didn't do that.

Type 3: Sentences that are related to the hearer's doing something.

Ex. 7-10 Would you take it down?

Ex. 7-11 Won't you stop whistling and keep quiet for a while?

Type 4: Sentences that are related to whether the hearer is willing to do something.

Ex. 7-12 Do you want to read this letter for me?

Ex. 7-13 Would it be convenient for you to lend me five *Yuan*?

Type 5: Sentences that are concerned with reasons for doing something.

Ex. 7-14 You'd better stand there where you are and don't move.

Ex. 7-15 You should read more and try to recite some best parts.

Anyway, some utterances showing requests may be very complex with more than one characteristic. That is to say, they may have two or more than two characteristics of the above-mentioned types.

In fact, an utterance usually does not perform only one illocutionary act. A speaker may put his or her intended meanings in just one utterance (i. e. the intentions may be various, ambiguous or vague), and the hearer may find it difficult to understand what actually the speaker means. So, it is hard to decide what act or acts it actually performs. Since the meaning of an utterance depends too much on context, the speech act theory alone fails to describe and explain it.

7.3 Conversational analysis

Conversations play an important part in our daily communication, so some sociologists and sociolinguists record and analyze how people talk with each other. They want to find out some regular patterns that naturally reoccur in people's conversations. So, generally speaking, conversation analysis is an approach to the study of natural conversation, especially with a view to determining how conversation works in different conventional settings and how participants manage the structures of their conversations. That is why some of their major findings are related to the structural features of conversations.

7.3.1 The structural features of conversation

1. Adjacency pairs

When one kind of utterance is followed by another kind of utterance that is special and typically expected to come after the former utterance, this kind of relation or fact is called **adjacency pairs**. For instance, a greeting is usually followed by another greeting; a question is followed by an answer; a refusal or acceptance comes after an offer, and there are so many other cases. "Adjacent" means "near", "next to" or "close to". They are adjacent because they hold closest relation to each other. What different speakers say is ordered as the first and second part.

Sometimes, the first and second parts may be directly adjacent, i. e., they come closely next to each other, but sometimes they are separated from each other by another adjacent pair or other pairs. For example,

Ex. 7-16 A^1. Hello! May I speak to your manager?

B^2. Are you from London?

A^2. Yes, I am.

B^3. Do you have an appointment with our manager?

A^3. Yes, I do.

B^1. OK. Right away I'll give him a call.

In principle, the number of the pairs put between other pairs can be limitless. Anyway, since human beings in general cannot memorize so many of them, and for some other reasons, people usually insert at most three or four adjacency pairs.

2. Preferred second parts

In practice, a first part, or a question, may have two or more than two answers or second parts. For example,

Ex. 7-17 A. Do you know that boy in black suit?

B. (a) Do you need to know?

(b) Yes.

(c) What's that got to do with you?

(d) Why do you ask me such a question?

(e) Do you think I should tell you about him?

(f) Tell me if you know him.

(g) Do you know the girl in red?

(h) Hehh, well, sorry. I'm really glad to answer your question, but I'm afraid I can't. You know I'm a stranger here myself, and I haven't come into contact with many people here. Maybe you can ask the man over there, or you may as well ask the boy himself...

Since there are different answers to the same question, the status of them are not the same or equal. They have different meanings and values, so which one or ones do people prefer? They may be satisfied with some of the answers, but dissatisfied with others. It is found that the preferred second parts are more usual and more normal with less specific information. They are usually most directly related to the first parts in terms of meaning, like answer (b) in the above dialogue. Researchers also find that dispreferred second parts share many characteristics, or they have much in common. For instance, they give more information than needed, or they give seemingly irrelevant information. They often have elements of delay (such as the mouth fillers of "well", "let me see", "you know", "Hehh, Um..."), elements of apology (see the last answer in the above dialogue), and elements of explanation or appreciation or of other kinds when the information given is relevant (also see the last answer in the above dialogue).

3. Presequences

When the first and second parts are regarded as **sequences** (that is to say, they are put in order according to time, or which comes first and which comes after), it will be found that some sequences are used to prefigure or make sure if some other actions or events are likely to take place. The information they have seems to have nothing to do with central or key information, but they turn out to be closely related to each other when the key parts appear. For example, one may ask about other things before he finally invites his pen pal to a party:

Ex. 7-18 A. Are you going out tomorrow evening?
B. No, not really.
A. Will you be free then?
B. Yes, I think so.
A. How do you like my classmates?
B. Yeah, I like them. Why?
A. Will you please come to our party tomorrow evening, then?
B. Yes, I'd like to. That sounds like a great idea.

In this pre-invitation, the parts that come before the last two utterances are used to check or make sure if some preconditions (B's being free and willingness to come) exist for the invitation. Those parts are necessary parts for a presequence. A presequence usually has the following four turns or moves:

Turn 1: a question which is used to check if some precondition exists for some specific potential actions to be preformed in Turn 3. (e. g. as in the above-mentioned example, whether being free, whether B has a good impression of the classmates, etc)

Turn 2: an answer indicating that the precondition exists (or it doesn't exit, as it depends). (affirmative answers to the questions)

Turn 3: the actual action appears or takes place if the precondition exists, otherwise no action. (invitation)

Turn 4: response to the action in Turn 3. (acceptance of the invitation)

7.3.2 Conversational implicature and the Cooperative Principle

1. Conversational implicature

As we have discussed in previous discussions, pragmatics helps one accurately interpret what a speaker intends to mean through his or her utterance. In various contexts, the literal meaning of an utterance may be different from what is really meant by the speaker who makes the utterance. The intended meaning that is not covered in the literal meaning is called implicature, which is believed to be prevalent in everyday conversations. As Horn (2004: 3) defines it, a conversational implicature is "a component of speaker meaning that constitutes an aspect of what is meant in a speaker's utterance without being part of what is said".

It is held that a sentence in itself has a fixed and clear meaning, but when it is used in a certain context by a certain speaker for a certain purpose as an utterance, its real meaning changes. That is to say, a conversational implicature derives from its context. But how does a hearer manage to work out the implicature hidden behind the literal meaning of what is said? How does a speaker, in giving a reply to a question, try to mean something by just saying something else? How do other people correctly or incorrectly understand a conversation? And why do some replies, which are seemingly irrelevant to the questions, in fact make sense and successfully convey certain implicatures? All these questions need to be answered satisfactorily. One answer, among many others, is the Cooperative Principle (CP) proposed by an American philosopher and logician named P. Grice (1975).

2. The Cooperative Principle (CP)

We know that a speaker may quite often mean a lot in his utterances besides the literal meaning of what he says. But how do we know a speaker means more than what is said? How can we get the implied meaning exactly? How can a speaker try to mean more than what is said? Grice (1975) believes that there must be something that controls and determines the production and comprehension of these utterances. To make the conversations move on smoothly, people need to observe some shared principles, especially the so called Cooperative Principle. To be more specific, it is his thought that, in principle, people willingly cooperate by obeying or following a set of special rules, which he calls "assumptions", when they have conversations, and, they in that case mean just the literal meaning of their utterances. But when the rules are violated, or when people do not obey the rules in their conversations, either consciously or unconsciously, conversational implicature appears. One thus may realize that they mean more than merely the literal meaning of their utterances. Grice calls the set of rules the Cooperative Principle, because he thinks people can carry on their conversation only when they are willing to cooperate with each other in their conversations; if they do not, the talk cannot be carried on. He describes the Principle as a general one consisting of four maxims, simplified as follows:

The General Principle: Make your contribution such as is required, at the stage at which it occurs, by the accepted purpose or direction of the talk exchange in which you are engaged.

The Maxim of Quantity: Give information as required for the conversation (not much but not less).

The Maxim of Quality: Say what you believe to be true and that you have enough evidence for.

The Maxim of Relevance: What you say should be relevant to your conversation.

The Maxim of Manner: What you say should be brief, clear, put in good order and avoid obscurity and ambiguity.

3. Violation of CP and conversational implicatures

Grice believes that conversation participants nearly always follow the principle in their talk, but they do not obey the rules so closely. In fact, for some reasons, the maxims are often violated. When they are violated, conversational implicatures appear, and people mean more than what they say literally. In this sense, conversational implicature refers to the extra meaning that is not contained in the utterance. Usually, people violate the maxims intentionally or on purpose. If a speaker and a hearer share much background knowledge in common, it will be possible for them, especially the hearer, to understand the extra meaning and make out why and how the speaker violates the maxims. Let's see the following examples and understand how the violation of the four maxims respectively affects the meaning of the utterances.

Ex. 7-19 A. Do you know where Prof. Wang lives?

B. Yes. Somewhere on the campus. (e. g. , rather than "*Yes. No. 25 of Zhongshan lane.*")

Both A and B know Prof. Wang lives somewhere in the university, so A wants to know the specific address in detail, but B gives a general answer and withholds the very information A requires. And he does that on purpose, because he does not want to tell A the address of the professor. The Maxim of Quantity is violated, and the implicature is thus produced.

Ex. 7-20 A. I'm wondering if I can use your laptop for a while?

B. I'm afraid it's broken. (e. g. , rather than "*Yeah. Please do.*")

Both A and B know that the laptop is working properly, but B says something that he himself knows to be false and violates the Maxim of Quality. The implicature produced is clear, "I'm not willing to lend you my laptop."

Ex. 7-21 A. Do you think that Ms. Rold is married?

B. Did you enjoy the movie last night? (e. g. , rather than "*No, I don't think so.*")

Both A and B may have their own understanding of Ms. Rold's marital status, but B asks A another question instead without answering his question. B's question is obviously irrelevant to A's question, so B violates the Maxim of Relevance on purpose. The implicature is "I don't wish to talk about other people's private life in such a rude manner."

Ex. 7-22 A. Your name and title, please.

B. Jack Powell. Associate editor and professor. (*Maybe he is an associate editor and associate professor.*)

B should give a definite and clear answer rather than an ambiguous one, so he violates the Maxim of Manner. It can be figured out that he is trying to win a false reputation or fish for fame and compliments.

Sometimes, a speaker may know that he is going to violate or is violating some Maxim, so he may say something to give a hint to the hearer or remind him. That will help the hearer understand the speaker better. We call this "licensing violations of the maxims", because it is like that the speaker has a license to violate the maxims, or he has his reasons for violating the maxims. Let's cite some examples. When one knows he is going to violate the Quality Maxim because he knows he is not sure about what he is going to talk about, he may make it clear by saying, "I don't remember the details, but it seems that..." or "I was told that...", or "I guess it's a sort of special device...". When it comes to the Quantity Maxim, he may say, "Well, I well know that I should give you a brief account, but it's really a long story to tell, and it's really important..." When the speaker is aware that what he is going to talk about is irrelevant to the conversation topic, he may use some special ways to make his topic turn direction smoothly. He may say, "Yes, what you said just now really reminds me of..." When he is conscious of his possible violation of the Manner Maxim, he may say, "I'm afraid I've mixed you up. Let me put it in a simple way..."

That happens often in our daily conversations. We can see that the use of these licensing remarks shows clearly that the Cooperative Principle is playing a very important role in conversation. We also know that people use such remarks just because they share the same psychological activities, as they think it is important for them to be polite and cooperate with each other in their community.

Last but not least, if conversational implicature is considered a type of implied meaning, which is deduced on the basis of the conversational meaning of words together with the context, under the guidance of the CP and its maxims, one can find it easy to make sense of the major features of it, i. e. its calculability, cancellability, non-detachability, non-conventionality and indeterminacy (Levinson, 1983: 114-118).

7.3.3 The Politeness Principle

Grice's maxims of conversation rely on the cooperative principle. That is, in conversations, participants should stick to the above-mentioned four maxims, or conversational implicatures may occur. But it is demonstrated that in conversations, participants do violate these maxims. One may wonder, why must they obey the cooperative principle in verbal communication? And why do they intentionally violate the principle by choosing to communicate in an indirect or a seemingly irrelevant way instead of giving a direct and clear reply? The Grician theory fails to answer these questions satisfactorily, but many theorists point out that the answer is related to politeness. In other words, people violate the cooperative principle mainly because they intend to be polite in conversing.

Various politeness theories have been proposed. For example, Robin Lakoff (1973) argued that much conversation interaction is governed by what she called the politeness principle. She defined this further by specifying three rules or maxims that speakers usually observe: 1) Don't impose; 2) Give options; 3) Make your receiver feel good. According to Brown & Levinson (1978, 1987), politeness involves us showing an awareness of other people's face wants, and face refers to our public self-image. There are two aspects to this self-image: positive face and negative face. The former refers to the want of every member that his wants be desirable to at least some others. The latter refers to the want of every "competent adult member" of a society that his actions be unimpeded by others. However, researchers argue about the nature of politeness as it can be observed as a social phenomenon in all cultures. Therefore, it is hard to define politeness as it differs among cultures. And this facts leads to the heated discussion about such questions as "what is politeness?", "What are politeness strategies?" and "what are acts that threaten other people's face?". However, the Politeness Principle proposed by

Geoffrey Leech (1983) has been considered the most reasonable and influential theory so far.

1. The Politeness Principle (PP) and its maxims

In the centre of this concept does not stand the information of a conversation, but the effect of what is said on the people. In everyday situations we primarily use language for various communicative purposes, for example, to get information, to gain knowledge about a topic or to reach a variety of goals. To effect successful communication, one has to follow some important strategies. Beside the Cooperative Principle, there exists another Politeness Principle which has above all been developed by G. Leech. The principle is a series of maxims, proposed as a way of explaining how politeness operates in conversational exchanges. According to Leech, politeness is defined as forms of behavior that establish and maintain comity. That means the ability that participants in a social interaction have to engage in interaction in an atmosphere of relative harmony. Referring back to Searle's categories of illocutionary acts, Leech points out a subdivision into negative and positive politeness. The negative politeness belongs eminently to the directive group, while positive politeness is dominant in the commissive and expressive group. In stating his maxims, he uses his own terms for two kinds of illocutionary acts. He calls *representatives* "assertives", and calls *directives* "impositives".

Leech (1983) proposed the Politeness Principle which is formulated in a general way from two aspects: 1) to minimize the expression of impolite beliefs; 2) to maximize the expression of polite beliefs. The six maxims are stated as follows:

(1) **Tact maxim** (in directives/ impositives and commissives)

A. minimize cost to other

B. maximize benefit to other

(2) **Generosity maxim** (in directives and commissives)

A. minimize benefit to self

B. maximize cost to self

(3) **Approbation maxim** (in expressives and representatives/assertives)

A. minimize dispraise of other

B. maximize praise of other

(4) **Modesty maxim** (in expressives and representatives)

A. minimize praise of self

B. maximize dispraise of self

(5) **Agreement maxim** (in representatives)

A. minimize disagreement between self and other

B. maximize agreement between self and other

(6) **Sympathy maxim** (in representatives)

A. minimize antipathy between self and other

B. maximize sympathy between self and other

It is clear that each maxim is accompanied by a sub-maxim, which is of less importance. These support the idea that negative politeness (avoidance of discord) is more important than positive politeness (seeking concord). In fact, Tact maxim and Generosity maxim form a pair, just like the two sides of a coin. Tact maxim states how one treats others and Generosity maxim states how one treats himself. See in the following instances the differences in politeness due to the effects of the two maxims:

Ex. 7-23 A. Could you possibly take me home? vs. Take me home.

B. You must have dinner with me. vs. I must have dinner with you.

Approbation maxim and Modesty maxim are related in the same fashion. Compare the following examples:

Ex. 7-24 A. What an outstanding performance! vs. You could be more careful!

B. Please accept this small gift for your birthday! vs. Accept this large gift for your birthday!

And see in the following examples, respectively, how Speaker B tries to agree with Speaker A, and how Speaker B shows sympathy with Speaker A:

Ex. 7-25 A. I have brought some apples here.

B. That's great. It's my favorite. (vs. Oh, My God! That's too bad.)

Ex. 7-26 A. My sister lost her purse in the market.

B. Oh, it's most unfortunate. (vs. Oh, I'm glad to hear that!)

It should be noted that not all of the maxims are equally important. For instance, tact influences what we say more powerfully than does generosity, while approbation is more important than modesty. One should also note that speakers may adhere to more than one maxim of politeness at the same time. Often one maxim is on the forefront of the utterance, with a second maxim being invoked by implication. If politeness is not communicated, we can assume that the politeness attitude is absent.

Leech holds that the Politeness Principle can rescue the Cooperative Principle in that they supplement each other and combine to account for the facts that people violate the Cooperative Principle mainly because they intend to follow the Politeness Principle. It is commonly believed that the Politeness Principle itself is universal among cultures, but the politeness maxims might be different across cultures. Therefore, polite beliefs may vary from culture to culture and consequently such a basic asymmetry may cause politeness problems in cross-cultural communication. But still there are interrogations as to how motivated every human being is in saving others' face and being polite in conversations, and some researchers just wonder if participants really stick to these six maxims in verbal interactions or even other human interactions as Leech believed.

2. Characteristics of the Politeness Principle

Participants in social interactions must know the pragmatic features of the linguistic means they use in following the Politeness Principle. When conversing, they should be well aware of the gradations of the principle, bearing in mind the grades in politeness of linguistic means and knowing what grades to use when obeying the principle.

A. Gradations

Grades of politeness can be demonstrated in various linguistic expressions. In fact, all the grades form a continuum. Generally, the grade of politeness is in direct proportion to the degree of indirectness of such expressions. One should know how to use them appropriately in specific contexts, i. e. , he should be able to use them properly to effect successful communication and achieve the desired goals. See the following examples:

Ex. 7-27 a. Lend me your dictionary.

b. I want you to lend me your dictionary.

c. Will you lend me your dictionary?

d. Can you please lend me your dictionary?

e. Would you mind lending me your dictionary?

f. Could you possibly lend me your dictionary?

In this continuum, the grade of politeness in the six utterances increases in order, and they are supposed to be used to the right persons in the right contexts. If one uses a most formal expression to a generally most familiar talking partner in an informal context, or vise versa, their relation might be spoilt because special implicature is believed or suspected to have occurred. For example,

Ex. 7-28 I was wondering if you could possibly be so kind as to lend me your dictionary for just a few minutes?

It is clear that the division of grades of politeness of linguistic means is in nature a matter of deciding how to use linguistic expressions to perform various speech acts in a polite way.

The grades of politeness are also manifested and measured by employing the cost and benefit scale. In general, to follow the Politeness Principle implies benefiting others as much as possible and cost oneself as much as possible. By doing that, one makes others feel respected and in turn wins favor from them. Therefore, the more respectful one is to others, the more polite his linguistic expression is. In this sense, another continuum of politeness grades can be established according to this scale. However, this continuum does not demonstrate the grades of politeness of linguistic expressions, but the ones based on how much others are benefited or how much one is cost. For example, the grades vary much in the following imperative utterances according to how much the hearer is benefited:

Ex. 7-29 a. Sweep the floor.

b. Pass me the salt.

c. Sit down.

d. Look at that.

e. Enjoy your stay here.

f. Have another apple.

From these utterances one can see clearly that the degree of politeness vary in accordance with how much a hearer is benefited and how much a speaker is cost. Generally speaking, the more the hearer is benefited, the more polite the utterance is; the more the utterance is polite, the more the speaker is cost. In addition, it calls our attention that both the grades of politeness of linguistic expressions and the gradations of the Polite Principle are closely interwoven in real-life verbal interactions and of service for the following of the principle. Though an imperative utterance might sound impolite, it may be polite if the hearer is benefited. In this way, the speaker still obeys the Polite Principle.

B. Conflicts

Since there are so many maxims and sub-maxims that play roles in deciding the Polite Principle, it is only natural to expect them to conflict in one's effort to follow the principle. For example, Tact maxim may conflict with Generosity maxim, Modesty maxim may conflict with Agreement maxim, and Agreement maxim may conflict with itself. For example,

Ex. 7-30 A: Let me carry the luggage for you.
B: Oh, thank you.

Ex. 7-31 A: (An English native) You have drawn a wonderful picture!
B: (A Chinese student) Oh, not at all. You are kidding.

Ex. 7-32 A: English is a difficult language to learn.
B: Indeed, but its grammar is quite easy.

In Ex. 7-30, if speaker A really wishes to carry the luggage for speaker B, he follows both Tact maxim and Generosity maxim of PP, and the Maxim of Quality of CP. But if he does not really wish to do that, he actually follows Tact maxim but violates both Generosity maxim and the Maxim of Quality because he offers to do that just in order to sound polite. In this case, Tact maxim conflicts with Generosity maxim. Similarly, in the cross-cultural interaction demonstrated in Ex. 7-29, Modesty maxim conflicts with Agreement maxim because both speakers follow PP in their special ways specific to their own cultures, which are different from each other in that regard. In Ex. 7-30, the affirmation of A's statement as a whole followed by partial negation of it indicates that Agreement maxim conflicts with itself because speaker B intentionally violates the Maxim of Quality first and then soon follows it, in each of which cases he tries to follow Agreement maxim of PP. Leech (1983) calls this feature of conflicts between the maxims "pragmatic paradoxes of politeness".

C. Appropriateness

The feature of appropriateness means that one should follow the Polite Principle by using linguistic expressions according to the demands of context. To be more specific, it means a speaker should decide the degree of politeness of his linguistic means in accordance with what is talked about, who the addressee is and the situation in which the talk takes place, taking into consideration the degree of benefit and cost to both sides.

A speaker should well choose his linguistic expression in right degree of politeness according to what is communicated in the interaction, especially in the light of his communication purpose. For example, when the speaker intends to make a request, he may be very careful in choosing the appropriate expressions to achieve that goal, with the degree of politeness varying according to whether the occasion is formal or how likely the request can be satisfied. Sometimes he may pay most attention to following the principle and use the expressions with very high degree of politeness. See the following utterances:

Ex. 7-33 a. Just give me one buck.
b. Let's take a seat.
c. Give me the knife, will you?
d. Is there any chance that you can help me to find a right place to stay for a couple of days?
e. I'm afraid it will be much nicer if it is a little bit more salty.

In that case, the speaker might violate a maxim of CP in order to follow PP, as in the utterance E, he intentionally violates the Maxim of Manner of CP in order to ask for some more salt in a polite manner.

Meanwhile, the speaker must consider his relationship with the addressee before choosing an appropriate linguistic form to use for his purpose. That is to say, the politeness degree of the linguistic expression should fit the relationship between the addresser and addressee, as expected culturally in a general sense. A too formal expression used between familiar friends or family members or a too informal expression used between an employer and employee would similarly cause offence, surprise or communication failure of other kinds. Let's refer back to Ex. 7-26. Generally a speaker will not say that to his close friend if he does not intend to convey anything special beyond just borrowing a dictionary from the friend. Similarly, a wife usually will not use the too formal expression as follows just in order to ask her husband to make or fulfill a little promise:

Ex. 7-34 I am wondering if I could possibly ask you about your promise to go out and have dinner with me?

And one is generally expected to know very well who will use which of the following expressions to ask for the permission to smoke when the speakers are a soldier and his officer:

Ex. 7-35 A: Mind if I smoke?

B: Excuse me, sir, but would it be all right if I smoke here?

What is equally important is that a speaker should also have clear knowledge about how to choose appropriate linguistic forms to suit the right occasions, when they are formal or informal or somewhere in between. For instance, when a speaker wants to ask for permission or opinions from others, he may use "Shall I..." when on a rather formal occasion or "Do you want me to..." when on an informal occasion. Similarly, introduction making between people on occasions of different degree of formality vary accordingly. Look at the following examples:

Ex. 7-36 a. Shall I call a taxi for you?

b. Do you want me to call you a taxi?

Ex. 7-37 a. Hi, Tom! Come and meet my friend John.

b. I don't think you've ever met my friend John before. This is John, and this is Tom...

c. Hello, Professor! Shall I introduce you to Dr. Levin, Dean of Faculty of Linguistics?

d. Professor Smith, please allow me to introduce Dr. Levin, Dean of Faculty of Linguistics.

Understandably, inappropriate use of linguistic forms without considering the degree of formality of the occasion where an interaction takes place will usually cause offence or other undesired results as it violates the Polite Principle. And in following the principle speakers need to pay adequate heed to the three features of it and choose appropriate linguistic forms to effect successful communication.

Exercises

1. Decide whether the following statements about speech acts are true or false.
   1) The key constituent of an explicitly performative utterance in the performative verb, because the meaning of the performative verb is the essence of the illocution.
   2) A theory of meaning mainly aims to account for the meaning of a speaker's speech acts.
   3) Every declarative sentence can be true or false in certain context.
   4) Performatives are formally marked and easily identifiable while speech acts are not.
   5) There seems to be no very direct relation between speech act and the forms of words used. Nor can we identify speech acts with sentence types.
   6) The first stage in establishing the meaning of a speech act is to establish that the utterance act has taken place, then the second stage is to identify the sense or senses of what the speaker has said or asked or told the hearer to do.
   7) Most of what people say is aimed toward the success of illocutionary acts, as the purpose of speaking is often to cause an effect in the hearer.
   8) The maxims of Cooperative Principle are never to be violated in people's daily conversation.
2. Tell whether the following utterances are performative (P) or constative (C).
   1) "I promised Tommy to lend him my bike."
   2) "I admit that I made a blunder then."
   3) "I congratulate you on your latest promotion."
   4) "I've permitted him to use my dictionary."

5) "The management of the library advises the readers not to take the books out of the library without permission."

3. What type of illocutionary act do the following utterances involve?
   1) "I suggest that you see a dentist as soon as possible." ______
   2) "I will pay you the money I owe you next time." ______
   3) "Passengers are reminded that flight No. 2284 leaves here at 7:00 sharp."

      ______
   4) "Shut up! Leave me alone!" ______
   5) "I'm very sorry to hear that you've just lost your pet dog." ______
   6) "Can I fetch the purse for you?" ______
   7) "Don't come a step nearer, or I'll shoot." ______
   8) "I bet you a dollar I can jump that puddle." ______
   9) "There is a spider on the collar of your T-shirt." ______
   10) "Thank you for what you've done for me during my stay in Shanghai."

      ______
4. Can we insert "hereby" into the following utterances without changing the meaning? If "yes", fit it in.
   1) "I must take leave of you."
   2) "I sentence you to ten years of hard labour."
   3) "All passengers on Flight No. 42 are requested to proceed to Gate Seven."
   4) "I don't grant your request for more loans."
   5) "I charge you with attempting to murder a policeman."
5. Give the INDIRECT illocutions to express the illocutionary force given in the following sentences.
   1) Suggesting that the hearer should phone his mother on her birthday.

      ____
   2) Offering some candies to a friend. ______________
   3) Promising to take the child to a movie the next day. ______________
   4) Requesting politely the hearer not to make too much noise. ______________
   5) Apologizing for stepping on the hearer's foot. ______________
   6) Warning the hearer of the scorpion on his back. ______________

7) Ordering the hearer to keep quiet. ______________

6. Study the following utterances and tell what illocutionary force each of them has.
   1) "You can shut up now!" ______________
   2) "Sugar is not good to your teeth." ______________
   3) "Do you want a lift?" ______________
   4) "Will you recite me a poem?" ______________
   5) "I bet that the Republican will win." ______________
   6) "I pronounce you guilty as charged." ______________
7. Answer the following questions.
   1) In what way is semantics related to and different from pragmatics?
   2) What does context contribute to the understanding of utterances?

Chapter 8 Historical Linguistics

All languages change through time although the process is rather slow and it sometimes takes generations to witness any really significant change. **Diachronic linguistics**, or **historical linguistics**, is a sub-field of linguistics concerning the change of a language. It examines a language as it changes through time, which is in contrast to **synchronic linguistics**, a sub-field of linguistics that studies a language at a particular point in time. In other words, historical linguistics studies the historical development of a language and the ways language changes, which normally takes place at phonological, morphological, syntactic, and semantic levels. The historical study of a language is of great importance because it may help to reconstruct the earlier stages of languages and establish the genetic relationships among different languages, which may throw light on the causes that lead to the change of languages as well as the laws that govern the development of languages. All this is of great significance to our understanding of human languages.

8.1 A brief history of English language

English has undergone great, even fundamental changes throughout its development. Modern English speakers would find Old English simply unintelligible because it is so different from the language they speak. The following example of an Old English sentence with its translated version, which is a line from *Beowulf*, an epic written in the 8th century, may well illustrate this:

Ex. 8-1 Wolde guman findan pone pe him on sweofote sare geteode

(He wanted to find the man who harmed him while he slept)

Generally speaking, the history of English language is divided into three periods: Old English, Middle English and Modern English.

8.1.1 Old English (449—1100)

The history of the English language began with the migration of the Jutes, Angles, and Saxons from Germany and Denmark to Britain in the 5th and 6th centuries. Their Anglo-Saxon language is known as **Old English**, which is the ancestor of Middle English and Modern English.

Old English differs dramatically from Modern English in pronunciation, especially in the long vowels. Take the Old English word *hām* for example. The word *hām* is the same word as Modern English *home*, but the vowel [*ā*] is different: the sound [*ā*] has shifted to the sound [əu] in Modern English.

Other examples of vowel change:

Ex. 8-2 fūl——foul

blōd——blood

spēd——speed

Some consonants of Old English are also different from those of Modern English. For example, in Modern English, the sound /ʃ/ is represented by the letters *sh* while in Old English it is indicated by the letters *sc*, as in the word scēap(=sheep). In Modern English, a clear distinction is made between the sound [f] and [v] while in Old English the two sounds didn't exhibit any significant difference.

Besides the great difference in pronunciation, Old English and Modern English also display marked difference in morphology. In contrast to Modern English, which is an analytic language, Old English, which was a synthetic language, was highly inflected. For example, Old English had three genders (masculine, feminine, neuter) in the noun and adjective, and nouns, pronouns, and adjectives were inflected for case. Besides, Old English had a greater proportion of "strong verbs" (i. e. irregular verbs) than Modern English. Many verbs that were "strong" in Old English have become "weak" (i. e. regular) in Modern English, as is indicated by the following examples:

Ex. 8-3

	present infinitive	past singular	past plural	past participle
Old English	helpan	healp	hulpon	holpen

Modern English	help	helped	helped	helped

8.1.2 Middle English (1100—1500)

The period of **Middle English** is usually dated 1100—1500, i. e. , from the time of the Norman Conquest to the eve of the English Renaissance.

The Middle English period began with the **Norman Conquest** of England by Norman under the leadership of William the Conqueror in 1066. One of the most significant facts of the early part of this period, as far as the development of the English language is concerned, was the steady erosion of the Old English inflectional system. Actually, the dialects of the Old English had already shown tendencies towards dropping a great many of their inflections, and it was during the Middle English period that the whole sets of inflections became further weakened and less distinct, and some finally dropped completely from the language. The weakening of inflectional system naturally led to the change in syntactic structure. In the Old English period, the word order of a sentence was highly inflexible because the semantic relationship of words in a sentence could be indicated by means of inflections. In the Middle English period, however, the word order of a sentence became relatively stable because the semantic relationship of a sentence was denoted through word order rather than inflections. All this shows that during the Middle English period, English underwent a gradual (but dramatic as a whole) change from a synthetic language to an analytic language.

The Middle English period also saw a great influx of French and Latin words, which constitute a major part of English vocabulary. These borrowed words cover a wide range of fields including politics, law, military affairs, religion, science, as well as everyday life. The following is a list of words borrowed from French and Latin:

Ex. 8-4 Words borrowed from French: government, liberty, religion, baptism, plea, judge, army, fashion, pork, dinner, painting, etc

Words borrowed from Latin: history, homicide, rational, solar, ulcer, scripture, custody, immune, etc

Towards the end of the 14th century, there emerged a variety of English language which, in the course of the 15th century, won general recognition as standard in both speech and writing. With London dialect as its base, this variety of English, which is called standard English, began to be regarded as the standard national language of England and remained so when English developed into its modern form—Modern English.

8.1.3 Modern English (1500—the present)

The Modern English period extends from 1500 to the present time. It is generally accepted that this period is divided into two parts: the early Modern English period and the late Modern English period.

The early Modern English period extended from 1500 to 1700. During this period, a most important change in sound system of English, i. e. , the **Great Vowel Shift**, took place which produced far-reaching influence on the development of the language. The Great Vowel Shift chiefly involves the changes in the pronunciation of the long vowels in English, which is characterized by the raising of the tongue position of the long vowels; besides, the highest long vowels—the [i] and the [u] in back—became diphthongized, as is indicated by the following examples:

Ex. 8-5	Middle English		Modern English
	feet	[fe:t]	[fi:t]
	tooth	[o:]	[u:]
	ride	[i:]	[ai]
	house	[u:]	[au]

The Great Vowel Shift took place gradually and systematically, and it was largely because of this sound-shift that present English spellings of many words are not consistent with their modern pronunciations.

The late Modern English period, which started from 1700, was a time of stabilizing and purifying the English language. This period continued to see the disappearance of inflections, and the word order of English sentences became more and more fixed, thus making English move toward an analytic language. On the other hand, French and Latin words continued to find their way into English vocabulary. Besides, with the progress of the Industrial Revolution in the early part of the 19th century and the growth of the power of the British Empire, the English language itself was also very busy producing new words and expressions to meet the need of the time. As a result, the late Modern English period has been regarded as a time of rapid expansion of the English vocabulary in the history of the English language.

In brief, English has undergone great changes in its sound system, lexis, and syntactical structure during its long history of development. It is due to all these changes that English has been shaped to its present form.

8.2 Linguistic changes of English

All languages are subject to change, and English is no exception. What's more, historical linguistics has revealed that the change of language is, to a large extent, systematic and regular rather than disorderly and arbitrary. Generally, the change of a language can take place at such different levels as those of sound, lexis, morphology, syntax and semantics.

8.2.1 Sound change

1. Great Vowel Shift

The most prominent sound change in the development of English is the change of vowels which took place during the period of 1400—1600. This change, known as the **Great Vowel Shift**, involves seven long, or tense vowels, as is indicated in the following table:

Table 8-1

Sound change		examples	
Middle English	Modern English	Middle English	Modern English
[iː]	[ai]	[riːd]	[raid] ride
[uː]	[au]	[muːs]	[maus] mouse
[eː]	[iː]	[feːt]	[fiːt] feet
[ɛː]	[ei]	[grɛːt]	[greit] great
[ɔː]	[ou]	[brɔːken]	[brouk] broke
[oː]	[uː]	[goːs]	[guːs] goose
[ɑː]	[ei]	[nɑːmə]	[neim] name

The Great Vowel Shift had a great influence on the pronunciation of English language. As a matter of fact, it is largely due to this sound change that we find such a major inconsistency between the pronunciation and the spelling system of Modern English.

2. Sound loss

In the development of English language, some of its phonemes may be lost or disappeared. This is called **sound loss.** Take the sound [x] in Old English as an example. The words like *liht* (light), *niht* (night) and *siht* (sight) were once pronounced [li:xt], [ni:xt], [si:xt] respectively. This velar fricative, however, was lost between the time of Chaucer and Shakespeare. All the words that were once pronounced with a [x] no longer include this sound. In some cases the sound [x] has become [f], as in *laugh*, *enough*, etc; while in some other cases the sound has disappeared, as in *light*, *sight*, etc.

Sound loss can also occur in utterances at the cost of some unstressed vowels, as is reflected in the following examples:

Ex. 8-6 temperature ['tempərətʃə]→['temprətʃə]
laboratory [lə'borətri]→['læbrətori]
cabinet ['kæbənət]→['kæbnət]

3. Sound addition

While some sounds were lost in the course of the historical development of English, some other sounds were added to the original sound sequence. Take the sound [ʒ] for example. Old English did not have this sound. But when French words like *measure*, *pleasure*, *usual* and *rouge* came into English, [ʒ] came into English together with the words in which it occurs. Thus, we now have the two distinctive phonemes /ʃ/ and /ʒ/ in contrast with each other in Modern English.

8.2.2 Lexical change

It is generally accepted that change at lexical level is the most noticeable and eye-catching, which chiefly involves three dimensions: addition of new words, loss of words, and change in the meaning.

1. Addition of new words

English vocabulary can be enlarged either by word-formation or by borrowing.

1) Word-formation

Word-formation is concerned with the ways in which words are formed. It normally involves such processes as affixation, conversion, compounding, clipping, acronym, blending, back-formation and coinage.

Affixation is a word-formation process in which affix is added to the base. There are two types of affixation: prefixation and suffixation. Prefixation means the addition of a prefix to the base with or without a change of word-class while suffixation refers to the addition of a suffix to the base with or without a change of word-class. For example,

Ex. 8-7 Prefixation: un- → unfortunate/non- → non-standard/in- → insane/dis- → dishonest/mis- → misunderstand/mal- → malfunction/sub- → subtitle

Suffixation: -er → Londoner/-ess → hostess/-ship → relationship/-dom → freedom/-ful → spoonful/-ism → individualism/-ment → development

Conversion is a word-formation process by which a word is changed from one part of speech into another without the addition of an affix. For example,

Ex. 8-8 Verb → noun: dismay (v. to fill with dismay) → dismay (n. strong feeling of hopelessness)

Adjective → noun: daily (adj. every day) → daily (n. daily newspaper)

Noun → verb: coat (n. a covering spread over a surface) → coat (v. to give a coat to)

Compounding is a word-formation process of combining two or more words into one lexical unit. For example,

Ex. 8-9 sun + rise → sunrise

heart + breaking → heartbreaking

blue + print → blueprint

baby + sit → baby-sit

brain + wash → brainwash

Clipping is a word-formation process of cutting part of a word to form a new word. For example,

Ex. 8-10 e-mail←electronic mail
phone←telephone
Prof←professor
math←mathematics
hi-fi←high fidelity
bike←bicycle

Acronymization is a word-formation process by which a word is formed from the initial letters of a group of words. Words formed through this means are called **acronyms**. For example,

Ex. 8-11 CEO←chief executive officer
PC←personal computer
WTO←World Trade Organization
UN←United Nations
EU←European Union

Blending is a word-formation process in which a new word is made by using the parts or the full form of the two words and combining their meaning. For example,

Ex. 8-12 Chinglish←Chinese+English
brunch←breakfast+lunch
smog←smoke+fog
motel←motor+hotel
psywar←psychological warfare

Back-formation is a word-formation process in which a shorter word is derived by deleting an imagined affix from an already existing longer word in the vocabulary. For example,

Ex. 8-13 edit←editor
beg←beggar
televise←television
daydream←daydreamer
type←typewriter

audit←auditor

negate←negation

Coinage refers to the process in which new words are invented. The English vocabulary changes with the development of society. With the political, economic and social changes as well as the development of science and technology, new words have been constantly invented or coined, which contributes to the rapid expansion of English vocabulary. For example, *Xerox*, *nylon*, *Coke*, *Kodak* are all coined words.

2) Borrowing

English vocabulary has borrowed heavily from other languages, especially from Greek, Latin, French, Spanish and Scandinavian languages, among which the French may have played the most prominent role in this process due to the result of the Norman Conquest. Here are some examples of borrowed words:

Ex. 8-14 Greek: technology, hepatitis, neurology, electric, metaphor, tragedy, botany

Latin: history, inferior, rational, legal, solar, project, enterprise, tuberculosis

French: government, reign, court, army, guard, fashion, ballet, prestige, coup, baptism

Spanish: guitar, macho, tornado, junta, renegade

Scandinavian: anger, calf, husband, awkward, happy

German: waltz, quartz, nickel, swindler, hurrah, plunder

Italian: violin, trill, soprano, balcony, bust, granite, stanza

Dutch: dock, keel, smuggle, gin, loop

Hindi: ginger, shampoo, thug, punch

Chinese: wok, silk, kowtow, chopsticks

2. Loss of words

While new words are constantly entering the storehouse of the English language, one can also witness the disappearance, or the loss of some words, although this process is rather slow and gradual and is not as striking as the arrival of new words. Words such as *wherefare* (why), *wot* (to know), and *gyve* (a fetter) were once common during Shakespeare's time, but now they have disappeared from English language. Some other words, though still considered to be the members of English vocabulary, are obsolete or on the way out because of the discontinuity of the objects or concept they name. For example, since we no longer carry swords, the word *foin*, meaning "the thrust of a sword" is no longer in common usage. Words such as "soap flake", "wash board" and "rumble seat" are also of this kind.

8.2.3 Morphological change

Morphological change is chiefly brought about by the loss of inflections. The most noticeable morphological change in English can be found in the conjugation of verbs and the plural forms of nouns, which can be shown by the following examples:

Ex. 8-15		Middle English	Modern English
	verbs	didst	did
		hath	has
		speakest	speaks
		sayd	said
	nouns	wayes	ways
		seedes	seeds

Another dramatic morphological change of English concerns the loss of gender markings. Old English had a gender-marking system which divided nouns into three genders of masculine, feminine, and neuter. For example, "stan" (stone) was marked masculine, while "gief" (gift) and "deor" (wild animal) were marked feminine and neuter respectively. However, this gender-marking system has been greatly reduced during the development of the English language.

8.2.4 Syntactic change

1. Change in word order

In old English, word order was not so crucial because the language at that time was so highly inflected that the grammatical relations between words could be indicated by inflections. However, with the loss of inflections, new rules governing the word order enter the language. As a result, the word order of the language has changed considerably and has become relatively fixed. Take a look at the following example:

Ex. 8-16	Old English	Word-for-word translation
	Se man sloh þone keening	(* The man slew the king)
	Þone kyning sloh se man	(* The king slew the man)
	Se man þone kyning sloh	(The man the king slew)
	Þone kyning se man, sloh	(The king the man slew)
	Sloh se man þone keening	(Slew the man the king)
	Sloh þone kyning se man	(Slew the king the man)

The above six sentences on the left were all grammatically correct in Old English. Besides, they all express the same idea of "The man slew the king". However, on the right only two of their word-for-word translations (first two sentences with asterisks) are grammatically acceptable in modern English with each expressing a different idea, and the rest four simply do not make any sense.

2. Change in negation rules

In Middle English period, negation was expressed by putting negative particle *not* at the end of a sentence, for example, "I like it not" or "He saw you not". But in Modern English, *not* is put after finite elements, as in "I do not like it" or "He did not see you".

3. Change in comparison

In Middle English period, double comparatives and superlatives of English adjectives and adverbs were grammatically acceptable, as in *more gladder*, *more oftener*, *most slowliest*, *most beautifulest*, etc. In Modern English, however, we form the comparative by adding suffix *-er* to an adjective or by inserting *more* before it, and form the superlative by adding suffix *-est* or by inserting *most* before it, as in *gladder*, *more often*, *happiest*, *most beautiful*, etc.

8.2.5 Semantic change

Semantic change refers to the change in meaning, which may involve three dimensions: broadening, narrowing, and meaning shift.

1. Broadening

Broadening means the extension or generalization of the meaning of a word. Take the word *Solomon* as an example. This word used to mean "King of Israel in the 10th century B. C. who was famous for his wisdom". Today its meaning has been broadened and may denote any profoundly wise person. Another example is the word *tail*, which once referred to "the tail of a horse". However, it is now used to mean "the tail of any animals". Here are some more examples of broadening:

Ex. 8-17 holiday: holy day→any day for rest

pipe: a simple tube-like musical instrument, played by blowing→a tube used for carrying liquids and gas, often underground

2. Narrowing

Narrowing means the restriction or specialization of the meaning of a word. For example, the word *corpse* originally meant "a human or animal body, living or dead". But later this meaning was narrowed and now it has specialized to mean "a dead body, especially of a human being". The word *girl* can be cited as another example. This word originally meant "a young person of either sex, a child, a boy, or a girl". Now it has come to mean "a female child, a young woman". The following are some other examples of narrowing:

Ex. 8-18 meat: food and drink→flesh of animals used as food, excluding that of fish and birds

starve: die→die of hunger

deer: any animal→a particular species

3. Meaning shift

Meaning shift includes two dimensions: meaning elevation and meaning degradation. The former refers to the semantic process in which a word acquires good implications while the latter means the process in which a word gains unfavourable meaning. For example, the word *minister* underwent the process of meaning elevation during its semantic development. This word originally meant "servant" which carries some unfavourable meaning. Now it has come to mean "person at the head of a department of the government", which bears commendatory meaning. By contrast, the semantic change of the word *wench* shows an opposite shift of meaning. This word once meant "a young woman or girl, especially in the country". Now it means "a lewd woman, prostitute".

Other examples of meaning elevation:

Ex. 8-19 nice: foolish or stupid→fine, kind, friendly
comrade: roommate → fellow member of a political party or organization

Other examples of meaning degradation:

Ex. 8-20 silly: childish or naïve→foolish
lust: pleasure→strong sexual desire

8.3 Language family and language typology

Scholars have long been aware that many of the modern languages of the world originated, in some sense, from more ancient languages. For example, it was known that Modern English developed out of Anglo-Saxon English spoken by the Angles, Saxons and Jutes, and that what we now refer to as the Romance languages—French, Spanish, Italian, etc—all had their origin in Latin. What's more, it has also long been noticed that our present languages may have evolved from some genetically related common sources, or proto-languages. In fact, the study of the relationship between different languages can be traced back to as early as the 18th century, the first half of which saw the emergence of the linguistic study of Sanskrit, the classical language of India, by European scholars. The study of Sanskrit was the first major incitement to early 19th century comparative and historical work of linguistics. Then in the latter part of the 18th century, a significant breakthrough was made by Sir William Jones, a judge in the British court in India, who, in 1786, read his famous paper to the Royal Asiatic Society in Calcutta. In this paper, Jones established beyond doubt the historical relationship of Sanskrit with Latin, Greek and the Germanic languages by pointing out that all of them bear "a stronger affinity, both in the roots of verbs and in the forms of grammar". (Quoted in Robins, 2001: 168) Jones's work paved the way for the development of historical and comparative linguistics, which dominated the linguistic study of the 19th century.

8.3.1 Historical comparative linguistics

Historical comparative linguistics is the comparative study of the relationships or correspondences between two or more languages and the rules that govern the historical development of these languages. It is *historical* because it deals with the histories of particular languages; it is *comparative* because it deals with the relations between languages. Historical comparative linguistics aims at developing and establishing the genetic relationships which exist among the world's languages and finally reconstructing the proto-language from which these languages were derived.

1. Grimm's law

The significant discovery of Sir William Jones made in the latter part of the 18th century ushered in the new age of historical comparative linguistics in the 19th century. During the first half of this period, scholars such as R. Rask, Franz Bopp, R. Schlegel, Jakob Grimm and Karl Verner made thorough studies from various perspectives and achieved fruitful results in revealing the genetic relationships between European languages. Among various findings in this period, the most important one may be **Grimm's Law**, which is a description of the regular sound correspondence in Indo-European languages formulated by German scholar Jacob Grimm. This law unveils for the first time the prominent correlations between the Germanic and other Indo-European languages of Europe (though his discovery is partly attributed to the work of R. Rask, a Danish scholar who first showed that, in their consonant sounds, words in the Germanic languages vary with a certain regularity from their equivalents in the other Indo-European languages). It is important in that it clearly demonstrates the principle that sound change is a regular and systematic phenomenon rather than a random process affecting only some words. Grimm described two consonant shifts involving essentially nine consonants. For example, according to the law, the ancient unvoiced *p*, *t*, *k* became the English unvoiced *f*, *th*, *h* and the Old High German *f*, *d*, *h*, hence the correlation between Greek *pod*, English *fod*, and Old High German *fuo*; and the ancient voiced *d*, *b*, *g* became the English unvoiced *t*, *p*, *k* and the Old High German stops *ts*, *f*, *kh*, hence the correlation between Latin *duo*, English *two*, and modern German *zwei* (pronounced *tsvai*).

2. Verner's law

Grimm's law shows that sound shift was highly regular and systematic. However, there are cases in which Grimm's law fails to explain. For example, Grimm's law states that the Indo-European *p*, *t*, and *k* sounds changed into *f*, *th* or *d*, and *h* in the Germanic languages. Verner, a Danish linguist, noticed that Grimm's law was valid whenever the accent fell on the root syllable of the Sanskrit cognate, but, when the accent fell on another syllable, the Germanic equivalents became *b*, *d*, and *g*. This was also the case with *s* and *r*. Therefore, Verner provided linguistic explanation of the apparent exceptions to Grimm's law, which first demonstrated the significant role that accent (stress) played in linguistic change in the Germanic languages. Verner's explanation of sound correspondence and some exceptions was later called **Verner's law**, which serves as a indispensable supplementation to Grimm's law.

The correspondence of sound shift between Indo-European languages revealed by Grimm's law and Verner's law is of great significance. It is because of this amazing sound correspondence that the linguists began to be aware of the fact that different languages were genetically related and each of them may be traced back to the same original (or ancestral) form of a language family. This original form of language, which has ceased to exist, is technically called **proto-language**. In brief, the linguistic achievements made in the first half of the 19th century made it possible for the linguists to probe into the genealogical relationships between different languages and, based on this, to classify them into different language families accordingly.

8.3.2 Language family

There are more than four thousand languages in the world. These languages can be grouped together by their distinctive shared characteristics, into subfamilies.

There are generally two different theories of setting up a language family: the family-tree theory and the wave theory.

1. Family-tree theory

Family-tree theory was first proposed in the middle of the 19th century by the German linguist A. Schleicher, who believed that language is an organism exhibiting periods of development, maturity, and decline, therefore it could be studied by the methods of natural science. Developing a system of language classification resembling a botanical typology, he traced groups of related languages and arranged them into a genealogical tree, which is shown in the following diagram.

The Indo-European Language Family Tree

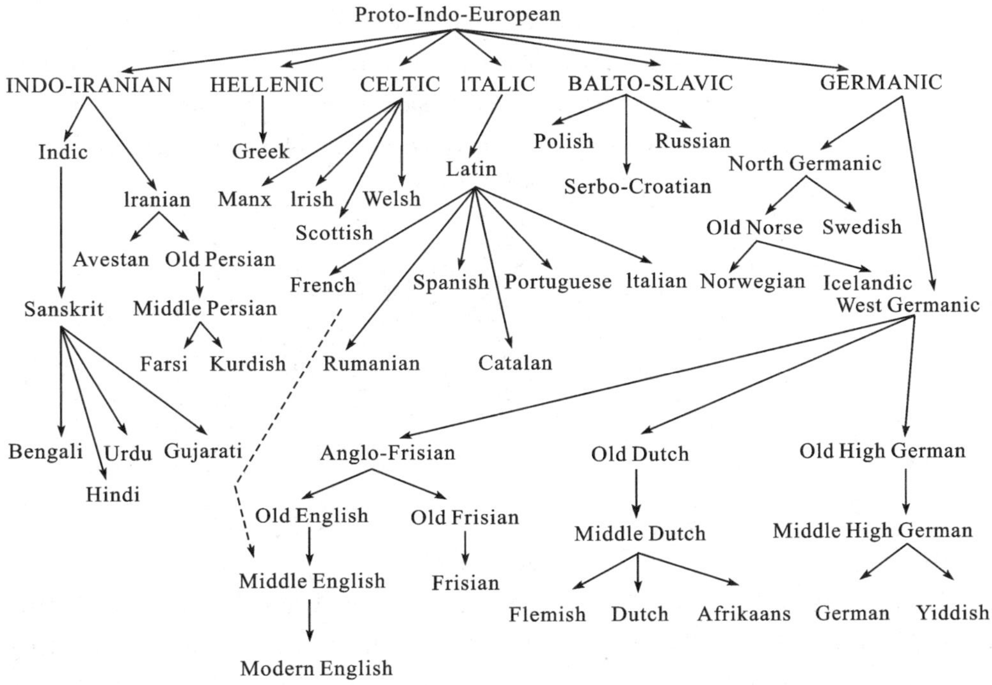

Diagram 8-1

Schleicher's family-tree model represents an important development in historical linguistics. It provides an easy and direct means of displaying the relations between the members of a linguistic family. However, it is open to certain objections. Languages do not sharply split at a given point in time corresponding to the division of a line in the tree, instead, a language splits itself gradually into various dialects or even separate languages, the departure of a dialect from its family must be a lengthy and gradual process, and it is difficult to make a definite split of one dialect from others, because as the differences between dialects are widening, the dialects will continue to influence each other. In view of the shortcomings of family-tree theory, another theory, i. e. , wave theory, was set forth by J. Schmidt.

2. Wave theory

Rather than replace it, J. Schmidt, a student of Schleicher, supplemented family-tree theory with his **wave theory**. This theory shows that a language may exist in different dialects that overlap each other in some aspects (e. g. sound, vocabulary, syntactic structure, etc). As the dialects evolve into separate languages, they continue to influence each other, as is indicated by the following diagram:

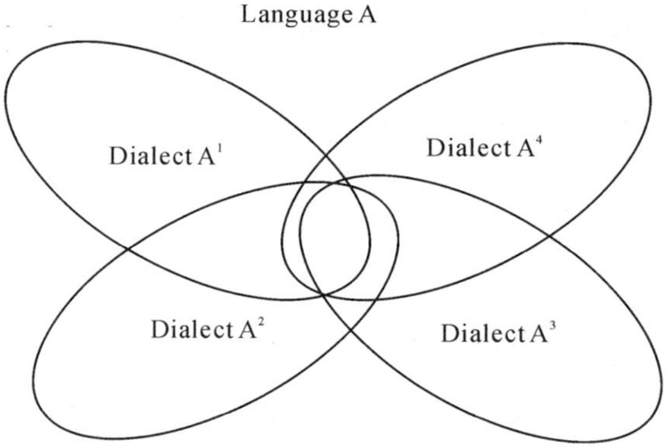

Diagram 8-2

Though the wave theory may have its merit in showing the influence between languages, it also has its limitation in that the variables in it are much more difficult to check and verify. Therefore, linguists continue to discuss family relationship among languages by tree model rather than wave model.

3. Language family

As has been mentioned above, languages can be grouped together into language families in terms of shared features which have been retained during the process of divergence from a common ancestor. To date, about thirty language families have been identified and recognized, among which four language families are considered to be the most important, i. e. , the Indo-European family, the Sino-Tibetan family, the Afroasiatic (or Hamito-Semitic) family, and the Austronesian family.

The Indo-European family, the biggest of all the language families in the world, is divided into the Germanic, Italic (or Latin), Slavic, Indo-Iranian, Baltic, Celtic, Hellenic, Albanian and Armenian subfamilies. It includes most of the European languages (about 150 languages) and many languages spoken in North India. The Sino-Tibetan family, the second biggest only to the Indo-Eurpoean language family in terms of the number of speakers, is normally classified into Sinitic (or Siamese), Tibeto-Burman, Miao-Yao and Zhuang-Tong subfamilies. It mainly consists of about three hundred East Asian languages. The Afroasiatic (or Hamito-Semitic) family has two subfamilies: Hamitic and Semitic. It is chiefly made up of classic Arabic and the Arabic languages and dialects of the Middle East and North African coast, and Hebrew and other related languages. The Austronesian family comprises up to a thousand different languages scattered over one third of the southern Hemisphere. English, the most widely used language of the world, belongs to the Low West Germanic branch of the Indo-European family while Chinese, the language spoken by the most population, is a major member of the Sino-Tibetan family.

8.3.3 Language typology

Language typology is concerned with the typological classification of languages. Based on the morphological and syntactic structures, different languages can be grouped into different types without any regard to either their historical origin or their present or past geographical distribution. Usually, languages are classified into the following four types according to their morphological characteristics:

a. **Isolating languages.** Isolating languages refer to those in which the grammatical relations of the words in a sentence are indicated chiefly through function words and word order rather than through internal inflections. Chinese, especially classical Chinese, is usually considered to be a typical isolating language for its complete lack of inflections. Vietnamese and several other Southeast Asian languages also belong to this type.

b. **Agglutinative languages.** Agglutinative languages are those in which words are typically composed of a sequence of affixes added to the root. Agglutinative languages have no internal inflections. In such languages, various morphemes are combined to form a single word with each element maintaining a distinct and fixed meaning. Turkish, for example, is a typical agglutinative language in which a word can be segmented into a root and several affixes with each affix carrying one grammatical meaning, and the boundary between affixes is clear-cut due to the absence of fusion, as is indicated by the following example:

Ex. 8-21	*ev*	house
	evim	my house
	evimde	in my house

The root *ev* means "house" in English, and the suffixes *-im* and *-de* refer to "my" and "in the" respectively. Therefore, the word *evimde* may be segmented into a root and two suffixes, and each of them carries a distinct meaning. Other languages such as Japanese, Korean and Hungarian also fall into the type of agglutinative languages.

c. **Inflectional (or Fusional) languages.** Inflectional languages are those in which morphemes in a word are fused together, and a word undergoes a change in morphological form when its grammatical function in the sentence is changed. Due to the presence of fusion of affixes, it is usually difficult to cut the word into its component morphemes. Latin, for example, is an inflectional language in that its verb is inflected for person, number and tense, as is indicated by the following examples:

Ex. 8-22	*amo*	I love
	amas	you love
	amat	he/she loves
	amamus	we love

Other languages like Ancient Greek, Sanskrit, German, and Russian can also be grouped into this type.

d. **Polysynthetic languages.** Polysynthetic languages are those in which a number of word elements are joined together to form a composite word that functions as a sentence does in the languages of other types. Actually, this type of languages may be considered as lying at the extreme end of the synthesis continuum with a very high number of morphemes per word (at the other extreme are isolating or analytic languages with only one morpheme per word).

It should be noted that the fourfold classification discussed above only represents a tendency, and no language falls neatly into one or another type. For example, we may say that Modern English is somewhat inflectional. But on the other hand, the inflectional morpheme —*ed* attached to the verb to form the past tense means only "past tense". Neither the singular and plural distinction nor the person distinction is specified in the inflectional morpheme —*ed*. This is, then, an agglutinative suffix. Again we may say Modern English is to some extent agglutinative, but on the whole, it is more isolating than inflectional or agglutinating. Therefore, typological classification of languages is relative rather than absolute. A language may possess more characteristics of one type of languages than those of other types.

The above classification of languages is chiefly based on the morphological features. It should be noted that languages can also be classified into the following two types on the basis of syntactic characteristics: synthetic languages and analytic languages. A **synthetic language** is one in which grammatical relations of words are indicated chiefly by inflections. Agglutinative, inflectional and polysynthetic languages, to a great extent, belong to this type of languages. By contrast, an **analytic language** is one in which grammatical relations of words in a sentence is showed largely by means of word order and function words rather than by inflections. Based on this classification, we may say that Latin, Greek, Russian, Old English and Turkish belong to synthetic languages while Chinese, Vietnamese and Modern English fall into the type of analytic languages.

8.4 Causes of language change

As is indicated at the beginning of this chapter, languages change in the course of time. Then why do languages change? It seems that there is no generally accepted answer to this question. Several theories of language change have been put forward, but none of them covers all the facts. In spite of this, linguists have come to the agreement that the following factors play the most important part in the development of languages.

8.4.1 Sociological factors

Sociological factors mainly involve such political or social events as internal/international political struggles, social changes, wars, colonialization, etc. A typical example of sociological factors is the Norman Conquest, a military event that marked the dawning of the Middle English period. Other examples include British colonial settlement, and the country's political, cultural and economic advances in distant lands such as North America, Oceania, South Africa, and India, which has led to the change of English into British, American, Australian, South African and Indian varieties.

The last century also witnessed great linguistic changes brought about by sociological factors. For example, the women's liberation movement which took place during the 1960s has produced a number of new words such as *chairperson*, *chairwoman*, *sexism*, *Ms.*, *spokesperson* while the international struggle during the latter part of the last century led to the coinage of such words as *superpower*, *hotline*, *globalism*, *mega-death*, *Watergate*, etc. In a word, with the rapid development of our modern society, linguists have become increasingly aware of the important role social factors play in the change of language.

8.4.2 Development of science and technology

The linguistic changes brought about by this factor are evident, which is chiefly showed in the expansion of vocabulary. For example, there were no such words as *telegraph*, *steamship*, *steam engine*, and *automobile* before the 17th century, and it was only in the 18th century, an age of rapid technological development brought about by the Industrial Revolution, that these words were coined and entered the storehouse of English vocabulary. It should be noted that, with the rapid development of modern science and technology, new words are being produced every day at an unprecedented speed. Words and expressions such as *nano*, *NMD*, *Dolly*, *big tent*, *White Watergate* etc are just the recent coinages which might be unknown even to some of the native English readers of the 1990s. In brief, new words appear in large numbers in the fields of science and technology, which has greatly enriched the English vocabulary.

8.4.3 Phonological and grammatical simplification

Many phonemes and morphemes lost their special features in the course of time because of "linguistic laziness" on the part of language users, which can be accounted for by the "theory of least effort", i. e. , we tend to exert as little effort as possible in our use of language. Here sound assimilation is a good example of phonological simplification. Sound assimilation refers to the physiological effect of one sound on another. In an assimilative process, successive sounds are made more or less similar or even identical to one another in terms of place or manner of articulation. For example, the Old English word *Engla-land* (the land of the Angels) came to be pronounced *England* through the assimilation of "la-la" sounds.

Grammatical simplification can often be found at the level of morphology. This kind of change, which is reflected in the loss of special status of some morphemes, has been called "internal borrowing" or "analogical change". In other words, we "borrow" from one part of the grammar and apply the rule generally. For example, by analogy to the plural formation of *foe/foes*, and *dog/dogs*, speakers started using *cows* as the plural of *cow* instead of the earlier plural *kine*. Similarly, by analogy to the past formation of *hand/handed*, and *finish/finished*, people began using *dreamed* as the past form of *dream* rather than the earlier form *dreamt*.

The use of the word *cheap* in place of *cheaply* may serve as another good example to illustrate the "theory of least effort". In theory, the distinction between these two words is clear: *cheap* is an adjective while *cheaply* an adverb, as is shown in the following two sentences:

Ex. 8-23 Fresh vegetables are very cheap in summer.
He sold the furniture cheaply.

However, *cheap* has been used as an adverb by more and more people, especially in colloquial English, for example:

Ex. 8-24 I was very luck to get it so cheap.

As a matter of fact, the use of the word *cheap* as an adverb has already found its way into English dictionary, and it is not impossible for its correspondent *cheaply* to gradually disappear from the English vocabulary and the same form *cheap* will be used both as adjective and adverb, just as the word *better* does at the present:

Ex. 8-25 I've got a better job.
Have another try. You can do better!

8.4.4 Children's language acquisition

Language may undergo some changes in the course of children's language acquisition. When children acquire their language, no one teaches them the rules of the grammar. Each child builds up his own grammar on his own generalized rules from the linguistic input he receives. In this way the child constructs his grammar step by step which will eventually become complex enough to come close to the grammar used by adults. The children's grammar, however, may never be identical with that of the adults', for he may receive linguistic input from many dialects of different styles used around him, and the features of these grammars may then merge, and certain rules may be simplified or over-generalized. The older generation may tend to use "variable" rules. For example, at certain times they may say "I don't know whom to give it to" but at other times they may also say "I don't know who to give it to". By contrast, the later generation may use only the *who* form of the pronoun in similar sentences. In such a case, the grammar will change.

From what has been discussed above, we can come to the conclusion that there is no single cause of language change, and English language changes in the course of time due to both internal factors (e. g. assimilation, analogy, etc) and external factors (e. g. the development of science and technology, etc). This is also the case with the changes that take place in all the other languages of the world.

Exercises

1. Decide whether the statements are true or false.
   1) English is more closely related to German than French.
   2) Scandinavian languages refer to Icelandic, Norwegian, Danish and Swedish.
   3) Old English was a highly inflected language.
   4) In early Middle English period, English, Latin, and Celtic existed side by side.
   5) The introduction of printing into England marked the beginning of modern English period.
   6) Modern English is considered to be an analytical language, and so is Chinese.
   7) The major factors that promote the growth of Modern English are advances in science and technology as well as foreign cultures and language.
   8) The most important mode of vocabulary development in Modern English is creation of words by means of word-formation.
   9) The most vigorous and on-going change in the historical development of English is the change in its grammar.
   10) In Old English syntactic relations such as agreement were heavily indicated by functional words and word order.
2. Discuss briefly what major sound changes have taken place during the development of English language.
3. Answer the following questions.
   1) How does a language undergo semantic change?
   2) What language families do Chinese and English belong to?
   3) According to their morphological structure, what type of language do Chinese, English, Japanese, Russian, and Latin fall into respectively?

Chapter 9　Sociolinguistics

Language is the major link between the individual and society. Therefore the study of language can never be divorced from the social context in which a language is used. Sociolinguistics is the study of the sociological aspects of language. In other words, it studies language in social contexts. As a sub-discipline of linguistics, it concerns itself with the part language plays in maintaining social roles in a community and language variation as well as language use in different speech communities, which include regional, ethnic and social groups. It is also concerned with the impact of extralinguistic factors on language use, such as age, gender, profession, and social status.

9.1　Variety of language related to the user

9.1.1　Notion of variety

We know that people use different types of language in different social contexts. A speaker may vary his language to some extent in accordance with such factors as the occasion on which the speech occurs, the addressor-addressee relationship, the subject matter, etc. For example, the type of language used by a professor in a classroom lecture would be totally different from the one he uses at home when he talks with his wife, and the following three sentences, which express basically the same idea but are in different forms, also illustrate the different use of language in different social contexts:

a. Would you please be so kind as to open the window?

b. Will you please open the window?

c. Open the window, will you?

Therefore we can find that the word "English" is merely a generalization of many different types of the language, hence the concept of "Englishes" or "varieties", which can be defined as the actual manifestations of the general notion of the language. Varieties are assumed to be related both to the language user and to the use to which language is put. Varieties related to the user are normally known as "dialects" and varieties related to use as "register".

9.1.2 Dialect

Traditionally, the term **dialect** denotes the type of language related to different geographical locations. However, now the notion of this term has largely been extended and it takes into account all variations of a language related to the user, which mainly involves regional dialect and social dialect.

1. Regional dialect

Regional dialects are the different varieties of the same language spoken in different geographical areas. Take English as an example. We know that Modern English has become an international language and is used as the first language by tens of countries in the world. As a result, varieties of the English language are gradually formed due to the differences existing in different countries which are located in different parts of the world and which have different social or cultural backgrounds. So there exist British English, American English, Canadian English, Australian English, South African English and so forth. They are all geographical dialects or varieties of Modern English. Even inside a country the national language may have different varieties. It is known that China is a country with a vast territory and a big population. Modern Chinese, as our national language, has many geographical dialects, such as the Northern Dialect (including the Beijing Speech, on which *putonghua*, or the Standard Spoken Chinese, is based), the Wu Dialect, the Xiang Dialect, the Min Dialect, the Yue Dialect, etc.

The differences between regional dialects are, to a large extent, brought about by the lack of communication due to geographical barriers such as mountains, rivers, or swamps. It should be pointed out, however, that the development in transportation and mode of communication has helped to decrease the stability of regional dialect, thus resulting in the decrease of geographical variation in language.

2. Social dialect

We know that people of different social classes, occupations, religious beliefs and educational backgrounds would speak differently, which is a reflection of the varieties of language related to social factors. This variety of language determined by social factors is called **social dialect**, or sociolect. Generally speaking, social dialect of a language is usually influenced by such factors as sex, social class (economic and political background), age, education, occupation, race, religious belief, etc.

9.1.3 Language variety and social class

A speaker's use of language is much influenced by his social status and educational background. For example, in the U. S. , the speeches of the upper-class speakers and those of the non-upper-class ones do not follow the same phonological patterns. For example,

Ex. 9-1	Upper Class	Non-Upper Class
	'yesterday	yester'day
	'inte'resting	inte'resting

The linguistic difference related to people's social class can also be found in the use of vocabulary. For example, people of higher class tend to use "big", refined and flowery words which are associated with social prestige while people of lower class are inclined to use "small", simple and common words, or even vulgar and slang words, although this difference in the use of vocabulary between people of different social status is not absolute and is merely a matter of degree on the part of the language users.

In grammar, a noticeable example of sociolect is the mistaken use of double negation such as *I can't eat nothing*, a structure closely related to the social status of the speaker, which can be shown in the following list:

Social class	the occurrence of double negation
Upper middle class	2%

Lower middle class	11%
Upper working class	38%
Lower working class	70%

The examples discussed above show clearly the great influence social class might have on the type of language used by people.

9.1.4 Language variety and race

Racial factors in English are best shown in Black English. For example, the phonology of Black English differs from Standard English in that it seems to have a sharper pitch variation and more pauses because longer sentences are usually cut into shorter clauses. Besides, with the drop of many inflections, morphology was greatly simplified, and so was syntax, as can be seen in the following list:

Ex. 9-2

Variable	**Standard English**	**Black Non-standard English**
Linking verb	He is going	He-goin'
Plural marker	I have five cents	I got five cent-
Third-person singular	He lives in New York	He live-in New York
Past tense marker	Yesterday he walked home	Yesterday he walk-home
Negation	I don't have any	I don't got none

9.1.5 Language variety and sex

It is not hard to notice that languages used by men and women are different to some extent. Generally, women use more linguistic items from standard English than men, therefore their speech comes more closely to the standard variety than the speech of men. For example, in pronunciation, men tend to pronounce /n/ for /ŋ/ and fewer women do so. In intonation pattern, women normally have a wider range in their intonation than men do. In lexical features, females tend to use uncertain, polite, or refined words while men usually use decisive, strong or even rough words. In syntactic features, women tend to use tag questions more frequently than men. All this indicates the different use of language between men and women.

The reason for the above-mentioned differences is subject to debate. Some linguists believe that women are more status conscious than men and, therefore, use more items associated with upper class speech (the prestige form of speech). Others argue that non-standard items are associated with masculinity and toughness, so men use them to identify themselves with these qualities.

9.1.6 Language variety and age

The type of language used by the older generation usually differs to some extent from that used by the younger generation, and certain linguistic features occur more frequently in the speech of one generation than in that of the other. For example, younger generation prefers to use newly-coined, or vogue words and slang expressions while older generation tends to use more stable or even out-dated ones. The causes of such differences chiefly lie in the different social attitude, value judgments, etc, between the two generations.

9.1.7 Idiolect

Every speaker has his own pet words and expressions and special ways of expressing his idea in language. This language variety used by an individual speaker is called **idiolect.** Therefore, idiolect is a personal dialect of an individual speaker characteristic of his geographical location, social and educational background, and personal preference in using the language. Idiolect involves such features as voice quality, pitch and stress patterns, the choice of lexical items, and grammatical structures, etc, which often reveal the personal identity of the speaker. Idiolect is also reflected in written language. For example, the choice of words and syntactic structure of one writer may differ greatly from those of another, which is closely related to the question of a writer's style. For instance, James Joyce's style of writing is different from that of Mark Twain, and Mark Twain's style differs from Jack London's. No wonder some linguists hold that, from the perspective of the sociolinguistics, you are, in many respects, what you say or write.

9.1.8 Standard dialect

Standard dialect is a particular variety of language that is not related to any particular group of language users, and is possibly used by any member of a speech community regardless of his social and geographical background, his sex and age. Standard dialect, which has a widely accepted and codified grammar and vocabulary, is often based on a selected variety of language. Usually it is the local speech of an area which is considered the nation's political and commercial centre. For example, the Standard English developed out of the English dialects used in and around London as they were modified over the centuries by speakers in the court, by scholars from universities and writers. Gradually the English used by the upper classes in the capital city diverged markedly from the English used by other social groups and came to be regarded as the model for all those who wished to speak and write well. In the United States, Standard American English (SAE), a form of language used in news program in the national media (known as "network English"), is also regarded as a form of standard dialect. In China, the central government stipulates *putonghua* (Standard Spoken Chinese), the standard dialect in China, as the standard common speech in the communication media and schools, and encourages its popularization across the country. In brief, in most countries, the standard dialect serves as a yardstick against which all other varieties are measured.

9.2 Variety of language related to the use

9.2.1 Register

Language is a means of communication, which is always carried out on a certain occasion, to a certain addressee, and for a certain purpose. The social life of human beings and the domain of their activity are various, and so is the relationship between people. It can be easily observed that language varies with the user and it also varies with the circumstances under which the language is used, i. e., according to the social context in which the language user finds himself. It's not hard for us to note that the same person uses different linguistic varieties in different situations and for different purposes. A lawyer in court might say, "The defendant wishes to inform the court that he is innocent." This would sound pompous, and inappropriate, in the street outside the court, and would probably be expressed by the same lawyer as, "He wants to tell you he didn't do it." Many sociolinguists have tried to work out models to describe the relationship between social variables and linguistic features. A well-known one of these is Halliday's register theory. According to Halliday, "language varies as its function varies; it differs in different situations"(Quoted in 戴炜栋,何兆熊,华钧,1989:144). The type of language that is selected as appropriate to a type of situation is **register.**

Halliday further distinguishes three social variables that determine the register: field of discourse, tenor of discourse, and mode of discourse.

1. Field of discourse

Field of discourse reflects the purposive role of the language user in the situation in which a text has occurred. It is concerned with the purpose and subject matter of communication, and it answers the question of "why" and "about what". Field of discourse may be technical or non-technical. Shopping, game-playing, and a personal letter are instances of non-technical fields. Technical fields refer to the specialized fields such as a professor of sociology giving a lecture in class or a physicist talking about the theory of relativity to a group of college students. Since field of discourse is concerned with the subject matter, it determines to a great extent the vocabulary to be used in communication. Besides, grammatical characteristics also seem to be determined by the field of discourse. This results in the recurrence of certain patterns, for example, in scientific writing in English, people tend to use the passive voice and lengthy pre-and post-modification of nominal heads for definition and precision as economically as possible in space; and in religious prayers, a high incidence of vocative nominal groups, imperative clauses and modal verbal groups.

2. Tenor of discourse

Tenor of discourse refers to the role of relationship in the situation in question:

who the participants in the communication group are and in what relationship they stand to each other. It answers the question of "to whom" the speaker is communicating. This dimension to a great extent determines the level of formality and the level of technicality of the language we use.

3. Mode of discourse

Mode of discourse mainly refers to the means of communication. It is concerned with "how" communication is carried out. Language can be either spoken or written, and different means of communication may have a direct influence on the register of language. For example, people often use such mouth-fillers as "err", "mm", and "hum" in their conversation to fill the gap of hesitation or uncertainty. These words in themselves are basically meaningless and seem to be redundant, but they enable us to get some idea about the attitude the speaker holds to the addressee or the things being talked about, and they also make the style of the language very informal. While in writing, people normally have enough time to organize the idea they want to express, therefore redundant words frequently found in speech do not often occur in writing, and this helps to make the style of the written language relatively formal.

The defining of the three variables mentioned above is of importance in that, in terms of these variables, any instance of communication can be analyzed. For example, a lecture on the theory of relativity in the department of physics at a university can be identified as:

field of discourse: scientific (physics)

tenor of discourse: teacher-students (formal, polite)

mode of discourse: oral (academic lecturing)

To sum up, the three variables are the features of the context of situation which determine the features of language appropriate to the situation, i. e. register. And they determine the register collectively, not in isolation.

9.2.2 Scales of formality

Language used on different occasions differs in the degree of formality, which is determined by the social variables, e. g., whom we are talking with, what we are talking about, and in what way the communication is carried out, etc.

An American linguist Martin Joos(1968) distinguishes five scales of formality, namely, (1) intimate, (2) casual, (3) consultative, (4) formal, and (5) frozen, as can be illustrated by the following examples:

Ex. 9-3 Frozen: Visitors would make their way at once to the upper floor by way of the staircase.

Formal: Visitors should go up the stairs at once.

Consultative: Would you mind going upstairs right away, please?

Casual: Time you all went upstairs now.

Intimate: Up you go, chap!

Frozen style, which is characterized by rigid language structure and precise expression of ideas, is normally used in technical writing (e. g. business letter, official document, legal document, etc) or very formal speeches.

Formal style is chiefly used in writing or public speech, the main purpose of which is to give information. Formal style is characterized by well-organized sentence structure and exact use of words and expressions.

Consultative style, which can be treated as a kind of "neutral" style, is the base of other different styles. It is characterized by precise diction, complete sentence structure, and full expression of ideas.

Casual style is normally used between friends, acquaintances or insiders. It has two features: one is the frequent use of slang; the other is the use of elliptical sentences, which is the most striking syntactical marker in differentiating consultative style and casual style.

Intimate style is used between people having very close relationship (e. g. between husband and wife); therefore, the communication can be carried out without participants' reference to anything about background knowledge. This style is characterized by the highly elliptical structure and the use of jargon.

Different styles of the same language can be characterized by differences at three levels, namely, syntactic level, lexical level and phonological level.

A look at the following two passages will reveal how language can vary at the syntactic level:

Ex. 9-4

Passage A

Although learning is judged to be required from teachers (and sometimes indeed it does), the real instructors may be found not so much in school or in great laboratories as in the student's own powers of insight.

Passage B

We think we learn from teachers, and we sometimes do. But the teachers are not always to be found in school or in great laboratories. Sometimes what we learn depends on our own powers of insight.

The reader will immediately sense that Passage A is more formal than Passage B. The use of passive and impersonal constructions as well as the "not so much... as..." structure in Passage A accounts in part for its greater degree of formality.

Variation at the lexical level is quite obvious, for example,

Ex. 9-5	Less formal	More formal
	fire	conflagration
	begin	commence
	building	edifice
	fat	corpulent
	thin	emaciated

Phonological variations can also be found in different contextual styles of an individual's speech. For example, contracted forms such as *isn't*, *didn't*, *shouldn't* etc, are often found in colloquial English while in formal speech they are seldom used. Besides, sound ellipsis (e. g. *cos*→*because*) and weak form (e. g. the weak form of articles) often occur in colloquial speech while in formal speech they could hardly be found.

9.3 Standard and non-standard dialects

9.3.1 Standard dialect

As has been discussed in the second part of this chapter, standard dialect is a particular variety of language. This variety has a widely accepted, codified grammar and vocabulary and is normally spoken by educated people and used in literary writing, official documents, news broadcasts, legal writings, etc. It is taught in schools, used in the army and government and propagated by the mass media. The political leaders and the upper social and economic classes of many countries use the so-called prestigious dialect—the standard dialect of their own language. The development of a standard dialect by modern states has been extremely important as a way for them to express their national identity in relation to each other; as a way of strengthening internal unity; and as a prerequisite for economic and political modernization. In Britain, the standard language evolved slowly over time; as the upper class of southeast England came to dominate the country, their way of speaking and writing gradually became the standard, accepted norm for the whole country.

Four processes have been identified in the emergence of a standard language:

a) Selection of the language: the selected language is usually an existing spoken variety of a dominant social group, as in Britain; or an artificial variety, for example Bahasa Indonesia; or even one with no native speakers like Hebrew.

b) Codification: dictionaries and grammars are written to establish the norm.

c) Elaboration of function: the standard is used in all official functions and in writing, therefore it is taught at school and used in news media.

d) Acceptance: people must accept the norm.

It should be noted that, although the standard language of many countries is also designated as the national or official language, these three types of languages do not always coincide. There are some languages in the world which are neither national nor official, though they are highly standardized. A country may designate a particular language as its official language which is not a national language. For example, a number of countries in the world have adopted English as their official language, but it does not and cannot serve as a symbol of nationhood or cultural identity for most of the citizens of those countries, who belong to a very large number of distinct ethnic and linguistic groups. Therefore, English in such a case is not the national language of the countries, although it is the standard and official language.

9.3.2 Non-standard dialect

Language varieties other than the standard are called non-standard, or vernacular, dialect. Some people hold that non-standard languages are substandard. However, this view is rejected by linguists because it suggests some inherent inferiority of these varieties. As a matter of fact, the view that the standard variety of language is superior to non-standard variety of language is by no means justifiable. From a historical point of view, the standard dialect of a language is not different in essence from its related non-standard dialects. All dialects of a language are equal in function, as they are equally expressive. So it is wrong to say that the standard dialect is superior to any other related dialects.

9.3.3 Lingua franca

There are many areas in the world populated by people speaking different languages. In such areas, where groups of people desire social or commercial communication, one language is often used by common agreement. Such a language is called a **lingua franca**. In other words, lingua franca is a variety of language that serves as a common speech for social contact among groups of people who speak different native languages or dialects.

The term "lingua franca" was first given by the Crusaders. But the language used by the Crusaders was not the first lingua franca in the history of mankind. In medieval times, a trade language based on Italian but mixed with French, Spanish, Greek and Arabic was called Frankish Language, which was a lingua franca. The term was generalized to mean any language similarly used. Any language can be a lingua franca. Today when we find a language which is commonly used by people whose native languages are different, we may describe it as a lingua franca. Therefore, all trade languages are lingua francas, such as Swahili, which is used and understood in nearly every market place in East Africa. English may be taken as "the lingua franca of diplomacy", and Latin and Greek were the lingua franca of

Christianity in the West and in the East respectively. Yiddish has long served as a lingua franca among all the Jews in the world when they get contact with each other.

9.3.4 Esperanto—an artificial lingua franca

With increasing international contacts many people have hoped for a universal language, in which people all over the world can communicate with each other. But no natural language can serve such a function, though some languages, say English, French and Spanish, are widely used by many peoples in the world. Since the 17th century, many scholars have been devoted to inventing planned lingua francas with the hope that they would get universal acceptance and satisfy international communication. But unfortunately, nearly all of them failed, because they are too abstruse, difficult and boring to learn.

In 1887, Dr. Zamenhof, a Polish scholar, invented an international auxiliary language which is named **Esperanto** after Dr. Esperanto. Esperanto, to some extent, is a successful artificial language and enjoys an increasing acceptance by people all over the world. It is said that Esperanto is now spoken by several million speakers in the world. At some international academic conferences Esperanto is also used as one of the languages in which scholars and scientists communicate with each other.

Esperanto is relatively simple for Europeans to learn because its words are derived from roots commonly found in the European languages, particularly in the Romance languages. It uses twenty-eight Latin letters, each having only one sound. Orthography is phonetic, all words being spelled as pronounced. The stress of every word is fixed with the second syllable from the last receiving the accent. Therefore one can pronounce all the words of Esperanto correctly if he has mastered the pronunciation of the twenty-eight letters. The main part of its vocabulary comes from Latin, Germanic and Greek languages. Grammar is simple and regular; there are characteristic word endings for nouns, adjectives, and verbs. Nouns have no gender and are marked by the ending *-o*; the plural is indicated by *-oj* (pronounced *-oy*), and the objective (accusative) case by *-on*, plural *ojn*; e. g. *amiko* "friend", *amikoj* "friends", *amikon* "friend (accusative)", *amikojn* "friends (accusative)". There is only one definite article, *la* (e. g. *la amiko* "the friend"), and no indefinite article. Adjectives end in *-a* (e. g. *bona amiko* "good friend") and take plural and objective endings to agree with nouns. Verbs are all regular and have only one form for each tense or mood; they are not inflected for person or number. There is an extensive set of suffixes that can be added to word roots to allow various shades of meaning or newly derived forms. As for the syntactic structure, it also enjoys simplicity and regularity. Therefore, it is easy for people, especially those who speak major European languages, to learn and master.

However, Esperanto is after all an artificial international auxiliary language. It cannot replace natural languages or serve as a mother tongue or the first language of all nations, for it is essentially a Romance-based language with Latin and Germanic influences. It, therefore, still remains a foreign language to speakers of all languages in the world.

9.4 Pidgin, creole, bilingualism and diglossia

9.4.1 Pidgin and creole

In most cases, a lingua franca is typically a language with a broad base of native speakers, and is likely to be used and learned by speakers whose native languages are of the same language family. But often in the world when sailors, traders or missionaries from one part of the world get contact with people residing in another area, they try to use their native language as a basis for a rudimentary language of few lexical items and simplified grammatical rules. Such a mixed language is linguistically called a **pidgin**, or a pidgin language. Therefore, a pidgin is a mixed or blended form of language (or a variety of language) which developed for some practical purpose, such as trading, among groups of people who did not know each other's languages.

The first recorded pidgin was the simplified Italian used by European crusaders and merchants who visited eastern Mediterranean ports in the Middle Ages. Because there were many French among these travellers, this pidgin was known as Lingua Franca. It should be noted that the expression "lingua franca" that is used today means something rather different: it refers to any language used for communication in multilingual settings, as has been discussed in the previous part. For example, English might be used as an international language. A pidgin is therefore a reduced lingua franca.

Originally "pidgin" referred to Chinese Pidgin English and was a modification of the word *business*. The appearance of pidgin languages since the 17th century followed the increase in European commercial trading and colonization. The establishment of these languages reflected the ethnocentric European view of the indigenous peoples as intellectually and culturally inferior. In his first encounter with the newly arrived European, the native may have attempted a few words in the European's language. The European, believing the other to be incapable of further learning, would respond in a similarly incomplete fashion. The native would assume that this simplified speech was the proper form of the language and so would continue to use the forms that he had heard, naturally adding some vocabulary and a few grammatical elements from his own language. This is not to suggest that pidgins have no grammar or that they are merely a variety of the indigenous language with borrowed European words inserted. In fact, pidgins are regarded as languages; although their structures are simpler than those of the languages from which they derive, they are complete. English pidgins spoken in different areas have been found to share the same underlying structure of English, although they may differ with regard to inflectional suffixes and other details.

Pidgins typically have a limited vocabulary and a very reduced grammatical structure characterized by the loss of inflections, gender and case. This "simplified" variety performs its functions as a communication medium in such situations as trading and employment.

When a pidgin develops beyond its role as a trade language and becomes the first language of a speech community, and is acquired by the children of that speech community as their native language, it is said to be a **creole**. Therefore, creole is a pidgin language that has become established as the native language of a speech community. Typically, a creole arises when the speakers of one language become economically or politically dominant over speakers of another language or languages, particularly if the latter are illiterate. At first, a simplified or otherwise modified form of the language of the dominant group comes to be used for communication between members of different groups. At this stage the communicating language is a lingua franca and, if simplified in its forms, a pidgin; when the lingua franca becomes the standard or native language of a community, usually of the less dominant group, the language has become a creole.

As a typically native language, a creole clearly has more linguistic functions than a pidgin and therefore is more varied in structure to enable it to fulfil its new functions. Besides, the vocabulary is vastly enriched, various kinds of inflectional structures tend to arise, and new syntactic-semantic concepts develop.

At present, there are about 90 pidgins and creoles in the world, most of which are found in Caribbean areas, African coast countries, and Oceania areas. Notable examples of creole are the English-based creole of Jamaica, and the French-based creole of Haiti.

9.4.2 Bilingualism and diglossia

1. Bilingualism

In many countries, regional variation is not simply a matter of two dialects of a single language, but a matter of two quite distinct and different languages. Some countries are officially bilingual (or multilingual) in the sense that they have two (or more) official languages. Canada, for example, is an officially bilingual country, with both French and English as official languages. Other countries, though not officially bilingual, have two different languages spoken within their borders. Most countries of the world fall into this latter category. In either case, two languages are used side by side with each having a different role to play; and language switching occurs when the situation changes. This constitutes the situation of **bilingualism**, as can be illustrated by the following list:

Ex. 9-6	Canada	English	French
	Belgium	Flemish	French
	Somali	English	Italian
	Rwand	Rwand	French

A bilingual speaker often uses two languages alternatively during a conversation with another bilingual speaker, a speech situation known as code-switching. For example, two people conducting business in English in Tanzania might suddenly switch to Swahili or, if they are fellow members of the same ethnic and linguistic subgroup, to a local vernacular, when the topic of conversation changes from business proper to more personal matters. Code-switching may also take place in a conversation when one speaker uses one language and the other speaker answers in a different language. Another instance of code-switching is the situation when a person begins his or her speech in one language and then changes to another language in the middle of the speech, or sometimes even in the middle of a sentence, a situation that occurs to all bilinguals at one time or another.

2. Diglossia

Diglossia, a term first introduced by Ferguson in 1959, refers to the coexistence of two different varieties of the same language in a speech community with each serving a particular social function and used for a certain situation. Usually, one variety is the literary or high dialect, and the other is the common or low dialect spoken by most of the population. The languages which Ferguson used as examples are Arabic, Modern Greek, Swiss German and Haitian Creole. Each of these languages has two varieties: the high variety (H) and the low variety (L), as is indicated in the following list:

Ex. 9-7

	High	Low
Swiss German	Hochdeutsch	Schweizerdeutsch
Arabic	Classical	Colloquial
Greek	Katharevousa	Demotic
Haitian	French	Creole

The situation of diglossia exists in many speech communities throughout the world. For example, in Greece, Katharevusa, heavily influenced by Classical Greek, is the prestige dialect and Demotic is the popular spoken language, and in Egypt, where there are two dialects of Arabic, the high, or classical, variety is used in lectures, religious speeches and formal political speeches, while the low variety is the local dialect of colloquial Arabic used in informal speeches. In China, there was a period of time when a high, classical form called 文言文(classical Chinese writing or speech) and low, spoken form called 白话文(vernacular Chinese writing or speech) were used side by side.

One of the most important features of diglossia is that the two varieties have their own special functions to fulfil, and each variety is the appropriate language for certain situations with very slight overlapping. In this regard Ferguson gives a sample listing the possible situations and the variety normally used:

Ex. 9-8

Situation	Variety
Sermon in church or mosque	H
Political speech	H
University lectures	H
News broadcast	H
Newspaper editorial	H
Speech in parliament	H
Conversation with family, friends	L
Folk literature	L
Caption on political cartoon	L
Poetry	H

Exercises

1. How is a person's use of language related to his social class?
2. How does the speech of a woman generally differ from that of a man?
3. Say briefly what you know about register theory.
4. Write three statements with the same content but in three different register forms, each appropriate for a particular context.
5. What is standard dialect? Is standard dialect superior to non-standard dialect? Why or why not?
6. What is lingua franca?
7. How is pidgin related to creole?
8. What distinction can you draw between bilingualism and diglossia?

Chapter 10 Psycholinguistics

Psycholinguistics is the study of psychological aspects of language. This branch of linguistics is chiefly concerned with such areas as language-thought relationship, short or long-term memory, and speech perception. Besides, much work in psycholinguistics has been done on the learning or the acquisition of language by children. Language is extremely complex, yet children learn it quickly and with ease, thus the study of child language is important not only for psychologists who are interested in cognition and learning of language but also for linguists concerned with the insights it can give about the structure of language.

10.1 Language and thought

10.1.1 Early views on language-thought relationship

The study of the relationship between language and thought can be dated back to as early as over two thousand years ago. Plato (429—347BC), the famous Greek philosopher, suggested that the categories of thought determine the categories of language, and hence language is regarded as the dress of thought, which means that language and thought are identical. This view, which is known as a mentalist view, was challenged by an empiricist view represented by Aristotle (384—322BC), a pupil of Plato, who argued that mankind could not have the same language and that languages were but signs of psychological experiences.

The debate between these two contrasting views continued into the 20th century. For example, Plato's view was echoed by Watson, an American psychologist and the founder of Behaviourism, who stated that language and thought were the same thing. According to Watson, thinking involved the same motor activities used in speaking. That is, when we "think aloud", it is called speech; when we "speak covertly", it is called thinking. Following Watson, the American linguist Bloomfield proposed a similar view. For Bloomfield, thinking was a system of movements that had been reduced from actual speech to the point where they were no longer visible (何兆熊,梅德明,1999:231).

However, the position that language and thought are identical can never be fully justified and we have too much evidence to refute it. For example, non-speaking humans such as those who are born deaf-mute or lose speech as a result of brain injury display complex thinking processes. In addition, if thinking and speaking were the same activity, we would not correct ourselves while speaking by saying, "I didn't mean to say that".

The most influential and also most controversial proposition on the relationship between language and thought has been what is known as the Sapir-Whorf Hypothesis.

10.1.2 Sapir-Whorf Hypothesis

In the study of the relationship between language and thought, Edward Sapir (1844—1939), a well-known American anthropologist, and Benjamin Lee Whorf (1897—1941), a student of the former, influenced by the Herder-Humboldt tradition of the relationship between language and thought, conducted investigations and made comparisons between languages, particularly between Indian language of Hopi and English, with respect to this kind of relationship, and consequently built up their hypothesis which can be summarized as follows(胡壮麟,刘润清等,1988:240):

a. One's thinking is completely determined by his native language because one cannot but perceive the world in terms of the categories and distinctions encoded in the language.

b. The categories and distinctions encoded in one language system are unique to that system and incommensurable with those of other systems.

Therefore, the **Sapir-Whorf Hypothesis** is chiefly concerned with two major assumptions: one is linguistic determinism, which means that language determines thought; the other is linguistic relativity, which means that there is no limit to the structural diversity of languages.

1. Linguistic determinism

Whorf's linguistic determinism is chiefly based on his comparative study between the Hopi language, an American Indian language, and English. He produced arguments in the 1930s that the language of American Indians led them to view the world differently from those who spoke European languages. Whorf claimed that the Hopi Indians of Arizona perceived the world differently from other tribes (e. g. the English-speaking tribe) because their language led them to do so (Yule, 1985: 196-197). For example, in the grammar of Hopi, there is a distinction between "animate" and "inanimate", and among the set of entities categorized as "animate" were clouds and stones. Whorf concluded that the Hopi believe that clouds and stones are animate (living) entities and that it is their language which leads them to believe this. Now, English does not mark in its grammar that clouds and stones are animate. So English speakers do not see the world in the same way as the Hopi do. In Whorf's words, "We dissect nature along lines laid down by our native languages" (Quoted in Yule, 1985: 197), i. e., one's thinking is completely determined by his native language.

2. Linguistic relativity

Sapir-Whorf's linguistic relativity may come from Saussure's notion of linguistic signs that there is no necessary or intrinsic relationship between the signifier and the signified. The basic notion of linguistic relativity is that there is no limit to the structural diversity of languages, including phonological, morphological, semantic and syntactic structures. There is, for example, no logical reason why the flower "lily" should be signified by the form "lily", and not some other possible form, as indeed is the case in other languages.

It is well acknowledged that the Sapir-Whorf hypothesis is a great contribution to the study of the relationship between languages and thought which are culture-dependent, and consequently it contributes a lot to the study of the relationship between language and culture. However, this hypothesis has given rise to a great deal of controversy and met with many criticisms. For example, some scholars point out that it is true that thought is influenced and shaped by language, but the point under question is: **to what degree** is the former influenced or shaped by the latter? If, according to Sapir-Whorf hypothesis, thought was completely determined by language and people who speak different languages had completely different ways of thinking or incompatible views of the world, then how could they share many of essentially the same basic concepts, such as time, space, number, matter, chemical elements, etc? And how could they come to the common understanding of the world and their mutual understanding in intercultural communication? Besides, there are many bilingual or even multilingual speakers in the world. If thought was completely determined by language, would these bilinguals (not to speak of multilinguals) have two different patterns of thinking in their brains or two incompatible views of the world and switch from one to the other as they switch from one language to the other? The answer is certainly negative. As far as language structure is concerned, Sapir and Whorf seemed to overemphasize the structural diversity of language or the variability in language diversity, failing to see the universal features of the languages in the world. As a matter of fact, more and more linguists have reached an agreement that most languages of the world, though different in their surface structure, share some universality in their deep structure. Therefore, the viewpoint that "there is no limit to the structural diversity of language" can hardly be fully justified.

Based on the critical view of the Sapir-Whorf hypothesis and the study of the relationship between languages and thought, most linguists nowadays have come to the common position that language and thought are, on the one hand, closely related to each other and, on the other hand, mutually dependent. Language does have some influence on thought, but thought in turn also influences the categories and structure of language. In brief, the influence of language on thought shouldn't be overestimated.

10.2 First language acquisition

10.2.1 Language acquisition

Language acquisition in general refers to a child's development of his first language, although sometimes the term is also used to mean the development of a person's second or foreign languages. Therefore, in a broad sense, language acquisition is concerned with how a person comes to understand and speak his first, or second, or foreign languages. The development of a first or native language (L1) is called **first language acquisition** (FLA), and the development of a second or foreign language (L2) is called **second language acquisition**(SLA).

The study of language acquisition is of great significance, for it enables linguists, psychologists and applied linguists to better understand the nature of human language and the development processes of language acquisition. We know that children acquire their native language naturally and successfully. However, that doesn't mean that, when they grow up, they could acquire a subsequent language the way they acquire their mother tongue. Although there is evidence that L1 learners and L2 learners follow a similar route of language development, L1 development and L2 development do not seem to involve identical processes and therefore, deserve separate treatment in our discussion. In the following part, we will examine the different stages at which children acquire their native language.

10.2.2 Stages in first language acquisition

It has been observed that children in different language areas of the world follow similar, possibly universal, stages of development in acquiring their languages, although there are individual differences in the onset and rate of language development. Starting from the prelinguistic cooing and babbling stage, children move through the one-word, two-word and multi-word stages, gradually acquiring phonology, morphology, syntax, vocabulary, semantics, and discourse skills of the adult language system as they grow. The following is a list which shows the stages in children's language acquisition(戴炜栋，何兆熊，华钧，1989：174)：

a) Around the age of three or four months—Children begin to babble speech-like sounds, such as /dɑ/, /mɑ/, /bɑ/, etc, and this period is called "babbling period".

b) Around the age of one year—Children attempt to carry out (or respond to) simple commands. They can also speak a few simple words, e. g. /papɑ/—papa; /dɑdɑ/—dada.

c) Eighteen months—This age usually marks the onset of speech. Their vocabulary consists of between three and fifty words, e. g. /dʌk/—duck.

d) Two years—This age is usually cited as the beginning of two-word stage, as they often utter two-word phrases which they have not imitated and which, therefore, are their own creation, e. g. /tukɑ/—two car; /budɑn/—blue van. Besides, children at this age can name most things which are familiar to them in their surroundings.

e) Two and a half years—Children's vocabulary extends rapidly, and they seem to be able to understand quite a lot said to him.

f) Three years—The vocabulary of the children at this age has extended to about a thousand words. The grammatical complexity of the utterance is about equal to that of colloquial adult speech.

g) About four years—Children have now mastered the essentials of their mother tongue.

What is noteworthy in first language acquisition is that, no matter what languages they may learn, most children normally acquire the basic essentials of language in the short period between the ages of 1.5 years and 4 years. This period is called the critical period for first language acquisition in the sense that language will not be acquired at all, or at least not with full mastery of it, unless it is acquired by the time the child reaches the age in question. Of course, some of the most complicated constructions, e. g. passives, may not be fully mastered until about ten years of age, and language learning may proceed throughout life as vocabulary increases, and skills in the appropriate use of language continually improve.

10.2.3 Children's development of linguistic system

1. Phonological development

It has been observed that the phonological development of children usually follows certain pattern no matter what language they are exposed to—they normally first acquire the sounds found in all languages of the world, and in later stages acquire "more difficult" sounds. For example, certain sounds will be produced (i. e. spoken) before others. So consonants such as /m/, /d/ or /p/ will be produced before /s/, /z/ or /θ/. In other words, the child must pass each stage before he can proceed to the next one. Thus, for example, the presence of palatal and velar sounds presupposes the presence of labials and dentals. But the presence of labials and dentals does not imply the presence of palatal and velar sounds. Similarly the three basic vowels /iː/ /uː/ /ɑː/ (front-central-back) form a minimum vowel system for the language of the world.

The following table shows the appearance of consonant phonemes in English, with respect to chronological age:

age (years)	consonant(s) acquired
2	p b m n w
2.5	d k g n h
3	f s l j
4	ʃ v z r tʃ dʒ
5	θ ð
6	ʒ

An interesting fact about children's phonological development is that, whether or not a child will speak a foreign language with an accent depends largely upon the age at which he/she learns the second language. A child who enters a foreign language speech community by the age of three or four (i. e. before he/she passes his/her critical period) learns the new language rapidly and without the trace of accent. Around the age of 10—13, the child loses his/her ability to learn a second language without an accent.

2. Vocabulary development

The vocabulary of a child during his/her first several years of growth expands rapidly. It is estimated that the number of basic words known by English-speaking school children of age six is around 7800. It should be noted that the vocabulary development of a child not only involves the rapid increase of the number of words but also the correct interpretation of the meanings associated with them. When a child learns a word, he does not just learn how to pronounce or spell it. He must learn the meaning of each form, and how each form is different in meaning from every other form. In other words he/she must learn the features of meaning associated with each word.

1) Overextension

Due to various factors, a child could hardly learn the meaning of a word "all at once". We can see this when the young child calls all adults "Mummy". In this case we can say "Mummy" has the meaning feature [+Adult].

If the child calls all women "Mummy", and refers to men in some other way, we can say that for him/her "Mummy" means:

$$\begin{cases}+\text{Adult}\\+\text{Female}\end{cases}$$

Therefore, the child in these two cases over-extends the meaning of the word "Mummy". Of course, with the development of the child, he/she will later acquire the conventional meaning of "Mummy", i. e.

$$\begin{cases}+\text{Adult}\\+\text{Female}\\+\text{Parent}\end{cases}$$

And in speaking he will be able to distinguish his mother from all other adult females.

The example discussed above illustrates that in the early stages, the child only knows one or two features of meaning; therefore he/she will use the word much more widely than an adult would use it. This incorrect wide use of a word is called **overextension.**

2) Precedence of perceptual features over function/social features

The semantic features of vocabulary may fall into two types: perceptual features and functional/social features:

Perceptual features

Perceptual features are those which are easily perceived by children at early stages, such as movement, shape, size and sound. The more perceptual features children perceive and recognize, the better their grasp of language will be. For example, as a result of the overextension of the meaning of the word "dog", very young children would take all the things having four legs as "dogs". Later, as they grow up, their perception of perceptual features develops, and they gradually learn to distinguish between "bark" and "mew", and therefore are able to distinguish between "a dog" and "a cat".

Functional/social features

It is normally acknowledged that, in children's cognitive development, perceptual features normally precede functional/social features which are characterized by particular social roles or purposes. Take the words "throne" as an example. From the perception point of view, "throne" denotes "a piece of furniture for someone to sit on", but from the point of view of social functions, the word means more than that, referring to "the ceremonial chair of a king, queen, etc", or, when used figuratively, "the rank of a king or queen". In their grasp of this word, children's understanding of its meaning normally proceeds from its designative meaning, which is related to perceptual features, to connotative meaning, which is related to functional /social features, because they would hardly be able to understand its functional/social features without an understanding of its perceptual features.

3. Grammatical development

Children around the age of two begin to be able to string words together, which marks the beginning of the first stage of grammatical development. Around the age of five, most of them will be able to grasp some of the basic categories of grammar.

Two-word stage

Around the age of two, children begin to produce two-word utterances, which is characterized by the absence of syntactic or morphological markers, that is, no inflections for number, or person, or tense can be found in their speech, and the two words they use usually express the idea of the whole sentence. For example, the following three pairs of two-word structures all express a child's demand or desire:

Ex. 10-1 More juice.

Give candy.

Want cake.

The following two pairs of two-word structures, on the other hand, indicate the idea of negation:

Ex. 10-2 No wet.

Not hungry.

It has been noted that in "noun+noun" sentences, the two words can express a number of different grammatical relations which will later be expressed by other syntactical devices. Thus, for example, *Mommy sock* can be used to show a "subject+object" relation in the situation when the mother is putting the sock on and the child is pointing to Mommy's sock, or to show possession, meaning "This is Mommy's sock".

Telegraphic period

About 6 months after the 2-word utterances begin, children may develop into a period of telegraphic speech, or telegraphic period. During this period, sentences are developed which contain three main elements, for example,

Ex. 10-3 Where dog gone?

Papa eat cake.

Kate clean car.

These sentences are examples of telegraphic speech. The term "telegraphic" derives from the observation that the child's speech throughout this period lacks inflections and function words (e. g. auxiliaries, prepositions, determiners and conjunctions), which is rather like the language of telegraphs. Therefore, the speech of a child at this period is characterized by the presence of content words which give us the information, and the absence of function words which by themselves tell us nothing. From the telegraphic period onward, the child will proceed from the two-word stage to later stages during which longer utterances will be produced, and his speech will come close more and more, in terms of word order, etc, to that of adult speech.

10.3 Theories on child language acquisition

Child language acquisition is a complicated subject. Linguists and psycholinguists have proposed various theories in their attempts to explain how children manage to acquire the adult's language, among which the most influential ones are reinforcement theory and innate linguistic competence theory.

10.3.1 Reinforcement theory

The reinforcement theory, based on behaviorist psychology, holds that language is learnt in much the same way as anything is learnt. The chief exponent of the behaviorist view B. F. Skinner(1957) argues that reinforcement of selected responses is the key to understanding language development. According to this theory, children learn to produce correct sentences because they are positively reinforced when they say something right and negatively reinforced when they say something wrong.

Though seemingly plausible, the reinforcement theory fails to account for the fact that children often construct their own rules in the process of their language acquisition. For example, when children begin to make negative sentences, at first they simply add a "no" or some negative morphemes at the beginning of their sentences, as is shown in the following:

Ex. 10-4 No want play toy.

They have never heard such a sentence spoken around them. But why do they produce the sentence above? This is because it is a simple and easy way to transform a declarative into a negative.

Some other linguists hold the view that child language acquisition is the result of imitation of the utterances spoken by the adults around them, which is called "imitation theory". Admittedly, imitation is to some extent involved in language acquisition, but the sentences produced by children show that children are not imitating adults' speech. If they were, from whom would they hear the "sentences" listed above as well as the "sentences" listed below?

Ex. 10-5 Cat run out.
I don't want some.

Even when children try to imitate what they hear, they are unable to produce sentences which cannot be generated by their own grammar. Suppose they are asked to imitate *Daddy went out*, but they would say *Daddy goed out*, because the first sentence does not agree to their own grammatical rules. Children at the age of about four can only acquire the regular rules for inflections; for instance, the past tense is formed by adding *-ed* to verbs.

From what has been discussed above, we can come to the conclusion that neither the reinforcement theory nor the imitation theory can account satisfactorily for the facts of language acquisition.

10.3.2 Innate linguistic competence theory

The innate linguistic competence theory, or the rationalist (or mentalist) theory, holds that children are born with an innate ability to acquire languages of a specific type. This theory is based on Chomsky's theory of speakers' innate linguistic competence, which is represented by the grammar (or rules) of a language. The generative-transformational grammarians believe that all languages are rule-governed. Children are born with (or genetically endowed with) a language acquisition device (LAD), which generate the rules of a language. Children use these rules to produce and understand infinite sentences, including those they have never heard of. Admittedly, the innate linguistic competence theory has played a very important role in revealing the truth of child language acquisition. However, it is still open to some criticisms. Some linguists argue that the theory of linguistic competence concentrates solely on children's innate or genetic factors and overlooks the social language environment which also plays a very important role in child language acquisition. Therefore the theory is not conclusive enough. In brief, child language acquisition is a very complicated subject in the study of psycholinguistics. There are still many problems open to further studies before we can fully understand the specific details of the language-learning device with which human beings appear to be born.

10.4 Error analysis and second language acquisition

Second language acquisition(SLA) is a new area in the linguistic studies which began to develop early in the 1970s. Though the exploration into the area is still in its infancy and it has not projected any approach or theory of SLA, some views or assumptions on the subject are of great value and have given great impetus to our English (as a foreign language) learning.

10.4.1 Acquisition vs. learning

Some linguists believe that the development of a first language in a child is a special process, which is different from the process by which a person learns a second language. According to American scholar Stephen Krashen (1987: 10), **acquisition** refers to the gradual and subconscious development of ability in the first language by using it naturally in daily communicative situations. "Learning", however, is defined as a conscious process of accumulating knowledge of a second language usually obtained in school settings, hence the distinction between "acquisition" and "learning". However, Krashen also noted that second language, though is more commonly learned, may also be acquired to some extent, depending on the environmental setting and the input received by the L2 learner. Therefore, Rod Ellis, a British linguist, holds that "I wish to keep an open mind about whether this is a real distinction or not, so I shall use 'acquisition' and 'learning' interchangeably, irrespective of whether conscious or subconscious processes are involved"(Ellis, 1985: 6).

10.4.2 Second language acquisition vs. first language acquisition

Second language acquisition stands in contrast to first language acquisition in several aspects. For example, while the first language is acquired, i. e. subconsciously, the second (or foreign) language is, more commonly, learned, i. e. consciously. It can also be noted that in acquiring their first language, children always concentrate on meaning, not on pattern, i. e. structure. The second language acquisition, however, concentrates on code, i. e. , the system of the thought. Besides, one learns his first language directly from reality. The second language is learnt in manageable sequence, i. e. , syllabus and course books. Furthermore, in first language acquisition children apply the rules subconsciously, while the second language learners, after a period of training, are able to verbalize the rules. Interestingly, we also discover the striking resemblance between first and second language acquisition—over-generalization. Children tend to over-generalize the rules, thus leading to errors, e. g. ,

Ex. 10-6 book—books child—childs

The same error, due to wrong hypothesis, is also found in the process of learning the second language, e. g. ,

Ex. 10-7 book—books sheep—sheeps

We shall deal with over-generalization in the latter section of this chapter.

10.4.3 Transfer and interference

In learning a second language, whether they learn the language consciously or subconsciously, learners have come to the task of acquiring a second language with their L1 knowledge. Naturally, learners will subconsciously use their L1 knowledge in learning a second language. This is known as **language transfer.**

Transfer can be positive or negative. It is apparent that for any two languages, there are similar patterns as well as different ones in their phonological, lexical, and grammatical systems. Presumably, **positive transfer** occurs when an L1 pattern is identical with, or similar to, a target language pattern. Conversely, **negative transfer**, a process more commonly known as **interference**, occurs when an L1 pattern is different from a target language pattern, which may lead to errors or inappropriate forms in the target language.

In order to identify the areas of learning difficulty, an inter-lingual contrastive procedure called **contrastive analysis** was developed. The contrastive analysis approach was founded on the belief that it was possible, by establishing the linguistic differences between the native and target language systems, to predict what problems learners of a particular second language would face and the types of errors they would make. Given this approach, it was hypothesized that L2 errors were predominantly the result of negative transfer, or mother tongue interference. For example, Chinese learners' frequent production of incorrect sequences like "Although... but..." and "he come tomorrow" is an instance of mother tongue interference. Such interference is found at all levels of language: pronunciation, morphology, syntax, vocabulary, and semantics.

With the framework of contrastive analysis, second language learning was believed to be a matter of overcoming the differences between L1 and L2 systems. This view has strong implications for SLA instruction—it suggests that the major task of second language teaching should be predominantly one of contrasting the native and the target language system, making predictions about the language items that would cause difficulty and the errors that learners are prone to make, and then of using these predictions in deciding on the type of language items that need special treatment in teaching.

However, when the contrastive analysis hypothesis was submitted to empirical investigation, it was found that a large proportion of grammatical errors could not be explained by mother tongue interference. In practice, errors predicted by contrastive analysis have often not occurred, whereas many actual errors, such as "goed" and "foots", are attributable to over-generalization instead of negative transfer. Practical experience suggests that interference from the mother tongue is not the only or major source of errors. One study shows that only 3 per cent of the subjects' errors could be classified as interference errors, while 85 per cent errors were developmental errors.

The consequence of these empirical studies is of great significance because it leads to the change of attitude towards learners' errors. The traditional view that errors in learners' language were negative and had to be eradicated was thus abandoned. The acceptance of such errors in learners' language reflects a fundamental shift in perspective of SLA. SLA is no longer viewed as a process of overcoming old speech habits and forming new ones but a process of constructing and modifying rules of communication. It is believed that an error produced in a learner's second language utterance may very well be development error and therefore, should not be looked upon simply as a failure to learn the correct form, but as an indication of the actual acquisition process in his learning process. Developmental errors, such as those resulting from over-generalization, often result from the effort on the part of the learner to construct and test general rules of communication in the target language.

10.5 Types of errors

10.5.1 Inter-lingual errors

Inter-lingual errors are mostly brought about by negative transfer, or language interference. These errors can be found at the levels of pronunciation, morphology, syntax, vocabulary and meaning and can be predicted by contrasting the grammatical or other systems of two languages.

1. Phonological interference

A lot of Chinese students have difficulty in pronouncing the sounds [θ] and [ð], and they tend to pronounce *three* [θri:] as *tree* [tri:] and *this* [ðis] as *dis* [dis]. This is caused by inter-lingual interference because there are no such phonemes as [θ] and [ð] in Chinese. Therefore, Chinese speakers use the nearest equivalents [t] and [d] in their first language system to replace [θ] and [ð], which results in phonological errors. Another example of phonological interference is the shortening of long vowels. The absence of such long vowels as [i:] and [ə:] in Chinese often causes trouble, and a lot of Chinese learners of English, when pronouncing these sounds, often take the easy way out and make these long vowels short vowels. Thus words like *sheep* and *meat* may sound like *ship* and *mit* respectively, and some learners never bother to distinguish between *fourteen* and *forty*.

2. Lexical interference

In learning English, Chinese students often produce utterances characteristic of "Chinese characteristics", or, in other words, "Chinglish". Take a look at the following examples:

Ex. 10-8 a. 他们过去常在星期五晚上去买东西。
They used to go out to buy things on Friday night.
(They used to go shopping on Friday night.)

"去买东西" in English is expressed by the phrase "go shopping" rather than "go to buy things", which is a typical Chinglish expression. The translation is a typical example of lexical interference of Chinese language.

Ex. 10-9 b. 这套家具价钱是多少?
How much is the price of this suite of furniture?
(How much is this suite of furniture?)

In English, the expression "how much" itself suggests "what is the price", so it's unnecessary to juxtapose "how much" and "the price" in a sentence, and "How much is this suite of furniture?" will do here.

3. Grammatical interference

Influenced by Chinese grammar, Chinese learners of English often produce ungrammatical utterances, for example,

Indefinite article deletion. Article deletion is a common error made by the Chinese learners. An investigation of errors in English composition of some pre-university students in Singapore shows that with regard to errors in the use of article deletion system, omission alone formed more than 50% of the errors in the category. The errors are perhaps attributed to the lack of L1 and L2 equivalence. Therefore the following sentences can often be found among the Chinese learners of English, especially among beginners:

Ex. 10-10 I would like to apply for driving license.
(I would like to apply for a driving license.)
Have you got bicycle?
(Have you got a bicycle?)

Subject+verb structure replaced by a single verb or complement. In Mandarin Chinese, often a verb or a complement is used as an answer to a question, for example:

Ex. 10-11 —你饿了吗?
—饿了。

As a result, some learners may transfer this feature of Chinese grammar into English and may utter sentences as follows:

(a) —Are you hungry?

—Hungry. (Yes, I am.)

(b) —Have you eaten?

—Eaten. (Yes, I have.)

Answers to tag questions. In Chinese, when answering a tag question with a negative statement, we normally use "是的" when the answer is negative and "不" when the answer is affirmative, for example:

Ex. 10-12 —你今天不出去,是吧?

—是的,我今天不出去。/ 不,我今天要出去。

Some learners may apply this feature of Chinese grammar to English and produce utterances as the follows:

—You are not going out, are you?

—Yes, I am not. / No, I am. (No, I am not / Yes, I am.)

10.5.2 Intra-lingual errors—over-generalization

Intra-lingual errors are those caused by the incorrect application of the rules within the target language. In other words, they are caused by **over-generalization.** It should be noted that, in second language learning, generalization, which is the use of previously available strategies in a new situation, often proves to be helpful in organizing the facts about the second language. For example, a learner may apply the rule of the verb *tell* in the sentence *Bill told me to leave at once* to other verbs and produce such correct utterances as *Bill asked me to leave at once.* / *Bill advised me to leave at once.* etc.

However, sometimes due to superficial similarities between some linguistic elements, a learner may apply certain rules in the wrong place, which results in intra-lingual errors. For example, he may apply the above mentioned rule to the verb *suggest* and utter the following sentence:

Ex. 10-13 Bill suggested me to leave at once.

(Bill suggested that I leave at once. /Bill suggested my leaving at once.)

This example illustrates what is commonly called over-generalization of target language rules, which is the result of particular learning strategies on items within the target language. Take a look at another example:

Ex. 10-14 The girl *is dressed in* a blue jacket.

↓

The girl *is worn in* a blue jacket. (The girl wore a blue jacket.)

Clearly here the Chinese learners are guided not by the grammar of their mother tongue, but by what they already know of English, and by their intuition.

10.5.3 Errors due to communication strategies

In learning a second language, a learner may find that sometimes the communicative demands made on him may far outpace his actual competence. Thus the learner may resort to some communication strategies by simplifying the syntax of the language so as to make the language into an instrument of his own intentions. Perhaps the clearest example of alterations in language structure as a result of communication strategies is to be found in various types of pidgin English. For example, a learner may use the word *yesterday* to denote past tense, and the word *tomorrow* to denote future tense, producing such utterances characteristic of pidgin English as: *We see an action program yesterday* or *I leave here tomorrow*. It should be noted, however, that communication strategies do not necessarily lead to errors. A Chinese learner of English, for example, needs to express intentions in the past and he is unable to fulfil it. What will he do? Since he has not acquired the grammatical means to do this, he has to find alternative ways of expressing the same content, by lexical means, through the use of a longer construction. Therefore, instead of saying: *I should have called you last night*, he might say, *I have the intention of calling you last night, but...*, thus fulfilling his goal of communication.

10.5.4 Performance errors

Performance errors are the ones made in the actualization of language due to his poor or inappropriate performance (usually caused by carelessness, anxiety, etc) rather than his competence. Performance errors are quite normal aspects of language use. A learner may produce a sentence like:

Ex. 10-15 The number of road accident recorded by the municipal authorities *are* greater this year than last year.
(The number of road accident recorded by the municipal authorities *is* greater this year than last year.)

The error in the first sentence is probably caused by the length of what the speaker is trying to produce. In other words, the error is caused by the speaker's memory limitation (performance) rather than his linguistic ability (competence). Therefore, in order to have a clearer idea of someone's competence in a second language, we need to have a much closer and more detailed look at his speech output and find out to what extent the speaker's linguistic system corresponds to that of the native speaker.

10.5.5 Errors due to cross-association

In English there are many words (or expressions) which are closely associated with each other in pronunciation, or spelling, or meaning. The close association of these words often leads to confusion on the part of the learners. Take the words *stalagmite and stalactite* for example. The two words are so much alike not only in spelling but also in pronunciation that students are often at a loss which one to use, or, if they are asked to make a choice between the two to suit a context, they often choose the wrong word. Sometimes they even use a hybrid word such as *stalagitite*, which is neither *stalagmite* nor *stalactite*, due to the close association of the two words.

Errors due to cross-association may be found not only at phonological, lexical and syntactic levels, but also at semantic level. For example, having learned the structure *too... to...* as in *It's too cold to go swimming*, a student may produce ungrammatical hybrid structure *It's very cold to go swimming* due to his cross-association between the words *too* and *very*, which are semantically related with each other to some extent.

Exercises

1. Discuss Sapir-Whorf hypothesis briefly and give your comments.
2. Different theories of child language acquisition have been set forth. Discuss two contrasting views with reference to the reinforcement theory and the innate linguistic competence theory.
3. What are the major differences and similarities between the first and the second language acquisition?
4. Explain some causes that lead to the systematic occurrence of errors in second language acquisition.
5. Judge whether the following statements are true or false.
   1) If parents try to teach grammar to a young child, they will not be successful.
   2) The young child is not *taught* to speak or to understand his language. There is no formal learning of grammar or pronunciation practice.
   3) At first a child does not inflect nouns and verbs.
   4) At the two-word stage, sentences are composed of content words, not function words.
   5) All normal children have almost equal ability in learning their first language, so do adults when they learn a second foreign language.

Answers to Exercises

Chapter 1

1. 1) arbitrary 2) psychological 3) linguist 4) communication 5) design
   6) productivity 7) scientific 8) general 9) Semantics 10) diachronic
2. 1)—5) T F F F F 6)—10) T F F F T
3. 1) Morphology studies the form of words. It identifies the smallest meaningful units of a language which are called morphemes and how these morphemes are arranged to form words.
   2) Syntax studies the internal structure of sentences and the rules by which sentences are formed. Sentences are not strings of words arranged at random order. Change in the sequence affects the meaning of the sentence. So syntax identifies the acceptable sequences in a language and the relationships between elements in sentence structure.
   3) Pragmatics is the study of the meaning of language in context. It deals with how language users use the language to achieve communicative effects.
   4) Scociolinguistics is the study of language and linguistic behaviours as influenced by social and cultural factors. It regards language as a social phenomenon. It's more concerned with investigating the relationships between language and society for a better understanding of the structure of language and of how languages function in communication.
   5) Psycholinguistics is the study of language in relation to the mind. It is viewed as the intersection of linguistics and psychology.
4. 1)—5) C B C D A 6)—10) B D C A C
5. 1) English, as a system, has "two levels of structures". The meaningful units at the "higher level", such as "teach" and "cheat", may also be arranged and rearranged, by certain "rules", into as many sentences as we need. It is the

same case with any other languages. This feature of language is what we mean by "duality".

Animals do not enjoy this feature in their communication system. They can transmit some information with different kinds of signals, but their signals are always at the "lower level", i. e. , they cannot set up a "rule" or "rules" to arrange their signals to fit in with the "higher level". To be more exact, there is only "one level" of signals in animals' communication system.

2) A scientific study of language is based on systematic investigations. Such investigations try to form language theories out of language facts/data. So, first of all, the linguist has to observe language facts, i. e. , to see how language is actually used; then he brings forth some hypotheses according to what he has observed. But the hypotheses thus formed have to be tested again and again. If the hypotheses can pass all tests, they are accepted as "theories".

3) The distinction between langue and parole was made by the Swiss linguist F. de Saussure early in the 20th century. Langue refers to the abstract linguistic system shared by all the members of a speech community, and parole refers to the realization of langue in actual use.

Langue is abstract in that it is not the language people actually use; it is a set of conventions and rules which language users abide by. So, langue is relatively stable, i. e. , it does not change frequently. Parole, on the other hand, is concrete and natural language events and varies from person to person.

Chapter 2

1. 1) Speech; writing
   2) production; transmission; perception
   3) articulatory; auditory; acoustic
   4) larynx; oral cavity; nasal cavity
   5) broad; narrow
   6) Consonants
   7) labiodental
   8) Nasal

9) Back

10) Diphthongs

2. 1)—5) F T F T F 6)—10) F F T T F

3. 1) Phonetics deals with speech sounds in isolation, and phonemics studies the system of speech sounds.

2) Speech sounds can be written down in a systematic and consistent way—phonetic transcription by using letter-symbols. It serves as an aid not only to phonetic study but also to language learning and teaching.

In order to record the sounds in speech some symbols are created and agreed upon in linguistics. Until present, many systems of phonetic transcription have been invented. One of these systems is the **International Phonetic Alphabet (IPA)**—a standard and internationally accepted system of phonetic transcription.

3) Different consonantal sounds result when we change the shape of the oral cavity by moving the lips and tongue, the articulators, and the place of articulation in the oral cavity.

According to the place of articulation, consonants are classified into the following groups: Bilabials: [p] [b] [m] [w]; Labiodentals: [f] [v]; Dental/Interdentals: [θ] [ð]; Alveolars: [t] [d] [s] [z] [n] [l] [r]; Palatals: [ʃ] [ʒ] [tʃ] [dʒ] [j]; Velars: [k] [g] [ŋ]; Glottal: [h].

4) According to the manner of articulation, consonants are classified into the following groups: Stops(plosives): [p] [b] [t] [d] [k] [g] [m] [n] [ŋ]; Fricatives: [f] [v] [s] [z] [θ] [ð] [ʃ] [ʒ]; Affricates: [tʃ] [dʒ]; Liquids: [l]—lateral sound [r]—retroflex; Glides: [w] [j]

5) The tongue may be put in different parts of the mouth: front, centre, back, hence the three classes of vowels:

Front vowels: [iː] [i] [e] [æ]

Central vowels: [ə] [ɜː] [ʌ]

Back vowels: [uː] [ʊ] [ɔː] [ɔ] [ɑː]

6) Vowels are more difficult to describe or classify than consonants because they are produced without any articulators touching or even coming very close to the points of articulation. The quality of a vowel is determined by the particular

configuration of the vocal tract when the vowel is produced. The articulation of vowels has much to do with the two articulatory organs: the tongue and lips. Different parts of the tongue may be raised or lowered. The lips may be spread or pursed. Therefore, the criteria according to which vowels are classified are mostly connected with the position of the tongue and the shape of the lips.

Chapter 3

1. 1) sound; patterns 2) phonemes 3) Allophones 4) assimilation
   5) suprasegmental 6) Word; stress 7) Tones 8) intonation
2. 1)—5) T T F F F 6)—10) T T F T F
3. 1) Phonetics and phonology, with the same root *phono-*, which means *sound*, are both related to the study of speech sounds, but they have different focus and approach to the subject. Phonetics is of a general nature; it studies all the speech sounds used in all human languages, dealing with the characteristics of speech sounds and providing methods for their description, classification and transcription. Phonology is the general knowledge of speech sounds of a language, concerned with the linguistic patterning of sounds in human languages, with its primary aim being to discover the principles that govern the way sounds are organized in languages, and to explain the variations that occur.

   Phonology aims at the system of sounds of a particular language. What applies to one language may not apply to another. Ways of combining speech sounds can be different across languages. With sufficient phonological knowledge of a certain language, a speaker is able to produce sounds that form meaningful utterances, to recognize a foreign accent, to make up new words, to add the appropriate phonetic segments to form plurals and past tenses, to produce aspirated and unaspirated voiceless stops in the appropriate context, to know what is or is not a sound in one's language.

   2) When people talk, their vocal tract produces continuous sounds which form words, phrases, sentences, and so on and forth. To analyze and describe speech sounds it is necessary to know what an individual sound is and how each sound differs from all others. The first task is, of course, to segment the speech

utterance into individual units. And these segmental units of speech are the phones of the language.

A phone is a phonic unit or segment. Phones are the actual sounds we produce. For example, the utterance "*Good morning!*" consists of the following individual phones: g, u, d, m, ɔ:, n, i, ŋ.

A phoneme is the smallest unit of sound that can distinguish meaning in a language. It is not a physical sound that can be pronounced but rather an abstract unit. It is a collection of distinctive phonetic features. Phonemes are usually put between two slashes: /p/ /b/ /i/ /e/.

3) Phonemes are abstract units and cannot be read out. Its realization in certain phonetic environments results in allophones, variants of the phoneme. An allophone is therefore a predictable phonetic variant of a phoneme. In English, each vowel phoneme has both an oral and a nasalized allophone. Allophones are put between two square brackets: [p] [p^h], [t][t^h], [k] [k^h].

4) The Assimilation rule assimilates one segment to another by "copying" or "spreading" a feature of a sequential phoneme on to its neighbouring segment, thus making the two phones more similar. Assimilation rules are mostly caused by articulatory or physiological process. Speakers tend to make articulation easier, or make it easier to move the articulators. According to nasalization rule, a vowel becomes or is nasalized in the environment before a nasal segment, for example, *bomb* [bɑ̃m].

5) The phonemic features that occur above the level of the segments are called suprasegmental features. Stress is the degree of emphasis or accent given to some syllables in relation to others. The stressed syllable receives more force in articulation than the unstressed ones.

Stress in English is phonemic, that is to say, it distinguishes meaning. The same word form, if read with different stresses, results in a difference in meaning or grammatical functions. For example, if the word *bluepencil* is read as [ˈblu:ˈpensil], it is a verb, meaning "to cross out anything not suitable from a piece of writing", while it is a noun, meaning a pencil in blue color if it is read as [blu:ˈpensil].

Chapter 4

1. 1)—5) TFTTT 6)—10) FFTFT
2. retroactive: retro-, act, -ive
   televised: tele-, vise, -ed
   unforgettable: un-, forget, able
   psychology: psych-, -ology
   holiday: holi-, day
   morphemic: morph, -mic
   deactivation: de-, act, vat-, -tion
   saltpetre: salt, peter
   befriend: be, friend
   margin: margin
   endearment: en-, dear, -ment
   unpalatable: un-palat-, -able
   grandmother: grand, mother
   mistreatment: mis-, treat, -ment
   airsickness: air, sick, -ness
3. a. terroriz*ed*: inflectional suffix
   b. un*civil*ized: derivational infix
   c. terror*ize*: derivational suffix
   d. *luk*ewarm: derivational prefix
   e. imposs*ible*: derivational suffix
4. 1) The morphological rule for forming an infinitive in Dutch is "Root+-en".
   2) The morphological rule for forming the Dutch past participle is "ge-+root+-d".
5. 1)

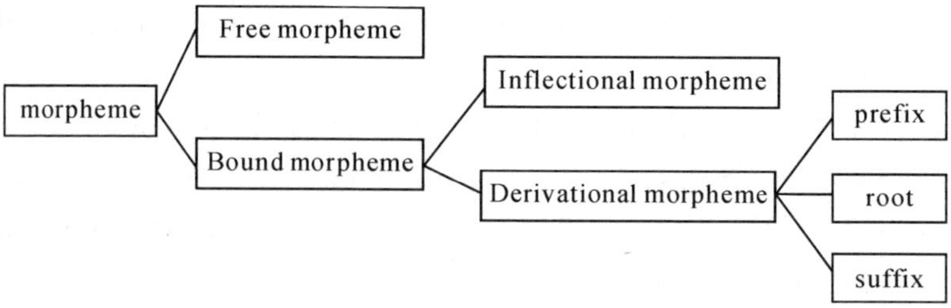

2) There are many inflectional suffixes in English. Their major function is to indicate the grammatical features of the word. For example, the plural suffixes like -s, -es indicates the plural meaning, -ing indicates the progressive aspect of the verb.

3) Orthographically, compounds are written in three ways: solid, hyphenated or open. Generally, the part of speech of a compound falls into the last element.

Semantically, the meanings of compounds are generally idiomatic, they are related to the meanings of their constituting elements, but are not the combination of them. The phonological rule can help to identify whether a combination formed by free morphemes is a compound or a free phrase.

Chapter 5

1. 1) Dick finally decided on the boat.
   ((Dick) ((finally) ((decided on) (the boat)))).
   ((Dick) ((finally) ((decided) (on the boat)))).
   2) The professor's appointment was shocking.
   (((The) (professor's appointment)) (was shocking)).
   (((The professor's) (appointment)) (was shocking)).
   3) The design has big squares and circles.
   (((The) (design)) ((has) ((big) (squares and circles)))).
   (((The) (design)) ((has) ((big squares) (and circles)))).
   4) That sheepdog is too hairy to eat.
   (((That) (sheepdog)) ((is) ((too) (hairy to eat)))).
   (((That) (sheepdog)) ((is) ((too hairy) (to eat)))).
   5) Could this be the invisible man's hair tonic?
   ((Could this) ((be) ((the invisible) (man's hair tonic))))?
   ((Could this) ((be) (((the invisible) (man's)) (hair tonic))))?
   6) The governor is a dirty street fighter.
   (((The) (governor)) ((is) ((a dirty street) (fighter)))).
   (((The) (governor)) ((is) ((a dirty) (street fighter)))).
   7) I cannot recommend him too highly.
   ((I) ((cannot recommend him) (too highly))).
   ((I) (((cannot recommend) (him)) (too) (highly))).
   8) Terry loves his wife and so do I.
   ((Terry loves his wife) (and) (so do I)).
   ((Terry loves) (his wife and so do I)).
   9) They said that they would go yesterday.

((They said that they would go) (yesterday)).

((They said) ((that they) (would go yesterday))).

10) No smoking section available.

(((No) (smoking section)) (available)).

(((No smoking) (section)) (available)).

11) Burning grass is dangerous.

((Burning grass) (is dangerous)).

(((Burning) (grass)) (is dangerous)).

12) The man watched the boy with a telescope.

((The man watched the boy) (with a telescope)).

((The man) ((watched) (the boy with a telescope))).

2. 1)

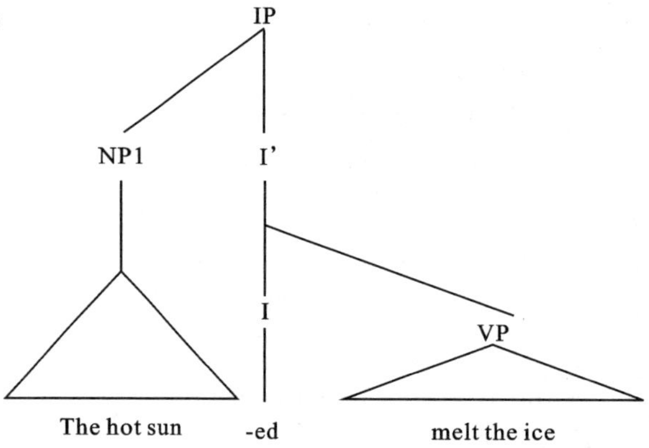

2)

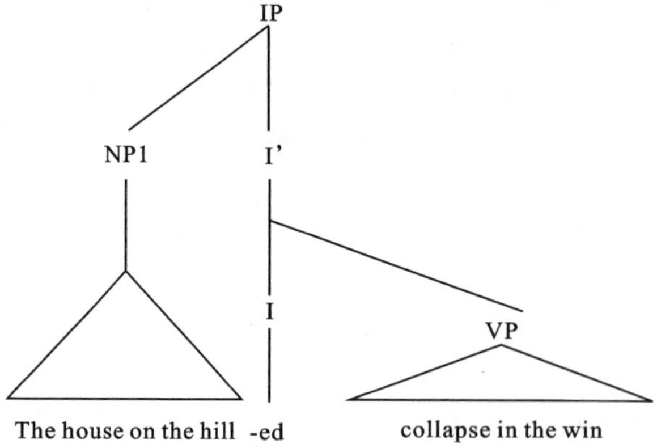

3)

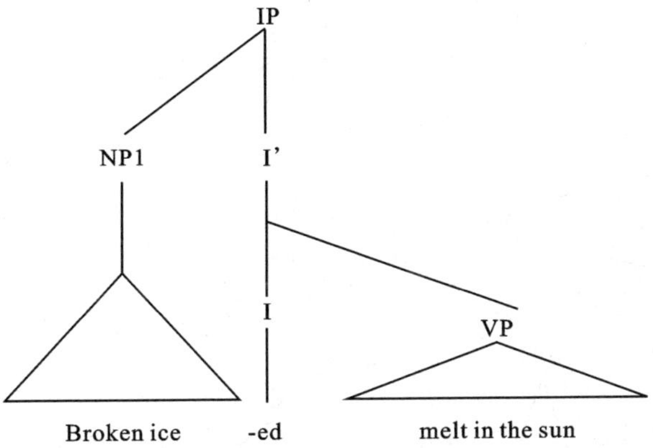
IP
NP1
I'
I
VP
Broken ice
-ed
melt in the sun

4)

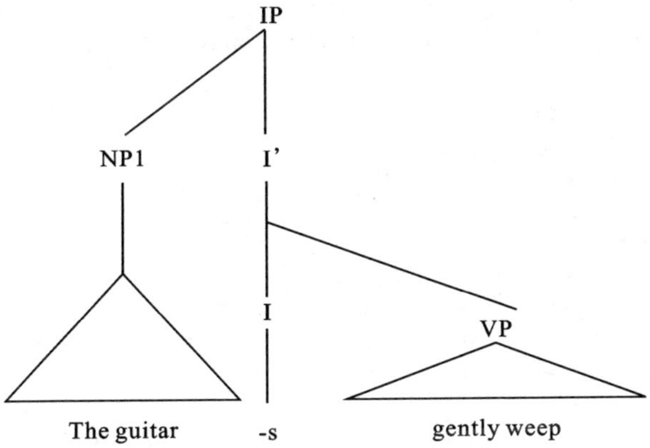
IP
NP1
I'
I
VP
The guitar
-s
gently weep

5)

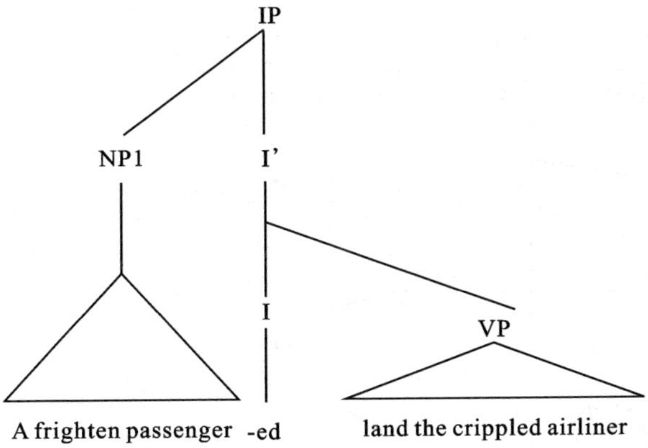
IP
NP1
I'
I
VP
A frighten passenger
-ed
land the crippled airliner

6）

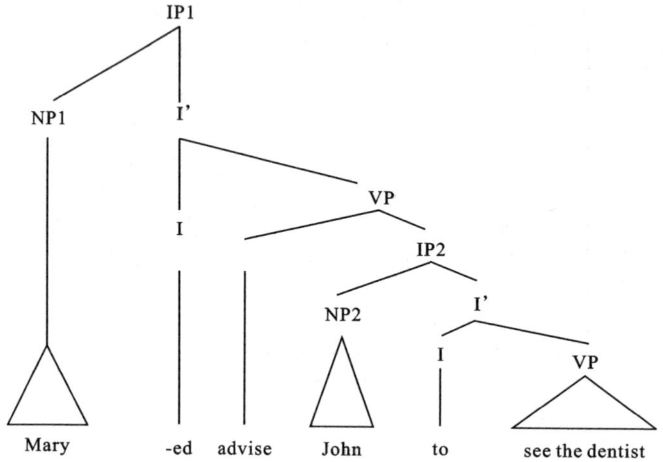
IP1
NP1
I'
VP
I
IP2
NP2
I'
I
VP
Mary
-ed
advise
John
to
see the dentist

7）

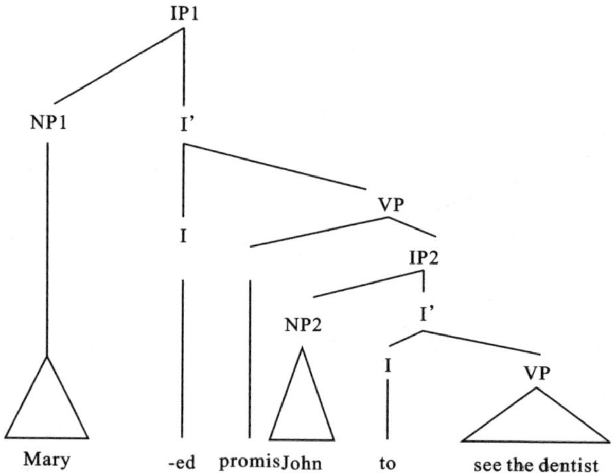
IP1
NP1
I'
VP
I
IP2
NP2
I'
I
VP
Mary
-ed
promisJohn
to
see the dentist

8）

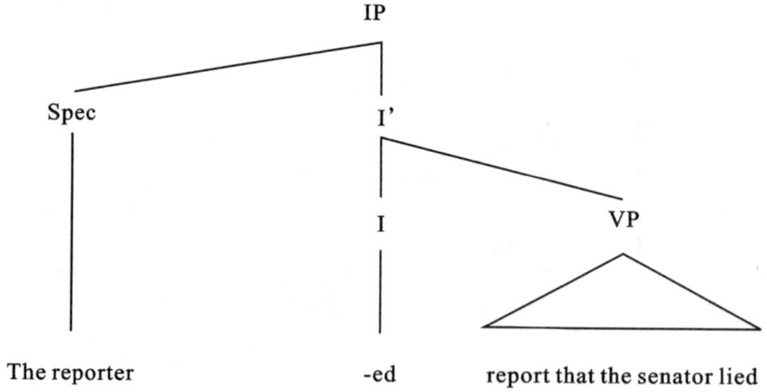
IP
Spec
I'
I
VP
The reporter
-ed
report that the senator lied

9)

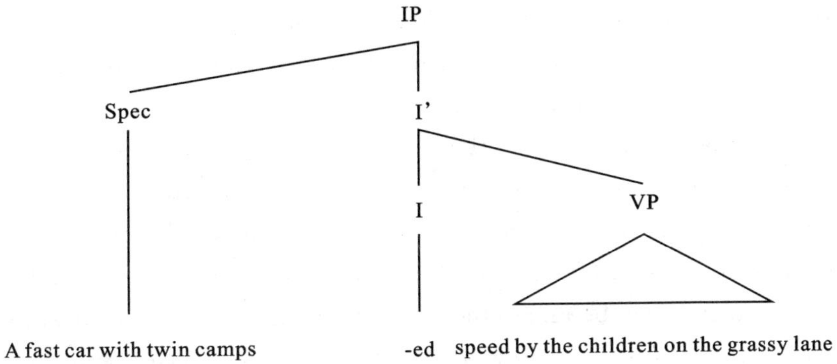

10)

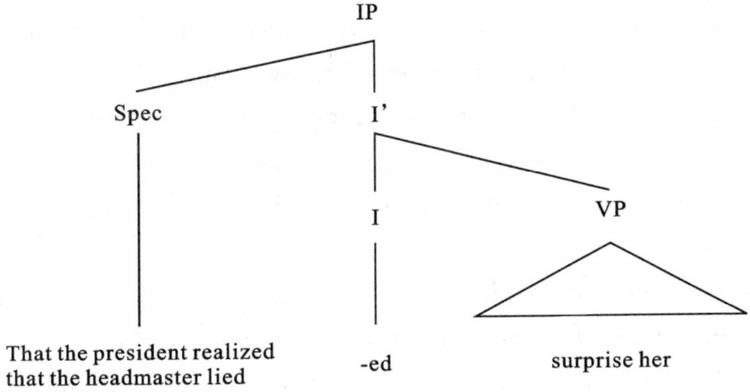

3. 1)—7) T T F T T T T

4. 1) The function of syntactic rules is to make the language users produce grammatical sentences, and to have the ability to judge whether a sentence is grammatical or ungrammatical. Generally, a sentence is considered grammatical when it accords to the grammatical knowledge in the native speakers' mind. That grammatical knowledge is shared by all the members in the speech community. They are a set of natural linguistic habits rather than artificial rules made by people.

The syntactic rules can not only help the speakers produce sentences which conform to grammatical rules, that is, sentences which are considered normal, natural or standard by the native speakers, they can also enable the native speakers to understand the sentences. All the sentences according with syntactic rules can be understood by the native speakers; if they violate the rules, they can not be understood, or understood properly by the native speakers.

2) Grammar is a broad term. It consists of all the rules related to words, sentences and even discourse.

Syntax mainly deals with the rules related to sentences. Sentences are constituted by words and phrases according to syntactic rules. The rules govern what kind of words can be used in the sentence and which part of the sentence they should be used in, i. e. , the function they can perform in the sentence. Syntactic category can be understood from two perspectives: the narrow one and the broad one. In the narrow sense, it refers to classes and functions of syntactic components, e. g. noun, verb, subject, verb phrase, etc; In the broad sense, it refers to the defining properties of these components: the category of noun, for example, involves number, gender, case and countability, the category of verb, involves tense, aspect, voice, and so on.

Grammatical rules are largely syntactical rules. Thus some linguists view grammar as syntax.

3) Chomsky, the founder of Universal Grammar, is much interested in the study of the similarities between languages rather than their differences. In other words, his theory is much more concerned with the finding of language universals. As the result of his research, Chomsky proposes that grammars of all human languages share a common framework, which he called a transformational grammar. According to Chomsky, this UG is a system of linguistic knowledge and a human species-specific gift which exists in the mind or brain of a normal human being. It is composed of two parts: a set of highly abstract principles (general principles) and a set of parameters. The former is responsible for generating phrases and restraining the power of Move α, the latter is responsible for the operation of general principles in certain ways, for example, according to which a particular grammar of natural language varies.

According to Chomsky, UG is an adequate grammar.

4) This is an open question. The troubles with transformations may involve the following:

a. How do we pin down the D-structure?

b. What transformational rules are to be used?

c. How can the same D-structure be transformed into different S-structures?

d. How can the same S-structure be transformed from different D-structures?

e. ...

Chapter 6

1. 1)—6) d a b b d a 7)—12) d d b d d a
2. 1) refers to 2) be sign of
   3) intend to convey 4) have (no) significance to
   5) be equivalent of 6) to imply
   7) intend 8) have in mind
   9) be equivalent to
3. 1)—8) U S S U U S S U
4. 1) Tom's mother, the dog
   2) Your books, the bed
   3) Jacky
   4) Lu Xun
   5) Premier Zhou En-lai, the workers, peasants, soldiers and intellectuals
   6) Hubei, Henan, Hunan
5. 1)—5) F T F F T 6)—10) T T T T F
6. 1) car, bus, lorry 2) sorrow, joy, excitement
   3) rose, lily, daffodil 4) loyalty, honesty, modesty
7. 1) dim, stupid, unpromising 2) poor, scarce, unfertile
   3) ugly, stingy, meager 4) wrong, left, inappropriate
   5) shallow, superficial, light
8. 1) → 2) → 3) ← 4) ← 5) →

Chapter 7

1. 1)—8) T T F T T T F F

2. 1)—5) C P P C P
3. 1) directive 2) commissive 3) directive 4) directive
   5) expressive 6) commissive 7) directive, commissive
   8) assertive 9) directive 10) expressive
4. 1) Yes. "I must hereby..."
   2) Yes. "I hereby..."
   3) Yes. "All passengers on Flight No. 42 are hereby requested..."
   4) No.
   5) Yes. "I hereby charge you..."
5. 1) Don't you think you'd phone your mother on her birthday?
   2) Would you have some more candies?
   3) I'll take you to the movie tomorrow.
   4) I am wondering if you could possibly keep the noise down a little.
   5) I'm sorry to have stepped on your foot.
   6) There is a scorpion on your back.
   7) Keep quiet!
6. 1) ordering 2) warning 3) offer 4) request 5) betting 6) sentence
7. 1) Semantics studies meaning of language as it is, or it gives no consideration to any extra-linguistic factor. People used to believe that meaning of language is stable, inherent and intrinsic, so they studied meaning in an isolated way. Later on, people came to realize that the context in which language is used actually determines the meaning of the language use. The meaning of language varies according to context. So pragmatics studies the dynamic relation of meaning of language use to the context. Whether the context is considered in the study of meaning differs the two branches.

   2) Generally speaking, context is viewed as a set of knowledge that the speaker and the hearer share. The knowledge can be divided into two kinds: knowledge of the language in use and that about the world, which includes the general knowledge about the world and the specific knowledge about the situation in which communication takes place. For instance, if one does not know of the person deictics (used to identify "who" like "you" and "our"), place deictics

(used to identify "where" like "this" and "that") or time deictics (used to identify "when" like "yesterday" and "next month"), he cannot make sure the specific meaning of the sentence "I will go to that town to visit you and our dog at this time next month". Look at another example. The sentence "How clever you are!" may mean a true praise or an irony in certain situation. In short, context contributes a lot to the meaning of language use.

Chapter 8

1. 1)—5) T T T F T   6)—10) T T T F F
2. Sound changes which have taken place during the development of English language involve Great Vowel Shift, sound loss, and sound addition.

   The most prominent sound change in the development of English is the change of vowels which took place during the period of 1400—1600. This change, known as the Great Vowel Shift, involves seven long, or tense vowels.

   Sound loss refers to the fact that, in the development of English language, some of its phonemes may be lost or disappeared. Take the sound [x] in Old English as an example. The words like *liht* (light), *niht* (night) and *siht* (sight) were once pronounced [li:xt], [ni:xt], [si:xt] respectively. This velar fricative, however, was lost between the time of Chaucer and Shakespeare. All the words that were once pronounced with a [x] no longer include this sound. In some cases the sound [x] has become [f], as in *laugh*, *enough*, etc; while in some other cases the sound has disappeared, as in *light*, *sight*, etc.

   Sound addition refers to the fact that, in the course of the historical development of English, some other sounds were added to the original sound sequence. Take the sound [ʒ] for example. Old English did not have this sound. But when French words like *measure*, *pleasure*, *usual* and *rouge* came into English, [ʒ] came into English together with the words in which it occurs. Thus, we now have the two distinctive phonemes /ʃ/ and /ʒ/ in contrast with each other in Modern English.
3. 1) Semantic change may involve three dimensions: broadening, narrowing, and meaning shift.

Broadening means the extension or generalization of the meaning of a word. Take the word "Solomon" as an example. This word used to mean "King of Israel in the tenth century BC who was famous for his wisdom". Today its meaning has been broadened and may denote any profoundly wise person.

Narrowing means the restriction or specialization of the meaning of a word. For example, the word "corpse" originally meant "a human or animal body, living or dead". But later this meaning was narrowed and now it has specialized to mean "a dead body, especially of a human being".

Meaning shift includes two dimensions: meaning elevation and meaning degradation. The former refers to the semantic process in which a word acquires good implications while the latter means the process in which a word gains unfavourable meaning. For example, the word "minister" underwent the process of meaning elevation during its semantic development. This word originally meant "servant" which carries some unfavourable meaning. Now it has come to mean "person at the head of a department of the government", which bears commendatory meaning. By contrast, the semantic change of the word "wench" shows an opposite shift of meaning. This word once meant "a young woman or girl, especially in the country". Now it means "a lewd woman, prostitute".

2) Chinese belongs to Sino-Tibetan (language) family while English belongs to Indo-European language family.

3) Chinese: isolating language
English: moderately isolating (and also a little inflectional /agglutinative)
Japanese: agglutinative language
Russian: inflectional language
Latin: inflectional language

Chapter 9

1. A speaker's use of language is much influenced by his social status. For example, in the U. S. , the speeches of the upper-class speakers and those of the non-upper-class ones do not follow the same phonological patterns. For example,

Upper Class	Non-Upper Class
'yesterday	yester'day
'int'resting	inte'resting

The linguistic difference related to people's social class can also be found in the use of vocabulary. For example, people of higher class tend to use "big", refined and flowery words which are associated with social prestige while people of lower class are inclined to use "small", simple and common words, or even vulgar and slang words, although this difference is not absolute and is merely a matter of degree on the part of the language users.

In grammar, a noticeable example of sociolect is the mistaken use of double negation such as *I can't eat nothing*, a structure closely related to the low social status of the speaker.

The examples discussed above show clearly the influence social class might have on the type of language used by people.

2. Languages used by men and women are different to some extent. Generally, women use more linguistic items from standard English than men, therefore their speech comes more closely to the standard variety than the speech of men. For example, in pronunciation, men tend to pronounce [n] for [ŋ] and fewer women do so. In intonation pattern, women normally have a wider range in their intonation than men do. In lexical features, females tend to use uncertain, polite, or refined words while men usually use decisive, strong or even rough words. In syntactic features, women tend to use tag questions more frequently than men. All this indicates the different use of language between men and women.

3. According to Halliday, "language varies as its function varies; it differs in different situations". The type of language that is selected as appropriate to a type of situation is register.

   Halliday further distinguishes three social variables that determine the register: field of discourse, tenor of discourse, and mode of discourse.

   Field of discourse reflects the purposive role of the language user in the situation in which a text has occurred. It is concerned with the purpose and subject matter of communication. It answers the question of "why" and "about what".

Tenor of discourse refers to the role of relationship in the situation in question: who the participants in the communication group are and in what relationship they stand to each other. It answers the question of "to whom" the speaker is communicating. This dimension to a great extent determines the level of formality and the level of technicality of the language we use.

Mode of discourse mainly refers to the means of communication. It is concerned with "how" communication is carried out. Language can be either spoken or written, and different means of communication may have a direct influence on the register of language.

In brief, the three variables above are the features of the context of situation which determine the features of language appropriate to the situation, i. e. register. And they determine the register collectively, not in isolation.

4. 1) We obtained some sodium chloride. (formal, technical)
   2) We obtained some salt. (formal, non-technical)
   3) We got some salt. (informal, non-technical)
5. Standard dialect is a particular variety of language. This variety has a widely accepted, codified grammar and vocabulary and is normally spoken by educated people and used in literary writing, official documents, news broadcasts, legal writings, etc. It is taught in schools, used in the army and government and propagated by the mass media.

   Standard dialect can not be seen as superior to non-standard dialect, as from a historical point of view, the standard dialect of a language is not different in essence from its related non-standard dialects. All dialects of a language are equal in function, as they are equally expressive. So it is wrong to say that the standard dialect is superior to any other related dialects.
6. Lingua franca is a variety of language that serves as a common speech for social contact among groups of people who speak different native languages or dialects.
7. A pidgin is a mixed or blended form of language (or a variety of language) which developed for some practical purpose, such as trading, among groups of people

who did not know each other's languages. When a pidgin develops beyond its role as a trade language and becomes the first language of a speech community, and is acquired by the children of that speech community as their native language, it is said to be a creole, which is a pidgin language that has become established as the native language of a speech community.

8. Bilingualism refers to the frequent use of two languages by a community. For example, some countries are officially bilingual in the sense that they have two official languages, as in Canada both French and English are used as official languages. While diglossia refers to the coexistence of two different varieties of the same language in a speech community with each serving a particular social function and used for a certain situations.

Chapter 10

1. Sapir-Whorf hypothesis can be summarized as follows:
    a. One's thinking is completely determined by his native language because one cannot but perceive the world in terms of the categories and distinctions encoded in the language.
    b. The categories and distinctions encoded in one language system are unique to that system and incommensurable with those of other systems.

    Therefore, the Sapir-Whorf Hypothesis is chiefly concerned with two major assumptions: one is linguistic determinism, which means that language determines thought; the other is linguistic relativity, which means that there is no limit to the structural diversity of languages.

    As far as linguistic determinism is concerned, most linguists nowadays have come to the common position that language and thought are, on the one hand, closely related to each other and, on the other hand, mutually dependent. Language does have some influence on thought, but thought in turn also influences the categories and structure of language. In brief, the influence of language on thought shouldn't be overestimated. As to linguistic relativity, it is generally agreed that most languages of the world, though different in their surface structure, share some universality in their deep structure, and the viewpoint that "there is no limit to the structural diversity of language" can hardly be fully justified.

2. The reinforcement theory, based on behaviorist psychology, holds that language is learnt in much the same way as anything is learnt. According to this theory, reinforcement of selected responses is the key to understanding language development. According to this theory, children learn to produce correct sentences because they are positively reinforced when they say something right and negatively reinforced when they say something wrong.

   Though seemingly plausible, the reinforcement theory fails to account for the fact that children often construct their own rules in the process of their language acquisition.

   The innate linguistic competence theory holds that children are born with an innate ability to acquire languages of a specific type. This theory is based on Chomsky's theory of speaker's innate linguistic competence, which is represented by the grammar (or rules) of a language. Children are born with (or genetically endowed with) a language acquisition device (LAD), which generate the rules of a language. Children use these rules to produce and understand infinite sentences, including those they have never heard of.

   The innate linguistic competence theory has played a very important role in revealing the truth of child language acquisition. However, it is still open to some criticisms. Some linguists argue that the theory of linguistic competence concentrates solely on children's innate or genetic factors and overlooks the social language environment which also plays a very important role in child language acquisition.

3. Second language acquisition stands in contrast to first language acquisition in several aspects. For example, while the first language is acquired, i. e. subconsciously, the second (or foreign) language is, more commonly, learned, i. e. consciously. It can also be noted that in acquiring their first language, children always concentrate on meaning, not on pattern, i. e. structure. The second language acquisition, however, concentrates on code, i. e. the system of the thought. Besides, one learns his first language directly from reality. The

second language is learnt in manageable sequence, i. e. , syllabus and course books. Furthermore, in first language acquisition children apply the rules subconsciously, while the second language learners, after a period of training, are able to verbalize the rules.

4. Omitted.
5. 1) T 2) T 3) T 4) T 5) F

Bibliography

Appel, R. , and Pieter Muysken. 1987. *Language Contact and Bilingualism* [M]. London: Edward Arnold.

Austin, J. L. 1962. *How to Do Things with Words?* [M]. Cambridge: Harford University Press.

Brown, Penelope & Stephen Levinson. 1978. Universals in Language Usage: Politeness Phenomena [A]. in Esther N Goody (eds). Questions and Politeness: Strategies in Social Interaction [C]. Cambridge: Cambridge University Press.

Brown, Penelope & Stephen Levinson. 1987. *Politeness: Some Universals in Language Usage* [M]. Cambridge: Cambridge University Press.

Chomsky, N. 1968. *Aspects of the Theory of Syntax* [M]. Cambridge, MA: The MIT Press.

Chomsky, N. 1995. *The Minimalist Program* [M]. Cambridge, MA: The MIT Press.

Crystal, David. 1987. *The Cambridge Encyclopaedia of Language* [M]. Cambridge: Cambridge University Press.

Ellis, R. 1985. *Understanding Second Language Acquisition* [M]. Oxford: Oxford University Press.

Fronkin, Victoria, Rodman, Robert and Hyams, Nina. 2003. *An Introduction to Language*[M]. 7th edition. Thomson Heinle.

Görlach, Manfred. 1991. *Englishes: Studies in Varieties of English 1984—1988* [M]. Amsterdam: John Benjamins.

Grice, H. Paul. 1975. Logic and Conversation [A]. In Speech Acts (Syntax and Semantics 3)[C]. P. Cole and J. L. Morgan (eds), 41-58. New York: Academic Press.

Grundy, P. 1995. *Doing Pragmatics*[M]. London: Edward Arnold.

Hock, Hans Henrich, and Brian D. Joseph. 1996. *An Introduction to Historical and Comparative Linguistics*[M]. Berlin and New York: Mouton de Gruyter.

Horn, Laurence R. 2004. Implicature [A]. In The Handbook of Pragmatics [C]. ed. by Laurence R. Horn and Gregory Ward. Oxford: Blackwell. pp. 3-28.

Hurford, J. R. and Heasley, B. 1983. *Semantics: A Coursebook*[M]. Cambridge: Cambridge University Press.

Krashen, S. D. 1987. *Principles and Practice in Second Language Acquisition* [M]. Englewood Cliffs, NJ: Prentice-Hall Internationale.

Ladefoged, Peter, and Ian Maddieson. 1996. *The Sounds of the World's Languages*[M]. Oxford, UK and Cambridge, MA: Blackwell.

Lakoff, Robin. 1973. The Logic of Politeness [A]. in Claudia Corum, T. C. Smith-Stark, & A. Weiser (eds). Papers from the Ninth Regional Meeting of the Chicago Linguistic Society[C]. Chicago.

Leech, Geoffrey. 1983. *Principles of Pragmatics*[M]. London: Longman.

Levinson, S. C. 1983. *Pragmatics*[M]. Cambridge: Cambridge University Press.

Lyons, J. 1977. *Semantics* (Vols. Ⅰ & Ⅱ) [M]. Cambridge: Cambridge University Press.

Lyons, J. 1981. *Language and Linguistics: An Introduction*[M]. Cambridge: Cambridge University Press.

Muysken, P., J. Arends, and N. Smith (eds). 1995. *Pidgins and Creoles: An Introduction*[M]. Amsterdam: John Benjamins.

Ouhalla, Jamal. 1994. *Introducing Transformational Grammar—From Rules to Principles and Parameters*[M]. London: Edward Arnold.

Palmer, F. R. 1981. *Semantics*[M]. Cambridge: Cambridge University Press.

Poole, Stuart C. 2000. *An Introduction to Linguistics* [M]. Beijing: Foreign Language Teaching and Research Press.

Radford, A. et al. 1999. *Linguistics: An Introduction* [M]. Cambridge: Cambridge University Press.

Robins, R. H. 2001. *A Short History of Linguistics* [M]. Beijing: Foreign Language Teaching and Research Press.

Romaine, Suzanne. 1994. *Language in Society: An Introduction to Sociolinguistics*[M]. Oxford: Oxford University Press.

Sampson, Geoffrey. 1980. *Schools of Linguistics—Competition and Evolution* [M]. London: Hutchinson.

Searle, John. 1969. *Speech Acts: An Essay in the Philosophy of Language*[M]. Cambridge: Cambridge University Press.

Searle, John. 1975. Indirect Speech Acts [A]. In Speech Acts (Syntax and Semantics 3) [C]. P. Cole and J. L. Morgan (eds), 59-82. New York: Academic Press.

Skinner, B. 1957. *Verbal Behavior*[M]. New York: Appleton Century Crofts.

Sperber, Dan and Deirdre Wilson. 1987. Precis of Relevance: Communication and Cognition [J]. Behavioral and Brain Sciences (10): 697-754.

Sperber, Dan and Deirdre Wilson. 1995. *Relevance: Communication and Cognition* (2nd ed.)[M]. Oxford: Blackwell.

Sperber, Dan and Deirdre Wilson. 2004. Relevance Theory [A]. in G. Ward and L. Horn (eds). Handbook of Pragmatics[C]. Oxford: Blackwell.

Sperber, Dan and Wilson, Deirdre. 1986. *Relevance: Communication and Cognition*[M]. Oxford and Cambridge, MA: Blackwell.

Todd, Loreto. 1990. *Pidgins and Creoles*[M]. London: Routledge.

Trask, R. L. 1994. *Language Change*[M]. London and New York: Routledge.

Trudgill, Peter. 1995. *Sociolinguistics: An Introduction to Language and Society* [M]. London: Penguin Books.

Wardhaugh, Ronald. 1992. *An Introduction to Sociolinguistics*[M]. Cambridge, MA: Blackwell.

Wolfram, Walt. 1991. *Dialects and American English* [M]. Englewood Cliffs, NJ: Prentice Hall.

Yule, G. 1985. Yule, George. 1985. *The Study of Language*[M]. Cambridge: Cambridge University Press.

Yule, G. 1996. *Pragmatics*[M]. Oxford: Oxford University Press.

Yule, George. 2000. *The Study of Language*[M]. Beijing: Foreign Language Teaching and Research Press.

戴炜栋,何兆熊,华钧. 1989. 简明英语语言学教程[M]. 上海:上海外语教育出版社.

何兆熊,梅德明. 1998. 现代语言学[M]. 北京:外语教学与研究出版社.

何自然. 1997. 语用学与英语学习[M]. 上海:上海外语教育出版社.

何自然. 1998. 语用学概论[M]. 长沙:湖南教育出版社.

胡壮麟,姜望琪. 2001. 语言学教程(第二版)[M]. 北京:北京大学出版社.

胡壮麟,刘润清等. 1988 . 语言学教程[M]. 北京:北京大学出版社.

胡壮麟. 2001. 语言学教程[M]. 北京:北京大学出版社.

胡壮麟,姜望琪. 2002. 语言学高级教程[M]. 北京:北京大学出版社.

姜望琪. 2000. *Pragmatics: Theories and Applications*[M]. 北京:北京大学出版社.

杰弗里·N·利奇编著,李瑞华,王彤福等译. 1987. 语义学[M]. 上海:上海外语教育出版社.

李福印. 2006. 语义学概论[M]. 北京:北京大学出版社.

李维光. 1995. 语言学[M]. 湖北省教育委员会师训处组编.

林承璋. 1997. 英语词汇学引论. 修订版 [M] . 武汉:武汉大学出版社.

林汝昌,李曼珏. 1993. 语义学入门[M]. 武汉:华中理工大学出版社.

罗·亨·罗宾斯著,李振麟,胡伟民译. 1986. 普通语言学概论[M]. 上海:上海译文出版社.

王刚. 1988. 普通语言学基础[M]. 长沙:湖南教育出版社.

伍谦光. 1982. 语义学导论[M]. 长沙:湖南教育出版社.

张维友. 1997. 英语词汇学[M]. 北京:外语教学与研究出版社.

左思民. 2000. 汉语语用学[M]. 郑州:河南人民出版社.

An English-Chinese Glossary

acoustic phonetics	声学语音学
acronym	首字母缩略词
acronymization	首字母缩略法
adjacency condition	毗邻条件
adjacency parameter	毗邻参数
adj-movement	形容词移位
affective meaning	情感意义
affix	词缀
affixation	词缀法
Afro-asiatic family	亚非语系,闪含语系
agglutinative language	粘着语
allomorph	语素变体
allophone	音位变体
ambiguity	歧义(多义性)
arbitrariness	任意性
articulatory phonetics	发音语音学
aspect	体
aspiration	送气
assertion	断言
assertives	断言类(以言行事)
associative meaning	联想意义
auditory phonetics	听觉语音学,感知语音学
Austronesian family	南岛语系
AUX-movement	助动词移位

availability	易得性,易想及性
back vowel	后元音
back-formation	逆构词法
bilabial	双唇音
bilingualism	双语(现象)
blending	拼缀法
borrowing	借用
bound morpheme	黏着词素
broad transcription	宽式标音法
case	格
case condition	格条件
central vowel	中元音
clause	分句,子句
clipping	截短法
code-switch	语码转换
cognitive meaning	认知意义
coinage	创新词
commissives	承诺类(以言行事)
communication strategy	交际策略
communication	交际/交流
competence	语言能力
complement	补语
complex sentence	复合句
componential analysis	意义成分分析
compound	合成词
compound sentence	并列句
compounding	复合法
conceptual meaning	概念意义
connotation	内涵(暗涵意义)
connotative meaning	内涵意义

consonant	辅音
constative	述愿陈述，断定陈述
context	语境
contextual meaning	语境意义
contextualism	语境论
contrastive analysis	对比分析法
conversational implicature	会话含意
conversion	词类转换
cooperative principle	合作原则
coverage	覆盖(面)
creativity	创造性
creole	克里奥语，混合语
critical period	(语言习得的)关键时期
cultural transmission	文化传承
declarations	宣告类(以言行事)
deictics	指示词，指示语
denotation	外延(字面意义)
denotative meaning	明指意义(字面意义)
dental	齿音
derivation	派生
derivational affix	派生词缀
derivational morphology	派生形态学
derivative	派生词
descriptive linguistics	描绘性语言学
design features	识别特征
diachronic linguistics	历时语言学
diacritics	变音符号
dialect	方言
diglossia	双语体现象
diphthong	双元音

directionality parameter	方位参数
directives	指令类(以言行事)
disambiguation	消除歧义
discourse	语篇
discourse analysis	话语篇章分析
distinctive feature	区别特征
double bar	双标杆
D-structure	深层结构
duality	二重性
embedded clause	子句
emotive meaning	情感意义
error analysis	错误分析
exophoric reference	外指
family-tree	谱系树
field of discourse	话语范围
field theory	语义场论
figure of speech	词藻(形象化说法)
finite clause	定式子句
finite verb	定式动词
finiteness	限定式
free morpheme	自由词素
fricative	擦音
front vowel	前元音
function word	功能词
fusional language	屈折语
generative semantics	生成派语义学
gerund	动名词
gerundial phrase	动名词短语
given information	已知信息
glide	滑音

glottal	喉音
glottis	声门
grammatical ambiguity	语法歧义
grammatical analysis	语法分析
grammatical meaning	语法意义
grammatical relations	语法关系
Grimm's law	格林定律
Hamito-Semitic family	闪含语系
hard palate	硬腭
historical comparative linguistics	历史比较语言学
historical linguistics	历史语言学
idiolect	个人言语特点,个人习语
illocutionary acts	施为性言语行为
illocutionary force	施为用意
illocutionary meaning	施为意义
illocutionary point	以言行事目的/意图
implication	蕴含(言外之意)
Indo-European family	印欧语系
inference	推理
infinitive	不定式
infinitive phrase	非限定性短语
inflection	曲折变化
inflectional affix	曲折词缀
inflectional language	屈折语
inflectional morphology	曲折形态学
interference	干扰
International Phonetic Alphabet	国际音标
interpretative semantics	解释派语义学
irony	反语
isolating language	孤立语

language acquisition	语言习得
language acquisition device (LAD)	语言习得机制
language family	语系
language typology	语言类型学
language variation	语言变异
larynx	喉
lax vowel	松元音
lexical ambiguity	词汇歧义
lexical categories	词类
lexical density	词汇密度
lexical meaning	词汇意义
lexical morphology	词汇形态学
lexicon	词汇
lexis	词汇
linguistic context	上下文
linguistic determinism	语言决定论
linguistic relativity	语言相对论
linguistics	语用学
liquid	流音
locutionary acts	表述性言语行为
locutionary meaning	表述意义
manner maxim	方式准则
manner of articulation	发音方法
matrix clause	母句
meaning components	意义成分
meaning in context	(语言在)语境中的意义
meaning in use	(语言在)运用中的意义
meaning potential	意义潜势(或可能性)
meaning shift	意义转移
meaning	意义

minimal pair	最小对立对
mode of discourse	话语方式
monophthong	单元音
morpheme	语素
morphology	形态学，词形学
Move α rule	移动 α 规则
narrow transcription	严式标音法
nasal cavity	鼻腔
nasalized	鼻音化
natural meaning	自然意义
negative transfer	负迁移
new information	新信息
non-finite clause	非定式子句
non-natural meaning	非自然意义
non-simple sentence	非简单句
number	数
object	宾语
oral cavity	口腔
overextension	扩展过度
over-generalization	概括过度
paraphrase	换说法
part of speech	词类
participle phrase	分词短语
performance	运用
performance error	语言运用错误
performative	行事性语句，言语行为(功能)
perlocutionary acts	成事性言语行为
person	人称
person deictics	人称指示词
pharyngeal cavity	咽腔

phone	音素
phoneme	音位
phonemic contrast	音位对立
phonetic feature	语音特征
phonetics	语音学
phonological rule	音位规则
phonology	音位学
phrasal categories	词组类
phrasal head	短语核心词
phrase structure rules	短语结构规则
pidgin	洋泾滨语
place deictics	地点指示词
place of articulation	发音部位
plosive	爆破音
polysemy	一词多义现象(关系)
polysynthetic language	多式综合语
positive transfer	正迁移
post-pose	后移
pragmatics	语用学
predicate	谓语
prefix	前缀
pre-pose	前移
prescriptive linguistics	规定性语言学
presequence	预示语列,前系列
presupposition	前提,预设
principle of relevance	关联原则
productivity	生产性
propositional meaning	命题意义
proto-language	原始语
psycholinguistics	心理语言学

quality maxim	真实准则
quantity maxim	量的准则
recursiveness	递归性
reference	指称(关系)
referential meaning	指称意义
referent	指称对象
regional dialect	地区方言
register	语域
relevance theory	关联理论
relevance	关联/关联性
representatives	阐述类(以言行事)
retroflex	卷舌音
Romance language	诺曼语
root	词根
rounded vowel	圆唇元音
Sapir-Whorf Hypothesis	萨丕尔-沃尔夫假说
second language acquisition	第二语言习得
segment	切分成分
semantic components	语义成分
semantic differential	语义微分法
semantic features	语义特征
semantic field	语义场
semantic stratum	义素层
semantics	语义学
sense relation	语义关系
sense	(词汇系统中)意义,词义
sentence meaning	句子意义
shared knowledge	共有知识
sibilant	咝音
signs	符号

simple sentence	简单句
single bar	单标杆
Sino-Tibetan family	汉藏语系
situational context	情景语境
social dialect	社会方言
sociolect	社会方言
sociolinguistics	社会语言学
sound loss	语音消失
speaker meaning	说话人意义
specifier	指示语
speech act theory	言语行为理论
speech acts	言语行为
speech community	语言社区
S-structure	表层结构
standard dialect	标准方言
stop	爆破音
stress	重音
suffix	后缀
synchronic linguistics	共时语言学
syntactic categories	句类
syntax	句法
telegraphic speech	电文语言
tenor of discourse	话语意旨
tense vowel	紧元音
theory of semantic fields	语义场理论
time deictics	时间指示词
tone language	声调语言
tone	音调;声调
transfer	迁移
transformational rules	转换规则

UG (Universal Grammar)	普遍语法
unaspirated	不送气
utterance meaning	话语意义
uvula	小舌
variety	语言变体,语体
velar	软颚音
velum	软颚
Verner's law	维尔纳定律
vocal cord	声带
voiced	浊化音的
voiceless	清音的
word-formation	构词(法)
x-bar	x 标杆